Emile Thomas

Roman life under the Caesar

Emile Thomas

Roman life under the Caesar

ISBN/EAN: 9783744723343

Printed in Europe, USA, Canada, Australia, Japan

Cover: Foto ©ninafisch / pixelio.de

More available books at **www.hansebooks.com**

ROMAN LIFE
UNDER THE CÆSARS

BY

EMILE THOMAS

PROFESSOR AT THE UNIVERSITY OF LILLE

———

ILLUSTRATED

———

G. P. PUTNAM'S SONS
NEW YORK & LONDON
The Knickerbocker Press
1899

PREFACE

WE shall never attain to a perfect knowledge of
Roman antiquity. It is too far removed
from us, and the greater part of the evidence which
might have preserved its memory has, unfortunately,
perished. What is left to us has either faded or else
fails almost entirely to reflect any of the essential
features of Roman life. Add to these losses our
own prejudices and bias; when we try to reconstruct
a picture of the ancient world, we inevitably falsify
it by introducing into it too much of the modern
spirit. Each succeeding generation flatters itself
that, by dint of repeated efforts, it has succeeded in
rendering the picture more faithful, unconscious of
the fact that it is merely following the caprices of a
passing fashion, and is, in the majority of instances,
swayed by the evanescent influences of its own
standard of taste. Thanks to recent excavations,
and to the advance achieved in the comparatively
modern sciences of epigraphy and archæology, we
have mastered a few points of detail and are proud
of our progress; but it seems very doubtful whether
we shall ever arrive at a clear and accurate general
conception of the ancient world such as we should

like to acquire. How can we restore to these lifeless texts the vital force and accent which once animated them ? How ever hope to recall, even by the
utmost effort of the imagination, the original colour
and pristine beauty of these faded frescos, these
mutilated statues, these crumbling bas-reliefs? Shall
we ever succeed in tracing anything more than a
faint and faltering image of the true Rome which
we feel lies hidden beneath all these books and
monuments ?

If I, in my turn, attempt the task, I do so with
my eyes open to the difficulties before me. The
picture I am about to draw will be necessarily an
incomplete one. I am sure to fall into many errors
in the course of these pages. The reader will perhaps forgive them, if he bears in mind that it has
been my object to write a popular, and, if possible,
a lifelike book; that while I have not failed to
profit wherever I could by recent researches, I have,
on the other hand, endeavoured to avoid excessive
detail in order that I might penetrate as far as possible into the life of the Romans as we conceive it
to have been—and what a gulf there is between our
conception of it and that of our fathers! Our
children will, in their turn, see it in quite a different
light, future discoveries making it necessary to add
or suppress some feature in one part or other of the
picture. What matters it ? We need not hesitate
to exert a single one of our faculties, whether of
criticism, memory, or imagination, to the utmost if
we may hope from this day forward to arrive at

some positive conclusion and to form a mental picture of Roman antiquity which, though perhaps inaccurate and imperfect in its details, shall be nevertheless well defined in its main outlines.

Undoubtedly our main difficulty lies in the fact that we are obliged to extract from monuments and books something which, strictly speaking, they cannot be said to contain. The Romans were like all other races; they did not trouble themselves to represent or record details which lay within the common knowledge of all [1]; now it is precisely these details of which we are often ignorant and which, since they are most characteristic of ancient customs, would prove of the utmost value to us. We must therefore seek to re-discover them, if need be, by guessing at them.

I do not mind confessing that in more than one part of the present work, I have realised how many things I was deficient in, which, had I possessed them, would have helped me to make this volume as correct in form and solid in foundation as I could have desired. In one place I wanted to be an archæologist, in another an epigraphist, and in numerous instances I should have liked to study in greater detail and at more leisure some problem of which I was able to divine the interest. But regrets of this nature are inseparable from any general review of a

---

[1] Vegetius, i., 8, makes a similar remark on the subject of military education : "illi res gestas . . . tantum scripsere, . . . ista quæ quærimus nota relinquentes" (authors confine themselves to the statement of events, omitting, as being well known, those very details which we desire to know).

large subject.　I have sought in every direction for anything which might help the reader to form an impression of the life of the ancients.　I have sedulously avoided hackneyed phrases and fictions of every kind; unless I am much mistaken, Gallus and Camulogenes have had their day.　Even schoolboys themselves have lost their liking for these scholastic fables; their curiosity no longer requires to be stimulated by such methods; they will, in my opinion, be fully justified if they demand that no factitious barrier of this kind shall be placed between the modern reader and ancient life.

Should anyone object, however, that the chapters of this book and the facts contained in them are not closely enough linked together, I know of a noble framework in which they might be set, and which would worthily hold nearly the whole material of the present work; I would take my readers straight to that villa of Hadrian near Tibur, which fell into ruins at the close of the Empire, and has since been so pitilessly ransacked by one generation after another, that hardly the bare bones of it now remain,[1] though scholars and artists of the present day are doing their best to restore it.

We know that the Emperor in question, a worthy and learned, if somewhat eccentric man, had erected there a sort of microcosm in which the characteristics of the most diverse regions were duly reflected;

---

[1] Cf. Juvenal, viii., 90. "*Ossa* vides rerum *vacuis exsucta medullis*" (Thou beholdest the bones of things from which the very marrow has been sucked).

in its " Poecile " we find the refinements of Greece, in its " Canopus " the weird customs of Egypt, in its " Hades " a crystallisation of popular superstitions, in its theatres the essence of the Greek and Roman character; in its baths, every form of public amusement, every refinement of private luxury which characterised the age. Where can we hope to find a more fitting frame in which to set our reconstruction of the life of the ancients ?

From the spoils of this villa, which are scattered broadcast at Naples, in Rome, and elsewhere, we know that it must have been enriched by all the magnificences of that period. We may people it as we please; in its chambers and under its porticos we may introduce a seething crowd of consuls, orators, tribunes and senators, poets and philosophers — these latter had a chamber to themselves, just as an alley was reserved for them at Chantilly; through this motley throng the Emperor passes, a man of a strong though somewhat inconsistent character. In a corner by himself sits young Marcus Aurelius, a serious youth,[1] and very sincere[2]; he is perhaps meditating over one of his future tests of conscience in the light of one's experience of things and men,[3] and doubtless estimates in a single

[1] Capitolinus, ii., 1, "a primâ infantiâ *gravis*" (of a serious mien from his earliest childhood).

[2] *Ibid.*, i., 10, Hadrian called him Verissimus (a punning allusion to the name of his father, Annius *Verus*).

[3] *Medit.*, x., 27: " Συνεχῶς ἐπινοεῖν, πῶς πάντα τοιαῦτα ὁποῖα νῦν γίνεται, καὶ πρόσθεν ἐγίνετο. . . . Καὶ ὅλα δράματα καὶ σκηνὰς ὁμοειδεῖς ὅσα ἐκ πείρας τῆς σῆς, ἢ τῆς

glance all the vanities before him at their true
worth.

These are some of the results which may readily
be attained by a little groping among the ashes of
archæology and history. But after all, even when
surrounded by these ruins, we must fall back, in the
long run, on imagination, and imagination cannot
carry us far across their confused remains. I shall
therefore most certainly refrain from guiding the
reader even to the threshold of the villa, and shall
merely content myself by naming one or two excellent guides for those who are not repelled by difficulties of detail.[1]

In an essay like the present, we shall, I think, be
well advised if we adopt a totally different method.
We must not confine ourselves in too narrow a space
or too short a period. The documents at our disposal would probably be too scanty, and we should
fail to obtain that general view of Roman life at the
beginning of the Empire of which we are especially
in quest.

To endeavour to include in this small volume

πρεσβυτέρας ἱστορίας ἔγνως, πρὸ ὀμμάτων τίθεσθαι, οἷον
αὐλὴν ὅλην Ἀδριανοῦ " (Forget not that in times gone by everything has already happened just as it is happening. . . . Place
before thine eyes whole dramas with the same endings, the same
scenes, just as thou knowest them *by thine own experience* or from
earlier history, *such, for example, as the whole court of Hadrian*).

[1] *Cf.* Boissier, *Rome and Pompeii*, or the work recently published
in German by a member of the German Institute at Rome, H. Winnefeld, Berlin, Reimer, 1895, containing thirteen plates and forty-
three engravings.

every form of life at Rome under the Empire, would be to attempt the impossible; Rome changed incessantly as years went by and new generations came on the scene: we must be satisfied to grasp the trend of these movements and to seize a few of their aspects. This must be our aim in the following chapters; in each of them we shall be transported into some well-known spot which has been fully explored, or we shall pause to examine some department of Roman life which has been made the subject of careful study and which may help us to form some idea of the remainder; within the narrow limits of Pompeii we shall learn what the excavations have to teach us concerning the everyday life of the ancients; the African contingent must be made to represent the other legions of the Roman army; and Pliny the Younger will have to sit to us as the model of a Roman gentleman of literary tastes at the close of the first century. I have naturally chosen my types from among those places, men, and institutions of which we possess the fullest knowledge.

I have avoided quotations wherever possible. It will be noticed, however, that I frequently quote from the *Historia Augusta*, a storehouse of information which is perhaps less generally known than others that might be named. I am quite conscious that it is not safe for the historian to draw too recklessly on this source.[1] I cannot, however, regard this as a good reason for allowing a host of charac-

[1] I have read and am greatly pleased with M. H. Peters's curious book, *Scriptores Historiæ Augustæ*, Teubner, 1892.

teristic touches which throw a searching light on customs and institutions, to lie buried in these poor biographies: for our present purpose it matters but little whether they were re-written by some writer of the fifth century, or drawn entirely from some ancient source.

In regard to the archæological portion of the work, I have in every case confined myself to a general view, leaving details and controversial matter on one side. To quote the words used by Stendhal [1] in reference to the baths of Caracalla: "There are times when these deserted ruins are a source of much pleasure; but, to my mind, they lose rather than gain in interest from complicated description." How many ruins and monuments there are to which even now—or, if you will, more especially now—the same remark may be applied.

[1] *Promenades dans Rome*, i., 209.

CONTENTS.

CHAPTER I.

xiii

CHAPTER II.

CHAPTER III.

Contents

Contents

CHAPTER VIII

Contents

CHAPTER IX

CHAPTER X

Contents

CHAPTER XI

Contents

Contents

ILLUSTRATIONS

Illustrations

ROMAN LIFE UNDER THE CÆSARS

ROMAN LIFE
UNDER THE CÆSARS

CHAPTER I

AT POMPEII

I

A BIRD'S-EYE VIEW

EVERY day that passes, our knowledge of antiquity receives some fresh addition, due to
the excavations that are now being carried on in
every direction throughout Europe. I need but
mention a single instance, that of Timgad,[1] where
works of this kind have been undertaken on French
territory and fully discussed in French publications.
The description of the forum of this little African
town which has been recently put forth, is most interesting and instructive. But if we would form an
accurate idea, not of the main current, but rather
of the everyday details of life in one of the ancient
Roman cities, we must turn to Pompeii, a town dis-

---

[1] *Timgad*, by MM. Boeswillwald and Cagnat, 1894.

covered in the last century. Let us, then, take Pompeii as the starting-point of our journey across the Roman Empire.

In order to attain a thorough knowledge of the Campanian city, our ideal course would be to go and live at Naples, to visit the ruins time after time and study them at our leisure, thus giving them the full attention they deserve. Unhappily, it is only the privileged few who can do this. It is true that a visit to the place itself, however hurried, will teach us more than many hours spent in poring over books and engravings. But those who have no opportunity of visiting the country must content themselves as best they can with maps and books. I append a bibliography of the literature on the subject for their benefit.[1]

Before we enter the town itself it will be well to note its boundaries—the narrow frame, if I may be allowed the phrase, which encloses the mirror into which we are about to look. And, first of all, we must not forget that here we need not hope to obtain a view of Roman life in its proper perspective. Pompeii was a town half Italian, half Greek, and

[1] In regard to illustrations, apart from those contained in atlases and dictionaries of antiquities, the reader may consult *Li Antiquità di Ercolano* (Naples, 1757–1792), the important works of Mazois and Roux, and the engravings of Piranesi, *Antiquités de la Grande Grèce*, vols. i. and ii. (1804 and 1807). In addition to the official reports and notices of the excavations contained in periodicals, the following manuals may be recommended : *Pompeia*, by Ernest Breton (Paris, Gide and Baudry, third edition, 1869), or the fourth (and latest) edition of a German work by Overbeck, revised by Mau, *Pompei* (Leipzig, 1884, Engelmann).

above all, a *small* town.   It will be necessary, therefore, to be very cautious and to˙ make all necessary
allowances in arguing from what we shall notice
here, as to what life in Rome, or in any other essentially Roman city, was like in the early days of the
Empire.

It will not take us long to find our bearings.   On
the south are the gates leading to Stabiæ and to
Nuceria; on the west the *Porta Marina ;* on the east
the Nola and Sarno gates; on the north those of
Herculanum, Vesuvius, and Capua.   The triangular forum, from which an extensive view is obtained,
and the two theatres will be found on the south-
west, close by the Stabiæ gate.   The amphitheatre is
on the south-east.   The *forum civile* lies almost in
the centre of the town, only a little higher up and
more to the westward, near the *Porta Marina.* From
the Herculanum gate a road leads to the tombs.   It
was here that the first attempt at excavation was
made, the Houses of Diomedes and those situated
in the north-western portion of the town having
specially engaged the attention of M. Mazois.   This
quarter was, however, merely a kind of suburb frequented for the most part by the country people.
At Pompeii, as elsewhere, the cemeteries lay outside the town, the inns being inside, close to the
gates; in the suburbs some of the houses seem to
have been half town, half country residences. Shops
were specially numerous in the more frequented
thoroughfares, such as those in the neighbourhood
of the forum, the baths, the theatres, and the gates.

The houses of the rich were not confined to any particular quarter, though the fashionable part of the town seems to have lain towards the north, a little above and to the left of the celebrated House of the Faun. None of the part which extends towards the east has yet been explored.[1]

To the north of the House of the Faun is that of the Labyrinth. The House of Vettius,[2] which was only opened out in 1895, lies to the east of the House of the Labyrinth.[3] It contains a fine *Lararium* (or chapel of the Lares), a number of paintings dealing with subjects similar to those already discovered, and last, but not least, a very beautiful peristyle. It will doubtless be duly admired by tourists, not only because every visitor likes to see the paintings and internal fittings just as they were when first brought into the light of day, but, more especially, for the following reason: Hitherto everything that has been found was at once carried off to the museum at Naples, with the doubly undesirable result that, while at Pompeii the houses stood stripped and bare and failed to present their

[1] In spite of the activity with which the work of excavation has been carried on ever since 1870, quite one-half of Pompeii, a great part of Herculanum, and nearly the whole of Stabiæ still remain buried.

[2] In this house have been found seals belonging to A. Vettius Conviva, and the same name occurs in the tablets of the banker Jucundus. In regard to the Vettii, *cf.* Willems, *Des élections municipales à Pompéi*, p. 100, n. 11.

[3] A detailed account of the results of these excavations, given by M. Mau, will be found in the first part of the *Mittheilungen Roms.*, xi. (1896).

true aspect, at Naples the paintings, sculptures, and
other works of art were scattered about anyhow and
deprived of the setting appropriate to them. In the
case of this house which has been recently unearthed,
everything has, as far as possible, been left absolutely
undisturbed. It is here, therefore, and here only,
that we have a chance of observing what a Pompeian
house was really like.

It is somewhat difficult to secure a bird's-eye view
of the town, owing to the fact that the littoral of
the Gulf of Naples lies but little above the sea-level.
In order to see Pompeii as a whole, we must either
climb the hills by which Naples is surrounded, or
make the ascent of Vesuvius. Unfortunately, at
this distance, though we can make out the white
walls, standing out like the headstones in a grave-
yard, it is impossible to obtain a clear general view.
On the other hand, if we go lower down, near the
sea-shore, we only see a part of the town from the
road leading from the amphitheatre as far as the station. On this side the walls overlooked the surrounding country, and the houses rose above the
walls in order that the inhabitants might command
a view of both land and sea.

I may add, in passing, a word or two on a question which has been the subject of much controversy
among scholars, viz., as to whether the coast-line
has undergone any change since classical times.
The sea is now a couple of miles away from the
town; is there reason to believe that it was much
nearer in days gone by ?

A kind of legend has grown up round this question.   To this day the guide who shows the visitor
over the amphitheatre assures him that the sea at one
time extended as far as this place, a circumstance
which enabled the Romans to include naval engagements among the spectacles in the arena.   The story
is still told of a naval engineer who, in the year
1831, discovered a plantation of cypress trees growing on a farm, and decided that they must be antique masts ; aided by a vivid imagination, he
jumped to the conclusion, and succeeded in per-
suading his contemporaries that he had come upon
the identical vessel in which Pliny had journeyed to
the foot of Mount Vesuvius.   He tried to unearth
it; but the supposed masts stood firm, and with
good reason—they were furnished with roots!

M. Ruggiero, who was till recently at the head
of the work of excavation, took advantage of the
operations in connection with the rectification of the
bed of the Sarno to definitely settle the question.[1]
He found remains of ancient buildings between the
sea-shore and the town, and after exploring the
doubtful region by sinking perpendicular shafts,
arrived at the conclusion that, in view of the plant-
ations and remains of buildings which are found
there, the coast-line to the east of the Sarno must
have been pretty much the same in ancient times as

---

[1] *Cf.* a paper on this question in *Pompei, Memorie* . . ., Naples,
1879, pp. 5 *et seq.* ; and on p. 33, pl. 1, the map of which a reduced
reproduction appears opposite. *Cf.* also the articles by MM. von
Duhn and Mau, *Rhein. Mus.*, xxxvi. (1881), pp. 136 *et seq.*

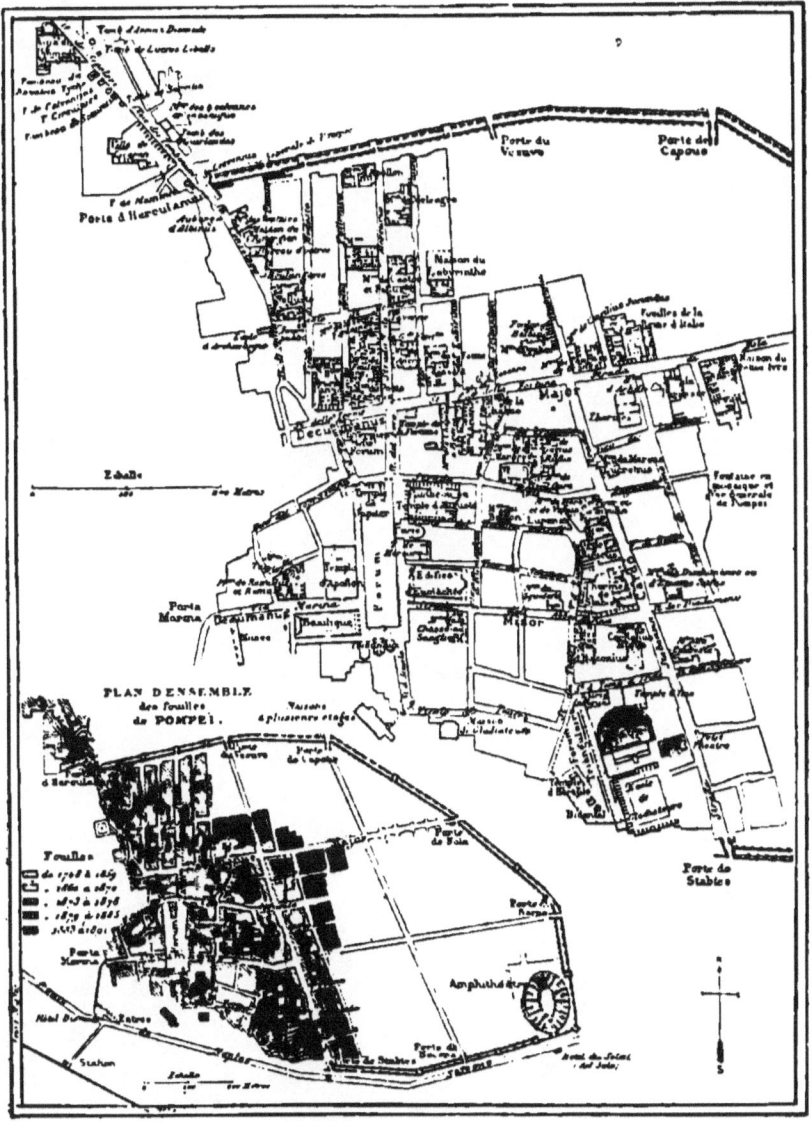

PLAN OF POMPEII.

it is now. To the west of the river, however, the
sea formed a curve, and must have approached about
half as near again to the walls as it does at present.
The amphitheatre has always been about a couple
of miles distant from the coast.

On entering the town, our first impression—and a
very important one it is, harmonising as it does with
a truth too often lost sight of by those who write
about Pompeii—is that everything is here on a small
scale.[1] Take the streets, for instance—some of
them are not more than 10 feet wide; so too with
the open spaces—the largest of them, the *forum
civile*, is barely 150 yards long, whereas the House
of Pansa, for instance, is 100 yards in length. We
are here in a small town which was valued by the
Romans merely for its position; they cared little
either for the town itself or for those who dwelt in
it. It boasts but one single monument of any size;
true, this is one which ministered to a ruling passion
of the Italian race, and which on high-days and
holidays attracted as many strangers as native resi-
dents or more; I refer to the amphitheatre, which
was capable of accommodating 20,000 spectators.

There can be no doubt that to the modern eye,

[1] Renan seems to have entirely forgotten that Pompeii was merely
a small town when he wrote the following sentence in his *Études
d'histoire religieuse*, p. 413 : " The antique life, serene and graceful
as it was within its narrow limits, lacked expansiveness in the direction of the infinite. *Take those charming little houses at Pompeii !*
how cheerful and complete they are, but narrow and confined ! On
all sides we find a sense of peace and joy : on all sides are pictures of
happiness and pleasure. But such things no longer content us."

accustomed to the spacious buildings of the present time, the most surprising features of Pompeii are the narrowness of its streets and the modest proportions of the houses and of nearly all the public monuments. But apart from the fact that the eye soon becomes used to the small and, as it were, reduced scale of everything,—which is the less apparent because universal; and making due allowance for the fact that under the blazing Italian sun this method of building is not without its advantages, we need but recall for a moment the minor towns of Southern France or of Italy, or the ancient by-streets of Rome, and Pompeii, even though it may not rank with the great cities of the world, will perhaps cease to impress us as a small place.

As might naturally be expected from the modest proportions of their town, the part played by the Pompeians in history was not a brilliant one. Originally Oscan, then Samnite, Pompeii, following the lead of Capua and Naples, at first threw in its lot with Hannibal, and afterwards with the Italian federation, in the hope that it might thus preserve its independence. At length, like the rest of Campania, it was forced to submit to the Roman yoke. Its final effort was the successful resistance it offered to the besieging army of Sylla in 89 B.C. On his return from Asia, however, the dictator despatched a band of colonists to occupy the rebellious town, which thenceforward bore the name *Colonia Veneria Cornelia Pompeianorum*. After this date historians have but little to tell us of Pompeii,

CORPSE FOUND IN POMPEII.

except on the occasion of the earthquake which destroyed a part of the town in A.D. 63, or in connection with the celebrated eruption in A.D. 79, which led to its total disappearance.

There is one incident, however, recorded by Tacitus [1] as having taken place B.C. 59, which shows the stormy and turbulent character of its inhabitants. A certain Livinius Regulus, who had been banished from Rome by the Senate, gave a gladiatorial show in the amphitheatre at Pompeii. A quarrel arose between the Pompeians and a number of spectators who had come over from the neighbouring town of Nuceria. Hard words soon led to stone-throwing and this to a regular pitched battle, terminating in a massacre in which the townspeople, being more numerous and better armed, had the best of it. The Nucerians made their way to Rome to display their wounds; the children and relatives of the slain loudly demanded vengeance. The Emperor referred the matter to the Senate, the Senate to the Consuls. The result was that the Pompeians were forbidden to hold any performance of a similar character for the next ten years. A similar penalty was inflicted on Antioch by Marcus Aurelius after the revolt of Avidius.[2] The punishment must have seemed a hard one to the inhabitants of a pleasure-loving town, whether Italian or Oriental. The Pompeians consoled themselves with the proud reflection that at any rate their victory over their

---

[1] *Ann.*, xiv., 17.   [2] *Hist. Aug., Avid.*, ix., 1.

neighbours was beyond dispute.   They erected monuments in remembrance of it, and, in 1869, a fresco was discovered near the amphitheatre containing a view of the amphitheatre itself with the figures of combatants struggling on the steps at its entrance and in the neighbouring thoroughfares [1]; there can be no question as to the event here de-

CARICATURE OF THE MASSACRE OF THE NUCERIANS.

picted—it is the memorable feat of arms in which the Pompeians took such pride.

Next to the narrowness of the streets and the small size of the monuments, the feature which is most likely to surprise the visitor is to see so many houses without roof or covering.   One is almost tempted to think that one has strayed into some town in North Africa where the mild and equable

[1] Cf. Overbeck-Mau, Pompei, p. 14, where this design is reproduced.

climate renders the use of roofing unnecessary.[1] Here, however, Vesuvius has been at work; prior to the great eruption, the houses possessed not only roofs, but even balconies. We must, therefore, endeavour to replace them by an effort of imagination, a task which presents no great difficulty except in the case of the larger buildings. Of these latter but little is left to suggest the character of the original decoration, and the restorations of modern architects are based largely on pure hypothesis.

Private houses are more easily recognised than in our modern towns, owing to the fact that all, or nearly all, the windows open on to the inner court. Facing the street, the façades of the houses in the commercial thoroughfares were occupied by shops (*tabernæ*) of but little depth; in the other streets the houses merely present a blank wall, seldom showing any attempt at decoration. Some writers have tried to explain this arrangement on sanitary grounds. It seems simpler, however, to suppose that the ancients, spending, as they did, the best part of their time out of doors, naturally desired when they came home to be screened on all sides from prying eyes.[2]

No doubt the streets lost a good deal in animation by this; especially since vehicles were practically never employed inside the town itself, and were only used when people went into the country. The only places, therefore, where any great signs of bustle or

---

[1] As, for instance, in the *Prætorium* at Lambæsa; *cf.* Boissier, *L'Afrique romaine*, p. 111, Eng. version, Putnams, New York and London.

[2] *Cf.* the Pompeian *graffito*, No. 2400.

activity were to be seen, were the public buildings, the porticos, and a few streets occupied by shop-keepers.

At first sight all the buildings in Pompeii seem to date from the same period. The reason for this is not far to seek. The town had suffered serious damage from the earthquake of 63 A.D., and had only just been rebuilt. Indeed, the operation of rebuilding had not yet been entirely completed when the town was buried under the ashes of Vesuvius. This uniformity is, however, merely apparent. If we look more closely, paying special attention to the nature of the materials employed, we shall find evidence of more than one rough attempt at restoration; through and beneath the Pompeii of A.D. 79 we come upon remains of one or even two earlier cities. The last restoration, which took place after the year 63 A.D., is easily recognisable. Apart from the inscription in the temple of Isis, which must have been entirely rebuilt,[1] we find that the Pompeians, moved by some strange whim, had represented on a bas-relief in the Temple of Jupiter the result produced by the earthquake. Here we see porticos all out of the perpendicular, triumphal arches tottering on their foundations, and even the Temple of Jupiter itself in a state of collapse.

Before proceeding to describe some of the private

---

[1] "*N. Popidius . . . ædem Isidis terræ motu conlapsam a fundamento p. s. restituit.*" (N. Popidius restored at his own expense the Temple of Isis, which had been entirely destroyed by an earthquake).

houses, and the mosaics, paintings, and sculptures with which they were embellished, it will be well to say a few words concerning the monuments.

II

THE PUBLIC MONUMENTS

First come the various forums, chief among which stands the *forum civile*, with its temples, its basilica, and other monuments; the *forum boarium*[1] we need but mention in passing, and in regard to the triangular forum I may remind the reader that it is placed on a slight eminence from which a view of the town and its environs is obtained.

Knowing what we do of ancient customs, the places of general resort and the public baths[2] next deserve mention. Until recently, only two *thermæ* were known to have existed at Pompeii. A third has now been discovered. The number of these establishments and the lavish manner in which they were fitted up shows us how large a place the practice of bathing in public occupied in the life of the ancients.

There were two theatres: a small one with seating accommodation for about fifteen hundred persons, and—a somewhat unusual circumstance—roofed in; the other, which has nothing to distin-

[1] The cattle-market.

[2] This does not, of course, include baths attached to private houses. Quite recently (1894) a villa has been unearthed in the environs of Pompeii in which the complete fittings of an installation of private baths have been discovered intact.

guish it from those found elsewhere, must have held from five to six thousand spectators.

I have already had occasion to refer to the huge amphitheatre situated within the walls to the extreme east of the town. It was here that the whole town assembled whenever a performance was about to take place. Here appeared the gladiators, who are so frequently alluded to in the *graffiti*,[1] and whose principal barracks lay to the south-west, within the ramparts. Here took place the combats of wild beasts (*venationes*), of which announcements are still to be seen on the walls, and to which the whole country round flocked in thousands. Here, too, the famous conflict with the Nucerians occurred.

First among the temples, a Pompeian would probably have placed that of Jupiter, which formed the south-eastern boundary of the *forum civile*. To our modern ideas the Greek temple near the theatres seems most deserving of attention. It is true that architects are not entirely agreed as to the purpose for which it was intended, or the date of its erection.

The Temple of Isis also attracts the notice of visitors. As I have already mentioned, it had only just been rebuilt in A.D. 79, but the materials employed in its reconstruction date back to the last century of the republic. This fact seems to show that long before the Egyptian goddess had secured a footing in the capital she already had a band of worshippers in this little Campanian town.

[1] This term is applied to anything found written on the walls.

The only barracks in the place seem to have been the House of the Gladiators,[1] a large and spacious building, which was apparently a constant resort of the townspeople.

It is hardly necessary to refer again to the shops, which opened on the street and were let on leases, nor to the dwellings of the artisan class. Among these latter may be mentioned the fullers, a guild which furnished numerous situations and characters to the writers of the national drama and popular farces (*togatæ* and *atellanæ*). One of the finest frescos discovered at Pompeii, which has been reproduced times without number, represents a number of fullers at work.[2]

In regard to the houses of the wealthy, I must refer my readers to archæological manuals, nearly all of which contain reproductions or restorations of the houses of Pansa, of Sallust, of the Questor, etc. We may now proceed to examine some of the works of art with which these houses were adorned.

III

PRIVATE HOUSES

Here, again, it is impossible for me to go into details. In a later chapter we shall have to inquire

---

[1] In one of the *graffiti* a gladiator is called *Suspirium puellarum* (Thou for whom maidens sigh); in another *Puellarum decus* (Thou that art the delight of maidens).

[2] *E.g.*, in Smith's *Dictionary of Greek and Roman Antiquities*, *sub verbum* "Fullo."

as to the place occupied by art in the life of the ancients. For the present we are concerned solely with Pompeii and the museum at Naples. What impression does this latter leave on us at our first visit ? Our first feeling is undoubtedly one of profound surprise at the number and profusion of works of art which have been discovered in a town of such limited size, mingled with a no less profound admiration of a certain number of them which are veritable masterpieces. We feel as though we had been transported into another world than ours, in which the feeling for art is far more keen and more widely diffused. Even the humblest dwellings at Pompeii seem to have possessed their share of ornaments and to have contained some object in which their owners took pride: statuettes, mosaics, paintings, we find them all in the smallest shops no less than in the houses of the wealthy. The subjects treated are of the most varied character; in one place, we find specimens of fine art, mythological pictures, and large and beautiful statues; in another, we come upon tiny *genre* pictures dealing with subjects such as a Mignard, a Boucher, or a Watteau might have painted—some of them, indeed, being decidedly improper; elsewhere we meet with purely decorative productions, marine paintings, landscapes, or superb vases of glass or enamel; a little farther on are parodies and caricatures: among them we find masterpieces such as the dancing Faun, the drunken Satyr, the Narcissus, the Medea, or the charming group of dancing-girls.

A STREET IN POMPEII.

Here, as at Tanagra and Mycenæ, the objects discovered have proved the apprehensions of the critics
to have been ill-founded, and have conclusively
demonstrated the manifold resources of ancient art.
In this admirable museum in which they are assembled, we may pay all these paintings and statues
our tribute of unqualified admiration, provided always that we are careful not to forget that they
come from a small provincial town, and that what
we have before us are, in the majority of instances,
frescos, or rather replicas, and reduced copies of
larger works which have been here adroitly adapted
to the less spacious surroundings in which they were
placed. For an art which is said to have been in a
" moribund " condition,[1] the Roman school of
painting, so far as we may judge from what we see
here, seems to have been decidedly healthy.

But let us descend from the general to the particular, and briefly examine the two methods in
which the originality of Pompeian art is most plainly
shown, viz., painting and mosaic work.

Mosaics were very popular in the first century
A.D.[2] They enabled a guest on entering a house to
gauge by this external sign the wealth of its owner[3];
the Pompeians had a special weakness for them.

[1] This is the expression employed by Pliny the Elder, xxxv., 29
(5, 11); *cf. ibid.*, 50 (7, 32).

[2] *Cf.* the special works on the subject, or Friedlaender, *Mœurs
romaines*, iii., pp. 218 and 301 (French ed.).

[3] Epictetus, *Dissert.*, iv., 7, 37: " Thou settest great store on
dwelling in the midst of mosaics (ἐν ὀρθοστρώτοις); . . . and
on the possession of harp-players and tragedians."

In proof of this I need quote but a single instance, that of the House of the Faun, which contains scarcely a single mural painting, while the stucco on its walls is made to imitate inlaid marble, and its mosaics are among the finest that have come down to us from ancient times.

The mosaics and—as we shall see later on—the paintings also, may be divided into two classes; to the first belong those which are purely decorative in treatment, while the second includes reproductions of important pictures.

Subjects treated in the grand style were well represented at Pompeii. The whole of one room in the museum at Naples is filled with mosaics discovered in the *triclinia;* the adventure of Theseus and the Minotaur occurs more than once; then there are scenes from plays; a troupe of actors rehearsing before a poet; the famous watch-dog with the inscription *Cave canem* (Beware of the dog!); and above all, the superb mosaic found in the House of the Faun, which represents the battle of Arbela, and is probably taken from some celebrated painting of this event. It furnishes the sole information we possess in regard to the antique conception of historical painting.

It is a very curious thing—especially when one remembers what has been said concerning the amphitheatre and the fresco representing the conflict with the Nucerians—that among all the Pompeian mosaics there is not, so far as I am aware, a single one dealing with scenes in the arena, armed or fighting gladiators, contests between men and wild beasts, weapons of various kinds, etc., such as are so frequently treated on almost every conceivable scale, and often with striking success, in the Roman mosaics in the

THE MOSAIC OF THE DOG.

Lateran collection, at the Villa Borghese and else-where. This cannot have been due to any lack of enthusiasm for contests of this kind on the part of the Pompeians; we can only suppose, therefore, that it had not yet become the fashion among them to treat such subjects pictorially.

Similarly, I have never noticed anything analogous to those curious African mosaics,[1] in which the various buildings and pet animals belonging to the master of the house are depicted with their names and his subjoined.

In so far as *genre* pictures are concerned, Rome and Naples are on the same footing; in both places we find the same themes, and in some instances the scenes treated mutually supplement one another. There is, moreover, an important passage in the writings of Pliny,[2] in which he describes the fashion that prevailed in this branch of art during the first century A.D., and even though we no longer possess the mosaics of Sosus of Pergamus, the acknowledged master in this particular line, yet we have still at Rome and Pompeii copies and imitations of his best work.

Let us inquire what new element it was that he introduced. The artists who preceded him had learnt by experience that, when mosaic was employed as a vehicle for decoration, the most appropriate subjects invariably belonged to the domain of what we call " still life "—flowers, fruit, or edibles. The main point was to arrange them skilfully, relieving the whole by the introduction of actors' masks, or other ornaments of the kind; it was in this skill in

---

[1] *Cf.* Boissier, *L'Afrique romaine*, pp. 156 *et seq.*, p. 160, note; or Tissot, *Géographie comparée de la province romaine d'Afrique*, i., p. 360, where there is a reproduction of a mosaic representing the stables of Pompeianus.

[2] Pliny, xxxvi., 60, 184.

arrangement that the chief talent of the artist in mosaic lay. Sosus was the first to conceive the idea of representing these trophies of the table as they appear *after* instead of *before* a repast; thus, although the objects themselves remained the same, they conveyed an impression of greater realism. It thus became the fashion to depict "unswept" rooms (*asarotos œcos*, or, more briefly, *asarota*). Pliny adds the further detail that in one of his mosaics Sosus had introduced a number of doves alighted on the ground near a fountain; "one of them is drinking, and the shadow of her neck is shown in the water. The others plume themselves as they sit perched on the edge of the fountain." So far, no picture or mosaic has been discovered which includes this subject in its entirety; but we possess nearly all of it in detached parts, of some of which more than one replica is in existence. From what we know of the methods employed by the artists of ancient times, it is probable that the masterpieces of Sosus were divided into parts, certain details being either changed or omitted. A subject thus modified was regarded as being practically new and original.[1] Nearly the whole of this work of Sosus has come down to us reproduced in this piecemeal fashion. Thus we find doves pluming themselves, pecking up food, or drawing after them a string of pearls, in quite a number of specimens preserved at Pompeii itself, at Naples, and in the museum of the Capitol. In regard to the *asarotos*

[1] Friedlaender, *Mœurs romaines*, iii., p. 297 (French ed.).

properly so called, there exists a very clever reproduction of it in a mosaic in the Lateran collection,
signed with the name of Heraclitus.

I am not going to examine the paintings at Pompeii in detail.[1] I do not possess the necessary
knowledge, and, apart from this, the space at my
disposal would not permit of it. In the following
pages I shall merely endeavour to convey a general
impression of them, first of all premising that I do
not profess to speak as an expert.

Once we have got over the first natural feeling of
surprise which the paintings at Pompeii produce in
those whose eyes are accustomed to the colours and
subjects of modern pictures, we find that they exercise a certain fascination even before we have become familiarised with the themes habitually treated
in them, and while we are still under the influence
of the shock produced by their defects and by the
deplorable state to which some of them have been
reduced. Alike at Pompeii itself, and in Naples,
they stimulate curiosity. They possess a charm of
their own, and impart a keen sense of pleasure.
There is, however, this difference between them and
the mosaics, that we instinctively feel that, being
much the more fragile of the two, they have lost,
and are losing every day, something of their original
colour and brilliancy.

---

[1] For technical details the reader may consult Helbig, *Wandge-
mälde der vom Vesuv verschütteten Städte Campaniens*, Leipzig, 1868,
and *Untersuchungen über die Campanische Wandmalerei*, ibid, 1873,
Cf. also Gall, *Pompeiana*.

During the last fifty years a considerable number of them have faded almost to the point of complete disappearance, and this, not only on the walls of the houses, but even in the museum at Naples. Nevertheless, we need but go over the houses which have been unearthed during the last few years and note the brilliancy of the new frescos, and especially of the magnificent *lararia*, to realise that these paintings, though their technique may not be in harmony with modern ideas, occupy none the less an essential and highly original place in the decoration of the Pompeian houses.

Their defects are obvious; the painters who dashed them off in a few days laid no sort of claim to originality; the originals which they followed reflected the taste of the age, but it was an age of decadence. In a word, we have here a type of what the art of painting in Italy had become towards the end of the first century, a type which, though it may not always represent the high-water mark of the art, is yet in the main faithful enough. That this is so may be clearly proved by a comparison of the Pompeian frescos with those found elsewhere, such, for instance, as the frescos in the House of Livia; the same remark applies if we compare them with the mosaics, statues, bas-reliefs, or vases of the same period. The result of such a comparison is in no way unfavourable to the paintings at Pompeii.

Moreover, in so far as landscape paintings are concerned, the works of classical authors supply us with several instructive points of comparison.

It is useless to deny that all the landscapes we see in the museum at Naples strike us as being weak and confused; they are deficient in nearly every one of the qualities demanded by modern taste; yet we may rest assured that they are representative of the subjects and " handling " which the fashion of the period demanded at the hands of the artists who worked in this line.   This is plainly shown by a very curious passage in the writings of Pliny, which offers a close parallel to that quoted a few pages back [1] on the subject of mosaics.

" In the time of Augustus," writes Pliny, " S. Tadius was the first to conceive the idea of painting, at small cost (*minimo impendio*), rooms exposed to the open air (*sub dialibus*), with frescos representing country houses during the vintage season; or the seashore, or the banks of a river, with ships and fishermen." [2]   The general effect must have been

---

[1] *Cf.* p. 20.

[2] Pliny, xxxv., 116: "S. Tadius divi Augusti ætate, primus instituit, amœnissimam *parietum picturam ; villas et portus, ac topiaria opera*, lucos nemora ;   . . .   littora qualia quis optaret ; varias ibi obambulantium species aut navigantium aut villas adeuntium asellis aut vehiculis ; jam piscantes aucupantesque aut etiam vindemiantes." *Cf.* farther on, Chap. VIII., near the end, p. 195 of the present volume.   According to a paper recently contributed by M. Gauckler to the *Académie des Inscriptions*, the mosaic work recently discovered at Hadrumetum represents a large seascape, surrounded by geometrical ornaments interspersed with fruit and flowers ; the scene is a stretch of water, abounding in fish, across which flit the vessels of fishermen armed with lobster-pots, tridents, and drag-nets ; on the threshold are two nymphs erect, supported by two ocean deities seated.

pleasing, especially as in these combinations of land-scape and figure subjects a vein of humour was fre-quently introduced (*argutiæ facetissimi salis*). The landscapes at Pompeii furnish an accurate illustration of what Pliny describes.

The Pompeian paintings contained in the museum

FLYING FIGURES FROM POMPEIAN PICTURES

at Naples are undoubtedly the finest of those that were discovered in former times, and on its walls they are safe from injury. It is only, however, when we see them at Pompeii that we can form a proper idea of their true character. The recent de-cision, under which the frescos lately discovered are to be left in their places, will probably do much to prevent people from forming erroneous ideas in regard to them.   When we see them in their proper surroundings, it at once becomes obvious that these pictures were primarily intended to be decorative, and that their size, their finish, and the class of subjects treated were carefully adapted to the place they were to occupy, and to the general character of the house for which they were intended.   They were

FLYING FIGURES FROM POMPEIAN PICTURES

treated in much the same way as we do our carpets, the colour and pattern of which are chosen with an eye to the general effect of the room in which they are to be laid.   The ancients probably attached no greater importance to them than we do to the products of Kidderminster or Brussels.   A small *genre* painting, for instance, with a humorous inscription, representing, it may be, a traveller asking for a drink (*da frigidam* [1]), would be enclosed in a tiny frame along with a number of others of the same type on the wall of some wine-shop; while, on the other hand, a large fresco dealing with an heroic subject would be used to decorate a *triclinium* or a peristyle.

The mythological paintings are somewhat puzzling at first; indeed, the guides themselves are sometimes at fault and commit the most amusing errors. The total number of subjects which are treated is, however, not very great; we soon find our bearings, and once we have taken the trouble to follow up the sequence of the designs, we notice that endless changes are rung on the same theme. In the houses recently unearthed, and especially in that excavated in 1895, the paintings are replicas of subjects which have already been found elsewhere at Pompeii; Cupids weaving crowns, or plying some trade; the infant Hercules and the serpents; Pentheus; the punishment of Dirce,[2] etc.

Once we have thoroughly mastered the gamut of themes familiar to the Pompeian mind, we are better able to appreciate the intentional variations introduced here and there by the artist, and the endless caricatures of serious subjects which are to be met with at every turn. The painter's fancy oc-

---

[1] " Give (me) a cool (drink)."

[2] The legend of Dirce seems to have become familiar to the Romans at an early date, since we find a *leno* in Plautus (*Pseud.*, 195) making allusion to it in a threat addressed to one of the women belonging to his establishment.

casionally led him to group round these academic
compositions a quaint yet graceful train of Cupids,
Fauns, and Centaurs, with all sorts of possible and
impossible animals.   These fantastic creations are
more in harmony with our modern taste, which in-
clines to place the dancing-girls and gambolling
fauns far above the other frescos.   I scarcely think
that the ancients looked at them from this standpoint; they were inclined to assign everything,
pictures included, to its proper rank.   I can readily
imagine them pausing longer before some painting
in the grand style, representing heroic or tragic personages, such as Theseus, Orpheus, Io, Dirce, or
Medea.   Their large, expressive eyes seem to dwell
in the memory of all who have seen either the originals or good copies of them.

IV

THE GRAFFITI

In order to see Pompeii as it actually was, we
should have to borrow a pair of those fairy spectacles
which possessed the power of annihilating time and
space.   It would be delightful thus to follow, in
miniature, the comings and goings of life among the
ancient Romans, and to be present at some one of
the great gatherings of the little town.   As a matter
of fact, we can still do so—to a certain extent; the
only difference is that in place of looking we must
be content to listen.   Apparently speech was not

enough for the Pompeians, for some of them must needs write, while others read, and there were not a few of both classes. We are acquainted with their language and the walls have preserved their words[1]; we have but to read in our turn. And what do we find on these walls? In the first place, ordinary inscriptions, such as dedications, vows, epitaphs,

CARICATURES

thanksgivings; but side by side or interlined with these are words, phrases, and verses such as the Pompeians bandied about between themselves, the walls of public buildings being constituted the indiscreet bearers of these singular missives. These *graffiti* show us the life of the Pompeians in all its naked simplicity. Their vices, their impulsive char-

[1] As some one puts it—rather brutally—the walls are "the writing-paper of the mob."

acter, their easy-going ways, and, now and then, their grace.[1] The needle of the etcher could draw no more truthful or accurate picture.

Graffiti have been found at other places besides Pompeii, during the recent excavations in the Palatine at Rome and elsewhere.[2] Wherever found, they have been carefully collected. Even in the Sahara, near the wells or in the oases, Berber inscriptions have been met with, scratched with the point of a dagger on the wall of some grotto or on the face of some cliff. In this way conversations begun eighteen hundred years ago have been repeated by an unexpected echo which has continued to reverberate down to our day.

In reviewing these Pompeian *graffiti*, how may we classify them ? Let us first dismiss one section of them—the largest, no doubt—which is to be found in volume iv. of the *Corpus;* I mean those which consist of obscene insults. These deal with depths of human depravity which can interest none but the guardians of the law or students of medicine. Pompeii was a Greek town, which served as a sort of receptacle for the overflow of the population of Rome; it is scarcely to be wondered at, therefore, that many things the reverse of edifying were to be seen and heard in its streets. Nowadays we carefully obliterate scribblings of this kind; but the

---

[1] A selection of Pompeian inscriptions and *graffiti* will be found in Wilmann's *Exempla Inscr. Lat.*, Nos. 1899 *et seq.*

[2] M. Correra has recently issued an excellent monograph on the *Graffiti di Roma.*

Pompeians would seem to have been less squeamish. We may take it, however, that the existence of these objectionable *graffiti* is a guarantee of the genuineness of the remainder.

It would be a mistake to draw a distinction between the *graffiti* in verse and those written in prose. The verses have rarely, if ever, any claim to literary merit; they are mere hurried, slipshod impromptus, quite unpretentious, written in a kind of rhythmical prose, the point being elaborated more or less according to circumstances. A more intelligible classification would be to divide the *graffiti* according to the implement and colour by which they were produced. Where the writing has been picked out in two colours, as in the case of the *graffiti dipinti*, it is evident that they were deliberate and prepared; on the other hand, where the work has been done with a piece of charcoal, a stylus, or simply scratched on the stucco with the finger-nail, the presumption is that it was spontaneous and unpremeditated.

And first of all let us note the enormous number of these *graffiti* which have been collected at Pompeii.[1] As might be expected, they are specially numerous in places frequented by the multitude—in the basilica, on the walls of the covered theatre, and on those of the amphitheatre. Here they run into one another and intermingle in such marvellous abundance that we can understand the wonder expressed by a wit, in each of these three places, at

[1] Volume iv. of the *Corpus* (1871) contains 3255 of them.

the walls being able to support the weight of the inscriptions that had been written on them.[1]

Very often they run in what is evidently a series,
in which each succeeding scribbler makes fun of his
predecessors.[2]   Though the first writer usually tries
to safeguard himself, he generally leaves an opening
for the next scribbler to add some more or less ingenious insult, which, read by a passer-by, has all
the appearance of an admission.[3]   So much the worse
for him who reads.   Occasionally, however, the inscription contains a wish for the reader's prosperity.[4]

Not only do the *graffiti* join on and run into one
another, they sometimes even overlap and cover
each other.[5]   This popular epigraphy offers a
counterpart to the palimpsest MSS.

But the *graffiti* have yielded something more

---

[1] 2487 : "*Admiror, paries, te non cecidisse* ruinis,
         Qui tot scriptorum tædia sustineas.*"
(I marvel, O wall, that thou hast not fallen in ruins, loaded as
thou art with so many stupid inscriptions.)

[2] For instance, the first scribbler writes : " Qui hoc leget, nunquam posteac aliud legat et *nunquam sit salvus*" (May he who
reads this never read anything else, and may he never enjoy good
health).

The next comer, continuing the sentence, manages to turn the
wish back against the original writer, thus : "Qui supra scripsit "
([May] he who wrote the above [never enjoy good health])."

A third scribbler signifies his approval : "Vere dicis ! " (Thou
sayest truly).   But to which of the two does his approval refer?

[3] 2360 : ". . . qui legit." (I omit the objectionable word which
occurs repeatedly ; but there are many others of the kind.) *Cf.* the
note on No. 1121 in the *Corpus.*

[4] 1679 : "Valeat qui legerit " (Good health to him who reads).

[5] *Cf.* 1118 and 1119 and the reproduction in Pl. iii., 6.

valuable than mere salutations or rude jests. Scholars have been able from this wealth of new material
to deduce many important conclusions in regard to
the public life of the Pompeians.

Thus, thanks to the election bills found on the
walls,[1] M. Willems has been able to draw a most
interesting picture of the municipal elections at
Pompeii[2]; nor are the Pompeians alone represented
on these occasions. The aboriginal inhabitants of
a neighbouring town intervene and support their
candidate; *e. g.*, the *Campanienses* mentioned in
Nos. 470, 480.[3] Even artisans of the humblest class
were conscious of their influence and paraded their
recommendations at every corner.[4] We are in-

---

[1] The usual formula was *Rogo* or *rogamus* (sc. ut duumvirum
faciatis) (I or we beg you to make . . . *duumvir*); the duum-
viri were the two chief magistrates of the town and occupied a position equivalent to that of the consuls at Rome ; very frequently we
find it written *o*(ro) *v*(os) *f*(aciatis), followed by the formula *d*(ignum)
r(ei) *p*(ublicæ) ; or a more emphatic recommendation : *Facio* (sc.
duumvirum).

[2] Paris, Thorin, 1887.

[3] It is true that some authorities give a different explanation of the
word ; according to M. Henzen it refers to the Campanians domi-
ciled in Pompeii, while M. Willems believes it to be a term applied
to the north-eastern division of the town.

[4] *E.g.*, the bakers (*pistores*), the fishermen (*piscicapi*), the dyers
(*offectores*), the barbers (*tonsores*), the cooks (*culinarii*), the appren-
tices (*discentes*), the joiners (*lignarii* or *lignarii universi*), the *Isiaci*
and *Venerei* (sc. servi ; according to Willems, p. 36, n. 2, the worshippers of Isis and Venus) ; the *vicinis rogantibus* (loafers or
"corner-boys") ; the ball-players (*pilicrepi*). To these regular trade
guilds may be added the associations of pleasure-seekers such as the
seribibi or "late-drinkers," the *furunculi* or pilferers, and *dormientes*
or sluggards.

variably assured that the candidate in question is
" a splendid fellow who deserves well of the republic " (v[ir] p[ræclarus] d[ignus] r[ei] p[ublicæ]); " an
excellent young man of the highest character"
(adolescentem or juvenem egreg. frugi or probum);
one who will be able " to wisely direct the helm of
state."

Once they were returned, the elected magistrates
were carefully looked after by their constituents,
and we come upon more than one stirring admon-
ition to some ædile who had neglected to discharge
his duties properly, or who had been wanting in
vigilance; viz., vigila ! or dormis ! (wake up! thou
art asleep!).

Similarly, the receipts discovered some years ago
in the House of the banker Jucundus have enabled
archæologists to elaborate a number of ingenious
and detailed theories in regard to public works and
the method of apportioning them among contract-
ors, and in reference to the nature of the agree-
ments customary in this small Campanian town.
We cannot, however, enter here into subjects of
this kind, since to do so would involve the introduction of a host of technical details.

In like manner, we must pass over all those
graffiti which possess, as it were, a merely extrinsic
interest which can be indicated in a single word; the
Oscan inscriptions, of high antiquity, but few in
number; and the Greek inscriptions, also far less
numerous than the Latin graffiti.   More characteristic, perhaps, are the records left by children on

EVORVMSICIHABEASLANCESSENSPER...

SCIAENAESIVEESTVDIOSISEDVORVMSIC...

QVOSFACTINCENIOSPECTATOR

ILNVENISMO...IVSNOTALVITSEPVMIVS

PPENTISIV SVSSICLVISIBIFORTE...

WALL-WRITING.

their way home from school; they have made their
marks on the walls by tracing in their regular order
the Greek letters α β γ, which they had, apparently,
just been taught at school.

Nor need we linger over commonplace, practical
details, such as the rows of figures or tally-scores
referring to the quantity of wool given out to the
spinners, or to the number of garments received by
the fuller for the purpose of cleaning; the dates of
the birth of domestic animals; the daily programme
of work for slaves; cookery receipts, etc. So, too,
with notices and advertisements, such as "An excellent inn will be found on the right!" and other
similar substitutes for the modern signboard. Such
inscriptions, if less elaborate, yet belong to the same
category as the Pompeian amphora, which bears the
legend

"LIQUAMEN OPTIMUM,"[1]

doubtless applied when it was laid down in the
cellar.

We find a counterpart to our modern posters in
the advertisements embellished with drawings which
inform passers-by of the day and hour fixed for
combats in the amphitheatre. The Pompeians seem
to have had a special enthusiasm for amusements of
this kind. In one bill a thrilling hunting spectacle
is promised, with every possible comfort for the
spectators, including awnings to protect them from
the sun. The names of the gladiators are given,

[1] "Exceptionally fine liquor."

accompanied by portraits.   This was a practice
probably borrowed from Rome, since we find it
mentioned by Horace.[1]   In the provinces, however,
it would seem that admiration for these seductive
works of art was not confined to slaves.   Other bills
describe missing articles of property, and promise a
suitable reward to the finders.

Among the *graffiti* which express some definite
sentiment, by far the more numerous—as might
naturally be expected—are those due to lovers.
Their general drift may be readily imagined—vows,
regrets, imprecations, denunciations ; nothing is
omitted, not even insults of the grossest type.
Here are a few specimens.   Insults in Greek such
as *Atimetus* (ἀτίμητος, dishonoured one!).   Insults
in Latin (only a certain number of them will bear
quotation): *glaber es* (thou art bold!), *senium* (old
fool!), *spado, plane spado* (eunuch!), *fur, furuncule*
(thief!).   Here is one of the mildest in the whole
collection: " *Ut percat rogo ; in cruce figaris* " (I
hope he may die ; may crucifixion be your fate!)

One of the less ill-natured methods employed by
these would-be wits was to mention two names, the
second of the two in the genitive, and to add the
word *cinædus* (minion) after them.

It must have been difficult to resist so simple a
means of revenge; a fragment of charcoal was all
one required; a caricature was easily added if the
text stood in need of a commentary.   Catullus
(xxxvii.) tells us that, once his verses have been

[1] *Sat.*, ii., 7, 96.

fixed to the wall of the *salax taberna* (disorderly house) in which his enemies are staying, they will sting them like scorpions. More than one Pompeian has availed himself of this method, and has done his best to drive the poisoned dart into his enemy or enemies.

But the scribblers are no less lavish of prayers and threats than they are of insults; it is an epitome of antique life—nay, an epitome of human life in more than one age. Thus we find such inscriptions as "*felix feliciter*"; "*successus*"; "*kalos*" (καλῶς); "*Plurimam salutem ubique*"; *Januarius* (sc. *kalendas*) *nobis felices multis annis*"; *Quid faciem vobis, ocelli Lusci ?*" [1]

We are not spared the inevitable tags from poems dealing with love and its torments, even the artificial metaphors of the amatory poets being frequently imitated.[2] Here again, as elsewhere, brevity is often the soul of wit: *e. g.*, Ψ (for ψυχή = my soul); καλος (How handsome thou art!); *vale, felix, euge* (Farewell! be happy! be of good cheer!). Side by side with these invocations and names such as *Aphrodite* and *Lalage*, we find the lament of a lover who is separated from his fair one.

[1] "May you be happy !" "Good luck !" "May all go well with you !" "Good health attend you everywhere !" "A happy New Year to us and many of them !" "What would I not do for you, dear eyes of Luscus ?"

[2] As, for instance, in the following distich—

"Quisquis amat, calidis non debet fontibus uti :
   Nam *nemo flammas ustus amare potest*."

(Lovers should avoid warm baths; for he who burns cannot enjoy the fire.)

Some of the verses are very charming; for instance, the well-known quatrain addressed to a mule-driver:

"Amoris ignes si sentires, mulio,
   Magi properares ut videres Venerem.
   Bibisti : iamus ; prende lora et execute.
   Pompeios defer, ubi dulcis est amor meus."[1]

It is evident that the Pompeians were a happy, careless people, who managed to extract as much enjoyment out of life as possible.

Besides the passion of love, other emotions such as vanity, malice, and plain common sense find apt expression; take, for instance, the following protest veiled under the form of an ironical compliment:

"Tu enim me doces?"

or

"Mulus hic muscellas docuit."[2]

In the following we have a sort of proverb which recalls to mind one of the tasks imposed on Psyche by Venus:

"Moram si quæris,
   Sparge milium et collige."[3]

In spite of, or, it may be, because of the fact that

[1] "Didst thou but feel the flames of love, mule-driver, thou wouldst hasten, that thou mightest behold Venus herself. Thou hast drunk : then let us go ; take your reins and shake them. On to Pompeii, where my dear one dwells."

[2] "What, are *you* to give me lessons !" "Look at this mule who has undertaken to educate the tiny flies." (There is probably an allusion to some popular fable here).

[3] "If you want to kill time, scatter millet seed, and pick it up again " (*i. e.*, seed by seed, or counting it as you go).

Pompeii, like Naples, was a place to which people went in quest of pleasure (*urbs otiosa*), imprecations on idle loiterers are common enough. Here is one, couched in rather halting verse, which was found written up above a serpent (and therefore presumably on the wall of a house belonging to some apothecary of ancient times), in a street of doubtful reputation:

"*Otiosis* locus hic non est ; discede, *morator*."[1]

This is a more elegant variant of the direct adjuration which occurs rather frequently:

"*Hic tu, quid moraris ?*"[2]

Some of the inscriptions are aimed at members of a particular trade ; the following is addressed to an innkeeper who

"Vendit *aquam*, bibit ipse *merum ;*"

or, in another place:

> "Suavis vinaria,
>   Sitit, rogo vos";

and

"Valde sitit Calpurnia. Tibi dicit val."[3]

A little farther on, a parasite, mindful of the

[1] "This is no place for idlers ; pass on, thou lounger !"
[2] "Here you ! What are you loitering for ?"
[3] "He sells water, but drinks wine himself." "Charming hostess, it is thirsty weather ; some wine, I pray you." "Calpurnia is very thirsty ; she makes haste to say 'good-day.'"

necessities of his profession, calls down all sorts of blessings on the heads of those who invite him to dinner, but has no words hard enough for those who neglect to do so.

Even philosophy of the type beloved by Mr. Martin Tupper is represented almost *ad nauseam*, as witness the following maxim:

"*Minimum* malum fit contemnendo *maxumum*."[1]

Elsewhere we find some conundrum (*zetema*) propounded, the answer to which occasionally baffles modern ingenuity.   This is a kind of pastime much in favour with children, and it is at the same time an unfailing characteristic of the literature of a decadent age.

At Pompeii, as at Rome, pompous formulæ and the style appropriate to inscriptions were both known and liked.   Now and then this style is parodied, as in the following:

"Pyrrhus Chio collegæ sal.
Moleste fero quod audivi
Te mortuum.   Itaque val."[2]

Compare with this the following burlesque epistle:

"Virgula Tertio suo: Indecens es."[3]

[1] "A trifling ailment if neglected may become very serious."
[2] "Pyrrhus to his colleague Chius.   I was much grieved to hear of thy death.   I therefore wish thee good health" (or "farewell"; there is an intentional ambiguity).
[3] "Virgula to her dear Tertius: Thou art unseemly."

The enraptured lover sometimes ventures on a pun:

"Commiseresce mihi; da *veniam* ut *veniam*."

This reminds one of:

"*Verus* hic ubi stat
Nihil veri." [1]

In another place some student of rhetoric has seen fit to scribble up an obscene parody on one of the finest passages in the orations of Cicero.[2] Another gives rein to his poetic fancy by dovetailing together two verses, one taken from Propertius, the other from Ovid:

"Candida me docuit nigras odisse puellas;
Odero, *si potero; sed non invitus amabo*." [3]

But on a previous page I have already quoted enough from the Pompeian poets to enable my readers to judge of their quality.

[1] "Have pity on me; pardon me and let me come to thee." (The play upon words here is quite untranslatable.) "Where *Verus* is, there is nothing *veracious*."

[2] Verr., v., 161. *Cf. Corpus Inscr. Lat.*, iv., 1261.

[3] "A blonde taught me to hate brunettes; I will hate them if I can, but loving would come much easier."

CHAPTER II

THE majority of travellers, on entering a town for the first time, instinctively make for the principal centre of public resort.

From it they draw their conclusions as to the number, wealth, and character of the inhabitants, and also as to the importance of the town itself. So, too, most people on arriving in Rome at once seek out the *forum Romanum*, this being the spot their minds are full of. They know that it was here that the orators " dwelt " who passed their lives in pleading causes and haranguing the populace; here were recorded the popular suffrages which decided the fate of the most distant provinces; here the glories of triumphal processions were displayed; here raged the infuriated mob amid the glare of blazing houses and temples; here soldiers and statesmen swayed by their speeches what was known as the Roman people (*populus Romanus*). The newly arrived visitor begins by concentrating into this tiny spot the crowded historical associations of half a

THE FORUM
in the first years of the Republic

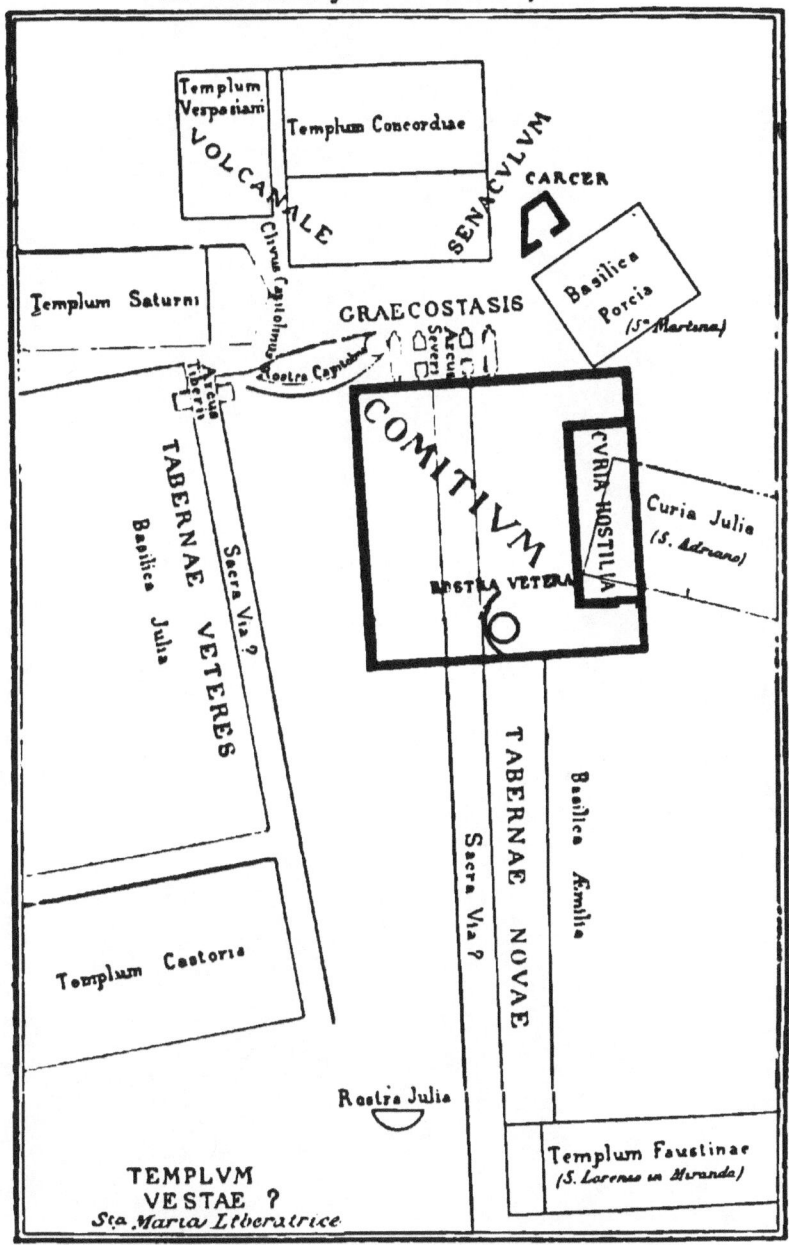

After Detlefsen

MAP OF FORUM.

score of centuries. As a matter of course, he is
doomed beforehand to disappointment.

This disappointment will probably tend to diminish by the time he has visited the other centres,
where Cæsar, Augustus, Nerva, and Trajan had
erected so many glorious monuments, of which but
a few wondrous columns now survive. In the case
of the *imperial forums*, we may hope to restore, by
sheer force of imagination, something of the general
effect of what once existed. What we may call *the*
forum, *i. e.*, the forum of the republic, has been less
fortunate. Though many of its monuments lie prostrate, the removal of the rubbish which once covered
it from the *Campo Vaccino* renders any mistake in
regard to its dimensions quite impossible; our fancy
is at once checked in its flight and brought to earth
stripped of all illusion: it is hopeless to think of
peopling so tiny a space with the memory of so many
great events.

I

*CONDITION OF THE FORUM TOWARDS THE CLOSE
OF THE REPUBLIC*

Let us try, then, to brush aside for a moment the
historic memories on which our illusions rested, and
endeavour, in the first place, to realise clearly what
it is that we have before our eyes. The excellent
article by M. Thévenat, recently published in Saglio's *Dictionary*, renders it unnecessary for me to
give a list of works on the Forum. I trust that the
plan annexed hereto, which is reproduced from that

of M. Dutert, will enable the reader to form a general idea of the forum and to follow clearly what I am about to say concerning it.

Let us begin with a chronological list of some of the buildings which serve as landmarks in its history. On the north stood the *Curia Hostilia*, said to have been built by King Tullus Hostilius; it was destroyed by fire during the obsequies of Clodius; was rebuilt, first by the son of Sylla, then by Augustus in the year 29 B.C., then again by Domitian, and finally by Diocletian. Hard by, but a little lower down, was the tribune from which orators were accustomed to speak. After the capture of the Latin fleet in 338 B.C., the tribune of the *comitium* was decorated with *rostra* (prows of vessels). Julius Cæsar moved them to the north-western extremity of the forum. At the opposite end, Augustus built the *ædes Divi Julii* and other *rostra* called the *Rostra Julia*. Of the two basilicas which occupied the north-eastern side of the forum, one, the *Basilica Porcia*, was built by the elder Cato in 184 B.C. It perished in the conflagration which destroyed the *Curia Hostilia* during the funeral of Clodius. The second, the *Basilica Æmilia*, built in the year 179 B.C. by the Censors M. Fulvius and M. Æmilius Lepidus, was reconstructed in the year 50 B.C. by L. Æmilius, and, later on, in the reign of Tiberius, it was restored and decorated by M. Lepidus.

On the opposite side of the forum, between the temples of Castor and Saturn, stood the *Basilica*

Julia. Begun by Julius Cæsar, this basilica was completed by Augustus, and was restored and enlarged after a fire. It was again restored by Severus (199) and by Diocletian (282) in consequence of two other fires. On the right of the basilica stood the Temple of Castor, of which three fine columns still survive; dedicated in 482 B.C. and restored in 119 by the consul L. Metellus Dalmaticus, it was rebuilt in the reign of Augustus (in the year 6 A.D.) by Tiberius and Drusus from the spoils obtained in the Germanic campaign. To the left of the Basilica Julia was the Temple of Saturn, eight granite columns of which still remain. It was here that the public treasury (*ærarium*) was kept.

In the intervening space, two monuments of a later date attract attention owing to the fact that they still remain standing, viz., the triumphal arch erected in honour of Severus and his sons after their victories over the Parthians in 203 A.D., and the column raised in honour of the Emperor Phocas by the exarch Smaragdus in 608 A.D.

Having now made the round of the forum, we may proceed to consider it as a whole.

In shape it was a somewhat irregular trapezium, rather more than 150 yards long and about 50 yards in width.[1]

---

[1] These were the dimensions prescribed by tradition. To be more precise, the forum was some 170 yards in length by from 38 to 51 yards in width at its broader and narrower ends respectively. Now, the *forum civile* at Pompeii measured 163 by 51 yards. It is a singular fact that this latter figure coincides with the maximum width of the *forum Romanum*.

According to Vitruvius, whose rule for the construction of a forum throws a vivid light on the
requirements of political life in ancient times, the
following is a list of the buildings by which it ought
to be surrounded : several temples, one or more basilicas, the public treasury, the gaol, and the *curia* or
senate-house.   And these are the very edifices which
we find in the *forum Romanum :* in the matter of
temples there is first of all the Capitol, then the
temples of Saturn, of Concord, of Castor, and Vespasian (the site of this last is marked by the fine
columns which stand on the left of the Temple of
Saturn).   As to basilicas, there were three large
ones, the Porcian, Æmilian, and Julian.   To complete the list we have the prison (*Tullianum*), the
Gemoniæ, and the *curia*. The triumphal arches, columns, and statues are, in a sense, mere accessories.

There is a sentence in the writings of Livy[1] which
throws a light on the condition of the forum at the
close of the Second Punic War.   At that time a
number of the buildings surrounding it[2] were set on
fire by a Campanian mob, who sought in this way
to avenge the overthrow of their country; the shops
which stood on the sites afterwards occupied by the
basilicas perished in this conflagration, viz., what
were known as the " old " shops (VII *tabernæ
veteres*) on the site of the *Basilica Julia*, and the
" new " shops, occupied for the most part by
money-changers (*argentariæ quæ nunc novæ*) on the

[1] Livy, xxvi., 28.
[2] " Pluribus simul locis et iis diversis, *circa forum.*"

site of the *Basilica Æmilia*. The fire also extended
to the space occupied by the prison, towards the
scalæ Gemoniæ, at the foot of the Capitol, between
the Temple of Saturn and the *curia*. In those
days this place was called *Lautumiæ*, probably because there had originally been quarries there. The
conflagration raged for a day and a night, and destroyed a large number of private houses; indeed,
the sacred buildings at the eastern extremity, close
to the foot of the Palatine, which were regarded as
central features of the city,—I refer to the *Regia*, or
dwelling of the *Summus Pontifex*, and the Temple
of Vesta,—only narrowly escaped.

This was the arrangement that prevailed in the
forum before the Greek civilisation had obtained a
foothold in Rome. But from that time forward,
advantage was taken of every occasion on which any
of the buildings were destroyed either by accident
or, as was more often the case, by fire, to enlarge
and beautify it. The forum had, at an early date,
become absolutely crowded with statues and profusely ornamented with columns. The honour of
having a statue erected to one in this place was
highly prized; the Senate regarded this as an excellent means of arousing among the citizens a kind
of rivalry which was productive of great benefit to
the commonwealth. The columns gave the place
an imposing aspect. Towards the close of the Empire, even the haughty Constantine, accustomed to
the splendours of Constantinople and other Asiatic
cities, stood still in amazement in front of the *rostra*

as he scanned the whole scene before him with wondering eyes.[1]

The regular *habitués* of the forum were not slow to take advantage of the pillars and statues with which it was adorned. Both at Rome and in the provinces they served as points of vantage from which one could see without being seen, and which rendered it easy to evade tiresome acquaintances or creditors.

From all points of the city the steps of the Roman citizen led him to the forum; the habit became stereotyped into a phrase; but once there, if he did not wish to be seen, he well knew how " to take refuge behind a statue or hide behind a column."[2] This practice throws an amusing side-light on ancient life, and is therefore well worth noting.

The Forum as the Centre of Political, Commercial, and Religious Life at Rome, where all Ceremonies and Festivals were Celebrated

Let us see if we cannot, by a closer examination, manage to discover here, in what was practically the

[1] Ammianus Marcellinus, xvi., 10, 13 : "Cum venisset ad rostra, perspectissimum priscæ potentiæ forum *obstupuit*, perque omne latus, quo se oculi contulissent, *miraculorum* densitate præstrictus " (When he had reached the *rostra* he contemplated the forum with wonder, recognising the evidence born by it to the former power of the Roman people, and gazing round him, stood amazed at all the marvels he descried).

[2] Sidonius, *Ep.*, i., 11, 7 : "*fugere post statuas, occuli post columnas.*" Apuleius, *Metam.*, iii., 1 : " *Columnis implexi . . . statuis dependuli . . . semiconspicui*" (Hidden behind columns . . . leaning from the statues . . . half concealed). *Cf.* also S. Basil and S. Ambrose, etc.

centre of Rome, just as Rome itself was the centre
of the Empire, some sort of picture of Roman customs and institutions.

1. It has been rightly pointed out that in all the
towns of antiquity the forum, as the principal thoroughfare of the city, was the natural centre of political, commercial, and religious life, and the scene of
all festivals arranged for the benefit of the populace.
Let us endeavour to ascertain how far the *forum
Romanum* complied with this fourfold purpose.

In the list of objects to which the forum was devoted, set forth above, one group stands out from
the rest. It is quite evident that the *comitium*, the
rostra, and the *curia*, and the Temple of Saturn (in
which were kept the tables of the law, the decrees
of the State, and the public exchequer), all of which
stand close together on the north-west, must here
represent the political element. The arrangement
of the buildings accurately reflects the relative importance enjoyed by each order in the body politic.
The *curia* (or senate-house) dominates all the others.
Here sat the members of the order which ruled
supreme in affairs of State—indeed, the only one
which counted for anything at first; a little lower
down came the *nobles*, who were the first to take
part in the task of government; then came the *plebs*
(or common people), to whom the aristocracy were
obliged to yield their share of power. It was in
this space of but a few square yards that the fiercest
of the struggles that marked the early days of the
republic were decided, such as the contests between

4

ultra-conservatives like Appius, who regarded themselves as the official champions of the ancient constitution, and men like Canuleius and Terentius,
who led the advocates of a new order of things in
their attack on the citadel of time-honoured privileges.   It took the popular party and their leaders
not merely years, but even centuries, before they
succeeded in obtaining a foothold on that rung of
the political ladder to which they aspired; by the
time the *plebs* became, or believed itself to be, victorious, and the *comitium* had come to be on a level
with the *curia*, the days of the republic were already
numbered.

We must not forget, however, that the forum
itself and all the various parts of which it was composed were overshadowed by the Capitol,[1] the true
seat and emblem of empire.   The Latin poets, when
they sought to claim imperishable glory for their
writings, invariably associated them in the sight of
posterity with this immovable citadel, which was to
remain for ever mistress of the world.[2]   Nor did

---

[1] The conspirators in Shakespeare's play (*Julius Cæsar*) are made
to declare with an ambiguity which is evidently intentional : " And
the high east stands, as the Capitol, directly here."

[2] Horace, *Odes*, iii., 30, 9 :

> ".   .   .   *dum Capitolium*
> *Scandet* cum tacita virgine pontifex."

(So long as the pontiff shall ascend the Capitol accompanied by
the silent virgin.)   And Virgil, *Æn.*, ix., 447 :

> " *Dum* domus Æneæ *Capitoli immobile saxum*
> Accolet, imperiumque pater Romanus habebit."

(So long as the house of Æneas shall stand on the immovable rock
of the Capitol, and a Roman leader shall retain the Empire.)

their prophetic instinct altogether deceive them. So long as the Empire lasted *Jupiter Capitolinus* held his ground; he showed a brave front against the new religion and the invasion of the barbaric hordes; but alas! what a pitiable end has been his, now that the vulgar tongue has degraded him into a *Campidoglio* (literally, " the field of oil "), who overlooks the *Campo Vaccino* (or field of the cows).

2. So much for the political element. Let us next inquire how the forum, in the beginning at any rate, came to be associated with the commercial life of Rome. In all the Italian forums there seem to have been two divisions placed side by side, one of which was devoted to public business, the other to commerce. To this fact may have originally been due the distinction between the *comitium* and the *forum* proper (literally, the market-place). At Rome, if any such distinction ever existed, it must have vanished at a very early date. The trading community did not fail, however, to secure a fairly extensive space for itself. The southern end of the trapezium formed by the forum was, as we have seen, at first occupied by shops pure and simple (*tabernæ veteres*). In the space left vacant on the north side were placed the offices of the money-changers (*tabernæ argentariæ*). These having been destroyed by fire, new ones were built in their place, known as the *tabernæ novæ*. These two rows of shops were later on abolished and replaced by two basilicas, on the north by the *Basilica Æmilia*, on the south by the *Basilica Julia*. Thus buildings

of a purely utilitarian character were obliged to make room for great public monuments. Similarly, at an earlier epoch, the public thoroughfare was used as a market, but, the space being insufficient, the markets were, later on, transferred elsewhere. In this way market-places for the sale of bread (*forum pistorium*), vegetables (*forum olitorium*), and fish (*forum piscatorium*) came to be established outside the forum proper.

3. On the other hand, we find that the forum continued to be the centre of religious life at Rome: as the city increased in size, religious edifices came to occupy more and more space there. Although there were plenty of temples built in other parts of the city, yet here in the space between the Capitol and the Temple of Vesta they never ceased to multiply, and were more and more magnificently decorated each time that it became necessary to rebuild them, until finally they formed a splendid fringe round the whole extent of the forum.

4. Lastly, we have the life of the streets. This was far more stirring among the ancients than it is with us, and the forum was the indispensable centre to and from which it ebbed and flowed. When any citizen of importance was buried, his ancestral images were paraded through it in solemn procession, and one of his relatives addressed the multitude from the *rostra*. On occasions like this, or on any of the public holidays when banquets or gladiatorial contests were held, it was in the forum that they took place. But how was it possible to see them in comfort ?

In a passage quoted by Pliny,[1] Varro tells us that above the *tabernæ veteres* there were galleries (*mænia*) covered with pictures dealing for the most part with incidents in the gladiatorial games. Elsewhere[2] we read of a certain *columna Mænia* (*i. e.*, a sort of raised platform or barbican); it had been erected in 318 B.C. by the censor C. Mænius. From its summit he, and his family after him, were enabled to obtain a view of the spectacles in the forum. These privileged spectators (and there were others besides the *Mænii*) were the objects of a good deal of envy, and C. Gracchus achieved great popularity by doing away with the scaffoldings that had been erected all round the forum which were let out for hire. By this measure, he rendered it possible for the poor to see all there was to be seen from these places without payment.[3]

Apart from the crowds on high-days and holidays, there was, of course, the everyday bustle of street life. In the course of time, however, the forum would seem to have been more or less deserted by traffic. In Rome, as in all other great cities, the world of fashion, with all the host of underlings it carried in its train, seems to have attached itself first to one place, then to another. In the time of Juvenal[4] its favourite haunts seem to have been the Temple of Isis in the *Campus Martius*, the Temple

---

[1] Pliny, xxxv., 113 and 25.
[2] Asconius in Cic., *Div. in Cæc.*, 16.
[3] Plutarch, *Caius Gracchus*, xii., 3.
[4] Juvenal, ix., 23.

of Peace in the *forum transitorium*, and those of
Cybele and Ceres on the Palatine; for, as the satirist bitterly remarks, '' where is there a temple to be
found which does not contain some woman of light
character ?'' (*nam quo non prostat femina templo*).

II

HISTORICAL MEMORIES ASSOCIATED WITH THE FORUM

We may as well admit the fact at once; this place
and the ruins it contains are not interesting in themselves; still less are they likely to affect us deeply.
They can only influence us through the channels of
memory and the imagination: the chief and sole
attraction of the forum lies in the history of its past.
Indeed, it is doubtful whether the case would be
much altered even if some enchanter's wand were
to give us back the whole or a part of the buildings
which once graced it, in place of the dozen or so of
columns and the few paving-stones now so jealously
guarded. It is not so much the buildings themselves
that appeal to us as the great events of which they
were witnesses: it was from this tiny oblong space
that the mighty influences which culminated in the
conquest of the universe first proceeded, and in the
days when Rome was free it was here that the fate
of nations either was, or was supposed to be, decided. These are the thoughts which occur to every
modern visitor, and it is with this aspect of the
forum alone that we need concern ourselves. We

must, therefore, hark back to those historic memories which we had put on one side for the moment; and after we have dealt with them, we shall have a word or two to say in regard to the narrowness of its dimensions which caused our first feeling of disappointment.

And first of all we will try to catch some echo of the voices which once resounded here, some memory of those eventful days that still live in the pages of history. The very name of the forum is suggestive of eloquence. Here the funeral orations were delivered; here magistrates, great statesmen, and, in later days, the emperors themselves, were wont to harangue the multitude. Here " dwelt " the orators, and those who aspired to become orators. It was in the forum that the famous semi-political trials of Verres and of Milo took place. Victorious generals, in all the pomp of their triumphal processions, marched across it; here the festivals and great games were held, when the multitude—a spectacle in itself—flocked in thousands to feast its eyes on the idols of the hour, the leaders who presided on such occasions, and on their paternal gods who were borne along in their chariots of state (*tensæ*).

In troublous times, life in the forum was strung to a higher pitch than ever. It furnished the battle-ground on which every question was decided. The opposing factions took up their positions long beforehand, or struggled for places at either extremity of the place and in the buildings adjoining it—in short, at every point whence those rushes and charges which swept through the crowd " like a torrent "[1] might be organised.   Sometimes they entrenched themselves a short distance away in one of the houses in the vicinity.   Metellus, when he wished to make headway against Saturninus and Glaucia, collected his partisans " like cattle " in his house on the Palatine.[2]   From this eminence they doubtless sallied forth at a given signal along the *Via Sacra* into the forum.

But the strategic points most keenly disputed were the temples in the forum itself, especially those of Saturn and Castor; other favourite points of vantage were the *rostra* and the entrance to the *curia*.   Political feeling ran very high, each faction employing troops of gladiators against the other; before long, stones would begin to fly and swords were drawn, and since the interests at stake were often considerable, we need not be surprised that now and then terrible scenes were witnessed, and that the earth more than once ran red with Roman blood.

The forum was the scene of numberless great events, including many which were not marked by bloodshed: here in this corner were burnt the bodies of Clodius and of Cæsar.   The place serves as a kind of frame for the history of the republic.   It was here that it drew its last dying breath.   Men prated ceaselessly of reason, justice, and liberty,

[1] Appian : " οἷον χείμαρροι."

[2] Glaucia once told him (*De. Or.*, ii., 263): " Villam in Tiburte habes, *cortem* in Palatio " (Thou hast a villa at Tibur, but in the Palatine a stable).

when, for a long time past, force had been the sole
arbiter of events; it is true that those who employed
it declared that they were merely " repelling force
by force." [1]

From the republican standpoint these are gloomy
memories. But the plebeians in the time of the
Empire, who only asked for something to amuse
them and plenty to eat, were scarcely more worthy
of our regard. The Emperor Aurelian, who seems
to have thoroughly understood them, in writing to
the prefect of the *Annona*, assures him that " no joy
could equal that of the Roman people after a good
meal." [2] About the same period someone proposed
that the people should be supplied with wine free of
charge. " In that case," replied the Prætorian
prefect, " the next thing they will ask for will be
fowls and geese." [3]

Cruelty was a feature in every age of Roman history, under the Republic and the Empire alike. If
we would assure ourselves of this, we need but turn
our eyes toward the *rostra* and that corner of the
forum which lay between the Capitol and the *curia*.
There were the *scalæ Gemoniæ*, to which the bodies
of executed criminals were dragged, and there, too,
the *gradus gemitorius*, or stairway of anguish. As
a rule, only the heads of criminals decapitated in
prison were exposed. But in the blood-stained days

---

[1] *Pro Milone*, 30 : " vi victa vis."

[2] Vopiscus, *Aur.*, 47 : " *neque* enim populo Romano *saturo quid-
quam* potest esse *lætius.*"

[3] *Ibid.*, 48, 8.

of Claudius the lifeless bodies even of women were cast down from here.   It was hither that the multitude came to view the dead bodies of Sejanus and his ill-fated children before they were dragged down to the Tiber by means of hooks.   It was hither that Vitellius was hurried amid the insults of the Flavian soldiery, who insisted on bringing him to the spot whence he had caused the body of Flavius Sabinus to be hurled.   It was on the *rostra* that the heads of those who had been proscribed under Sylla, under Marius and the triumviri, were exposed.   But enough of these painful memories. Let us endeavour, if possible, to banish them from our minds.

In the course of the last twenty-five years both the forum and Palatine have been cleared of the rubbish which had covered them, and at one time it seemed as though a good part, at any rate, of ancient Rome was about to be brought back to light. We owe a debt of gratitude to those who undertook this task, but I greatly fear that the result will, after all, leave very much the same impression as that produced on Montaigne at the sight of the old *Campo Vaccino* and the Rome of his day.   He thus expresses himself in a passage which is at once humorous and forcible [1]:

" We see nothing of Rome but the sky under which it stood and the foundations on which it rested; such knowledge as we have of it is of a purely abstract and

[1] *Voyage*, 1774 edition, ii., p. 114.

contemplative character; it is none of it derived through the agency of our senses. Those persons who affirm that we can, at any rate, see the ruins of Rome, go too far; for the ruins of such a terrible organism as Rome would reflect more honour and reverence on its memory; there is nothing left of Rome but its grave. The world, impatient at its long supremacy, had first of all broken and shattered every limb of that marvellous body, and finding that even after it lay dead, prostrate, and disfigured it was still repulsive, posterity proceeded to bury its very ruins [1]; the buildings of that bastard Rome which is now being dovetailed on to these ancient hovels, though they have much that is calculated to arouse the admiration of the present age, remind me more than anything else of the nests which sparrows and rooks are building in the arches and walls of those churches which the Huguenots have just destroyed in France."

III

THE SMALL SIZE OF THE FORUM: HOW IT IS TO BE EXPLAINED

But how came it that this so-called " nest " of Roman life was of such modest dimensions ? The forum, even when cleared of its rubbish, entirely fails to satisfy our preconceived idea of it. There

[1] Count Tyskiewicz (*Revue archéologique*, 1896, p. 132), in writing of the excavations undertaken by him at Rome and in the environs, mentions the following significant fact: " In the environs of Rome . . . the layer of deposit with which the earth is covered is not a thick one; it varies from 18 in. to about 4 ft. 6 in., whereas inside the town itself it is never less than 8 yards in depth, and is sometimes as much as 25 to 30 yards deep."

can be no question but that the space has always
remained the same: how was it, then, that this, the
most frequented spot in all Rome, was so limited
in area ? How did the ancients manage to crowd
into it all the buildings and monuments, not to
speak of the statues, which are mentioned in history?

Here again let us listen to what Montaigne says.
Even in his day people seem to have felt a difficulty
in finding places for all the edifices referred to by
ancient writers within so small a space:

" He [Montaigne] came to the conclusion, on good
evidence, that the shape of the mountains and declivities
had in no way changed since ancient times, and believed
that in many places we were walking on top of whole
houses. He declared that he was unable to understand,
in view of the scanty space and room available on any of
the seven hills, and particularly on the two most famous
ones of all, the Capitoline and the Palatine, how space
for so great a number of edifices can have been found
on them. He believed that no ancient Roman would
be able to find his way about the city if he were allowed
to revisit it." [1]

Montesquieu [2] seems to have received the same
impression, an impression which becomes all the
more forcible when we recollect that in addition to
the monuments there were numbers of complimentary statues which must have seriously encroached
on so confined a space. These statues were weeded
out from time to time by order of the Senate or of

[1] *Cf.* his *Voyage* (Roman ed. of 1774), p. 85.
[2] *Notes sur l'Italie* (recently published), p. 260.

the Emperor, the older and less popular ones being transferred to the *Campus Martius* or elsewhere.[1] But the ranks of this " nation of the dead " were continually receiving new recruits, and threatened to displace their living descendants unless these latter took steps to prevent it.

The first thing, then, to be noted, is that when we try to fit into the forum of a single period every-thing that was placed or built there in successive ages, we do but needlessly and unconsciously in-crease our difficulties and deceive ourselves. If we would know what the ancient forum was like, we must endeavour to restore it, epoch by epoch. We must bear in mind that the ancients themselves destroyed here quite as much as they built up. The forum was emptied every time it was rebuilt, and, for a space, the Romans had room to breathe freely.

Moreover, their ideas on this subject were in no way similar to ours. Suetonius[2] asserts that Augus-tus did not make his forum as large as he would have liked to, because he did not dare " to expro-priate too many people."[3] His successors were assuredly not troubled by any scruples of this na-ture: yet their forums do not strike us as being particularly roomy, and no attempt was made to en-large *the* forum *par excellence*, the *forum Romanum*. No doubt consecrated edifices, such as the Temple

---

[1] Suetonius, *Cal.*, 34 : "*propter angustias.*"

[2] *Aug.*, 56.

[3] " Forum *angustius* fecit, *non ausus extorquere possessoribus proximas domos.*"

of Vesta, the *Regia*, and other temples, formed so
many boundaries which could not be shifted. The
true explanation, however, is that so well expressed
by Vitruvius in the directions given by him for the
construction of a forum. The size of these places
was limited intentionally.[1] The ancients had no
rooted objection to a little crowding, a thing which
on great occasions could not possibly be prevented,
no matter what one did; on the other hand, too
large a forum, if sparsely filled, would have looked
empty,[2] and they were anxious to prevent at any
cost a feeling of desertion and solitude. All those
who took an interest or a leading part in public
affairs were certain of finding places; as to the
others, they were of no consequence. In a forum
of limited size people were able to hear better, the
place seemed more stirring, the town more populous
and influential. At any rate, this was the view
taken by the ancients.

But, in spite of all this, we find that in the time
of Cæsar and Augustus the want of additional forums
was so keenly felt that crowds collected in the new
ones even before the builders had finished them.

[1] Vitruvius, v., 1.

[2] We find the same idea expressed in one of Mæcenas's speeches
(Dion., lii., 30): "It is a mistake to provide larger buildings than
are necessary for assemblies of the people" (μητ' οἰκοδομημάτων
πλήθεσιν ἢ καὶ μεγέθεσιν ὕπερ τἀναγκαῖα χρήσθωσαν).

CHAPTER III

THE PALATINE

I

ITS HISTORY

THE origin of the name Palatine is a religious one; it was derived from the worship of *Pales*, the goddess of shepherds. But at an early date the name came to be applied generally to the Palatine[1]; the idea of empire seems to have become inseparably associated with those who dwelt there. It should be noted, moreover, that in spite of the enormous increase in the number of buildings which ended eventually by covering every available space in the city, and though there were more forums than one, there was only one " palace "; Rome— and the ancient world in general—knew of but one *Palatium*, the type of the sole authority from which everything else depended—''οὐκ ἀγαθὸν πολυκοιρανίη.'' [2]

---

[1] *Palatium* had already acquired this meaning by the time of Tacitus. *Cf.* also Dion Cassius, liii., 16.

[2] This line from Homer is said to have been quoted by Domitian (Suet., 12) when he was told that his brother's son-in-law had had his slaves dressed in white like those of the imperial household. The

It was there that the emperors dwelt; it was there that they were both made and unmade. Each one of them left some building behind him there, destroying, if necessary, some other edifice left by his predecessors; the early Cæsars, in particular, have left their traces behind them here. Let us briefly recall what they intended to do, what they actually did, and with what edifices their names are associated.

Augustus installed himself on the Palatine, which had been his birthplace and was, in his eyes, filled with memories of early Rome. His house, originally that of a simple citizen soon to be crowned with laurels, was enlarged in all directions by successive additions (*e. g.*, the houses of Hortensius, Catiline, etc.); it was finally rebuilt and decorated—a " house of marble " in the rising " city of marble "—and became the first of the palaces. When it was destroyed by fire in the year 3 A.D. and he was obliged to rebuild, in order that he might accept the contributions which were offered him on all sides, Augustus erected an edifice, the entrance (*propylaia*) to which on the *Vicus Apollinis* was regarded by the ancients as an architectural masterpiece. The peristyle which surrounded the *area Apollinis* was paved with white marble, and contained fifty-two pillars of *giallo antico;* between these columns were statues of the daughters of Danäus and their father. Opposite to them were equestrian statues of the sons

meaning is that it is not fitting that there should be more masters than one.

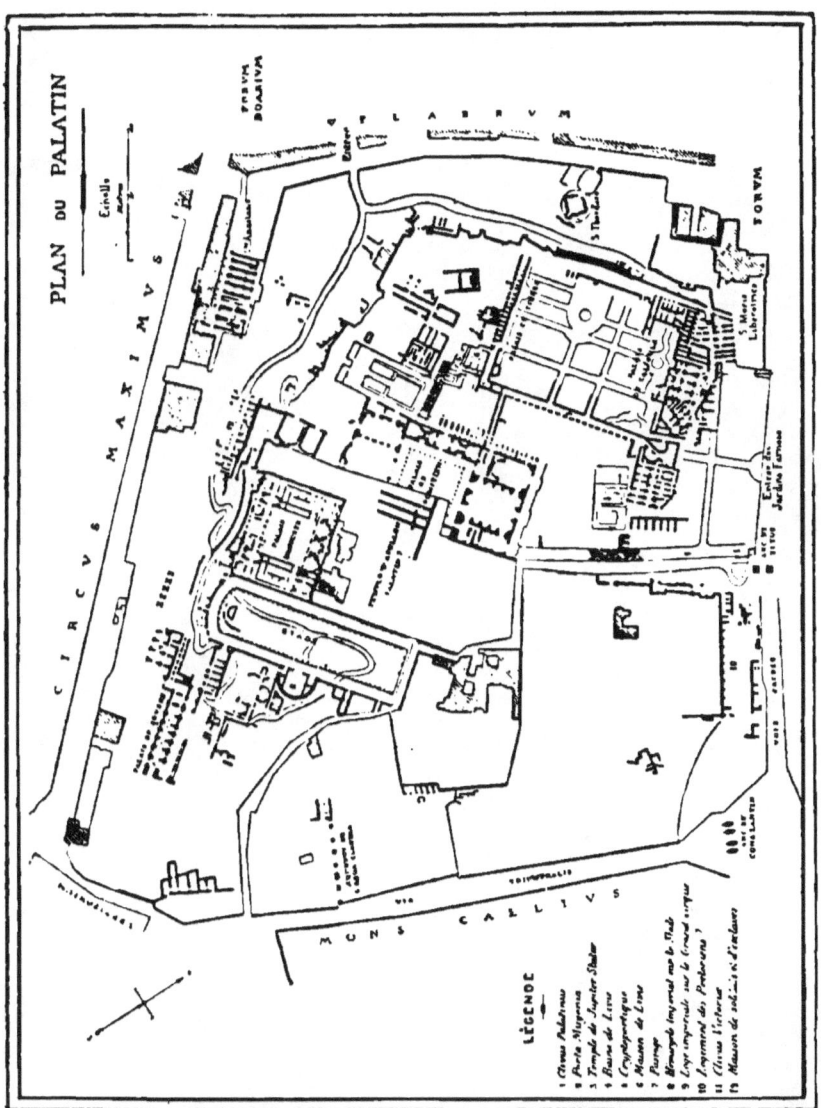

PLAN OF THE PALATINE.

of Danäus. On either side of the Temple of Apollo
stood libraries, one Greek, the other Latin, which
contained none but works of special merit, with
medallions of their authors embossed in either gold,
silver, or bronze. Between the libraries, and facing
the *propylaia*, stood the Temple of Apollo, which
was built entirely of Carrara marble, with bas-reliefs
of Parian marble from the studios of Greek sculptors. Its two doors, inlaid with ivory bas-reliefs,
represented, on one side, the destruction of the
daughters of Niobe; on the other, the rout of the
Gallic forces expelled from Delphi.

This first and truly imperial edifice was quickly
followed by others. The house of Livia, or palace
of Tiberius (*domus Tiberiana*), has survived to our
own time. Then Caligula carried out his insane
idea of connecting the Palatine with the Capitol by
means of a gigantic bridge. Domitian built his
stadium (or racecourse) here, his vast reception
chambers and banqueting rooms. On the south,
Severus erected his *Septizonium* (a palace containing
seven tiers of pillars placed one above the other).
Finally, there is scarcely a single stone on the Palatine, even down to a small Temple of the Sun on
the south side (to the north-east of the baths in the
vicinity of the *Via Sacra*), which does not remind
one of Heliogabalus.

Side by side with these imperial monuments, the
Palatine boasted, and the Romans took a delight in
exhibiting, monuments belonging to the time of the
kings and of *Roma quadrata*, such as the Temple of

5

Jupiter Stator, the *Porta Mugonia*, the *Porta Roman-ula*, and even the *Scalæ Caci*, a list which involuntarily carries the thoughts of the visitor back to legendary times.[1]   The Christian and anti-Christian inscriptions in the *Pædagogium* (chief among the latter being the caricature of Alexander adoring his crucified god, which bears the head of an ass), bring us down to a later period.

In the interval, the Palatine had, during the last days of the Republic, served as a dwelling-place for such illustrious citizens as Catulus, Scaurus, Crassus, Cicero, and Hortensius, not to mention Catiline, Claudius, and Antony, who also had houses there. Thus we find in this quarter of Rome a host of memories relating to the principal epochs in her history, some of them glorious, some disastrous.

At this date it is difficult, if not impossible, to distinguish the precise spot to which each of these memories ought to be assigned.   This is a matter which we must leave archæologists to settle, and even they do not attempt to deny the difficulty of the problem.[2]

[1] The legends associated with the various names mentioned here may be recalled in a few words.   The word *quadrata* contains an allusion to the supposed *square* (quadrum) shape of primitive Rome. The Temple of Jupiter Stator was built in fulfilment of a vow made by Romulus when Jupiter stayed (*sistit*, whence the word *Stator*) the flight of his soldiers in an engagement with the Sabines ; the *Mugonia* gate points to the pastoral character of the early Romans ; the *Porta Romanula* embodies the name of the race, and, finally, the *Scalæ Caci* recall the combat between Hercules and Cacus narrated by Virgil (*Æn.*, viii., 185 *et seq.*).

[2] In addition to the larger works dealing with the topography of

Until the year 1860, the Palatine had been covered with well-grown timber: it was the site of the beautiful Farnese Gardens, to which the Romans resorted for a breath of fresh air. The excavations have, however, entirely changed its appearance. With the exception of a single private estate of fairly large extent, the *Villa Mills*, one or two clumps of trees on the city side, and a thin wooded fringe of somewhat larger extent on the south, it now consists entirely of a pile of ruins, some of them dignified enough, but so confused as to give the casual visitor an impression of monotony. There are parts of it, however, the beauty of which cannot fail to strike even the least observant. Take, for instance, what is known as the *stadium* on the Palatine, which was built by Domitian and has now been unearthed by the *École Française;* the house of Livia, with its world-renowned paintings which furnish us with data that are simply invaluable to the student of ancient pictorial art and of the Pompeian frescos. Nor must we forget the admirable view obtainable in every direction: on the north we see the Forum, the Capitol, and the hills on the right bank of the Tiber; on the south the *Circus Maximus* and the boundless expanse of the Campagna. Historic memories here combine with the beauties of nature in a manner

Rome, and the extremely lucid and reliable chapter on the subject in M. Boissier's *Rome and Pompeii*,(New York, G. P. Putnam's Sons), I may refer the reader to other recent works such as Middleton's *Remains of Ancient Rome* and Lanciani's *Ancient Rome*. M. Deglane's articles on the *Palais des Césars au Mont Palatin* in the *Gazette archéologique*, 1888, pp. 124 *et seq.*, should also be mentioned.

which is particularly solemn and majestic.   As he
pauses before this stately panorama, the stranger
begins to understand the feeling which induces the
Romans to come here every day and in all weathers,
in order that they may feast their eyes upon it.

It is only natural that the specialist, and even the
scholar, should not be satisfied with this purely
æsthetic aspect, but must seek to identify the buildings erected by successive emperors, and the different
parts, or, at any rate, the general form of each, including the sites of the temples, of the libraries, and
of famous buildings, either ancient or modern,
which are mentioned by historians.   I cheerfully
abandon details of this nature.   It will be sufficient
to present here in a single group all the various
monuments which found a place in this " citadel of
the Empire." [1]   According to M. Deglane,[2] the general appearance of the hill must have been somewhat
as follows: In the centre stood the house of Augustus, with the sanctuaries which formed, as it were,
a part of it, namely, the temples of Apollo and Vesta;
near it was the palace of the Flavii, which joins on
to it after a fashion of the east, with its libraries, its
stadium, and its offices; then there were a number
of other sanctuaries, or houses, the precise character
of which is still a matter of controversy; on the
south stood the house of Livia and the Temple of
Jupiter Victor ; on the north the Temple of *Jupiter
Stator ;* farther on to the north-west were the palaces

---

[1] Tacitus, *Hist.*, iii., 70: "*arx imperii.*"
[2] *Cf.* the general plan given by M. Deglane, pl. 23.

of Tiberius and Caligula; on the extreme south-east the *Septizonium* of Septimius Severus.

The addition of one building after another in this way, together with the numerous conflagrations and the restorations by which they were followed, must, no doubt, have greatly altered both the general appearance and individual features of the Palatine. Still, even apart from the temples, there must have been some houses which the Romans did their best to maintain in their original state; for example, the house of Livia and the *Domus Augustana*. With the help of the foregoing notes, and more especially of the plan annexed hereto (p. 66), which is based on M. Lanciani's drawings, the reader ought, I think, to be able to form a general idea (quite sufficient for our purpose) of the buildings on the Palatine.

So much for the material part of our subject, which, contrary to the usual rule, we find to be richer in difficult problems than in definite information. On the other hand, when we come to deal with the imperial *régime* of which the Palatine was but a symbol, everything is as clear as noonday. The Empire was for so long a living reality, it made its influence so deeply felt, that we find traces of it on all sides. Let us briefly summarise what historians have to tell us on the subject, giving, where possible, a preference to characteristic anecdotes; let us see how it was that the masters of the world established their power here; what conception the emperors and their subjects had formed of this power, and how they came to retain it so long.

II

THE IMPERIAL RÉGIME

And first of all, how did the emperor secure possession of his throne ?

It was a case of " The emperor is dead! Long
live the emperor! " The new monarch, if he happened to be in Rome, went first of all to the Prætorian camp, and there obtained formal recognition
of his rights. In like manner he took the earliest
opportunity of assuring himself of the loyalty of the
provincial legions.[1] Armed with their support, he
knew that he would meet with nothing but formal-
ities and endless congratulations on the part of the
Senate. Once the family of the Cæsars became ex-
tinct, the new emperors were, almost without exception, military commanders. More than one of them,
had he been sufficiently outspoken, might have made
use of the phrase attributed to one of the Thirty
Tyrants,[2] " Comrades, you have lost a good general

---

[1] As a matter of fact, the Empire depended entirely on the army
and on the revenues levied by Rome from the wealth of her provinces.
Julius Cæsar, the founder of the new government, admitted this
himself (Dion Cassius, xlii., 49): " δύο τε εἶναι λέγων τὰ τὰς δυ-
ναστείας παρασκευάζοντα καί φυλάσσοντα καὶ ἐπαύξοντα
στρατιώτας καὶ χρήματα· Καὶ ταῦτα δι' ἀλλήλων συνεστη-
κέναι. . . . Περὶ μὲν οὖν τούτων καὶ ἐφρόνει, ἀεὶ καὶ
ἔλεγεν " (He declared that there were two things which conferred, maintained, and increased the power of a dynasty: *soldiers
and money;* and that these two things mutually supported one
another. It was ever thus that he felt and spoke on this subject).

[2] Saturninus, 23. Peter, *Hist. Aug.*, ii., p. 121, 19.

and have made a bad emperor." But if their eleva-
tion to imperial rank conduced, as their supporters
claimed that it did, to the general happiness, it
must in the case of many of them have led to their
own misfortune:

"*Felix omnia ; infelicissimus imperator.*" [1]

The previous emperor had now to be definitely
shelved. The simplest way of doing this was to
pay him divine honours. Under the Empire these
were dealt out with no sparing hand. We even find
the Senate decreeing them to Piso,[2] and to one of
the victims of the Thirty Tyrants. It was the regular thing for the deceased emperor to be promoted
to the rank of god; at his obsequies his soul was
invariably observed flying upwards to Olympus[3];
thenceforward he was styled *divus* and was served
by a brotherhood of priests (*sodales*) who bore his
name or surname.[4]

This cult of the imperial dead never lacked its
band of faithful worshippers; it was an easy and re-
munerative form of flattery. But we can readily
imagine that, from the very first, there must have
been a certain number of sceptics, and that the prac-

[1] "All things are happy ; the emperor alone is most unfortunate."
This is an epitaph which was inscribed on the tomb of Censorinus,
one of the Thirty Tyrants (*Trig. tyr.*, 33, 25 ; Peter, ii., p. 131, 22).
Felix omnia was doubtless a piece of bad grammar in general use
among the populace.

[2] Peter, ii., p. 119, 11.

[3] *Cf.* Chap. VI. of the present volume.

[4] *E. g.*, the *Helviani* in the case of *Helvius* Pertinax, and the
Marciani in the case of the Antonines (Spartianus, *Sev.*, vii., 8).

tice must frequently have been the topic of many a whispered jest. Soon the emperors themselves began to throw ridicule on the custom, and made a point of showing that they, at any rate, were not duped by it. Vespasian, when first attacked by the disease of which he died, exclaimed, " Woe is me; I fear that I am about to become a god!"[1] Caracalla masked his natural cruelty in a pun (which defies translation) in reference to his brother Geta : " Let him be a god, by all means, provided he dies first"(*sit divus dum non sit vivus*).[2] Once a conspiracy had proved successful, the murderer himself was generally the first to propose that divine honours should be paid to the victim. Out of consideration for the Prætorians, or merely as a matter of custom, a temple, Salian priests, and *sodales* were then assigned to him.[3]

It should be noted, however, that these honours were not rendered to all of the emperors. This is evident from a perusal of the titles given them in the biographies of Suetonius and in the *Historia Augusta*. The title of *divus* strikes us as ironical when associated with the name of a man like Claudius. Its absence from the names of Tiberius, Caligula,[4] Nero, and Domitian requires no explana-

[1] Suetonius, 23 : " Vae, inquit, puto, *deus fio.*"
[2] Spartianus, ii., 9.
[3] Macrinus did so in the case of Caracalla (Spartianus, xi., 5). The first step taken by Avidius Cassius when he rebelled against Marcus Aurelius, was to assume the title of *imperator*, and to assign to Marcus Aurelius that of *divus* (*M. Ant.*, xxiv., 5).
[4] Dion (lx., 4) explains that Tiberius and Caligula do not appear

tion. The only *divi* mentioned in the *Historia Augusta* are Claudius of Illyria and Aurelian.[1] But what possible value can the title possess in our eyes when we find that the historians, at any rate, do not apply it to the names of Alexander Severus[2] or Marcus Aurelius,[3] though such an application would have been the best means of investing it with some sort of value in the eyes of posterity. The fact is, the title of *divus* was well known to be purely complimentary; it was even more meaningless than the surname of *Pius*, given to Antoninus, and afterwards adopted by the emperors who succeeded him.

The newly elected monarch pardoned, or at any rate pretended to pardon, his adversaries.[4] As a matter of prudence, and in obedience to a kind of tradition, he emancipated his children and handed over to them their share in his estate.[5]

On the day on which he was proclaimed emperor,

on the list of emperors "whom we mention in our oaths or in our prayers"; but that, notwithstanding this, neither one nor the other of them was noted for his infamy.

[1] Aurelian is not described as *divus* in the inscriptions.

[2] Severus only appears as *divus* in a single inscription (Wilmanns, *Ex. Insc.*).

[3] It is true that Marcus Aurelius is accorded this surname in the inscriptions.

[4] Spartianus, *Hadr.*, xvii., 1. "Quos inimicos habuit . . . *tantum neglexit* ita ut uni, quem capitalem habuerat, factus imperator diceret : 'Evasisti'" (He showed such great indifference towards those who had been his enemies, that to one of them, who had been specially hostile to him, he remarked, after his accession to the throne, " Thou hast escaped—this time ! ").

[5] Julian (viii., 9) took this course. *Cf.* Antoninus's remark to his wife, which is quoted farther on (p. 85, note 2).

he became the recipient of a whole string of high-sounding titles : his wife and daughter became *Augusta*, his sons became Cæsars, and he himself received the title of " father of his country," the *imperium proconsulare* and the *jus quartæ relationis.*[1] It is true that he occasionally refused useless honours which savoured too much of mere adulation; thus Julian declined to accept statues of silver.[2] If the emperor bore a name expressive of any special virtue (*e. g., pertinax, severus,* or *probus*), it was the fashion to declare that he well deserved his title.[3] He was credited with having inherited all the virtues that had characterised his predecessors: with the bravery of Trajan, the piety of Antoninus, the moderation of Augustus.[4] It is a singular thing that one quality is never mentioned, though a most necessary one, which was possessed in a high degree by men like Claudius of Illyria and Aurelian, who proved themselves the saviours of the Empire when it was threatened with anarchy — I mean physical strength. Though it is true that Augustus did not possess it, it was conspicuously displayed by other emperors, such as Hadrian, who killed several lions with his

---

[1] Pertinax, v., 6; Julianus, iv., 5. This right entitled him to bring forward a motion before the Senate four times running : but it is doubtful whether any of the emperors found it necessary to do this in order to secure obedience.

[2] Julian., iv., 6. *Cf.* vi., 2, *et seq.*, where there is a curious debate between the Senate and Alexander Severus on the subject of his refusal of the titles of *Antoninus* and *Magnus.*

[3] *E.g.*, Spartianus, *Sev.*, xiv.

[4] Pollio, *Claud.*, ii., 2 ; Peter, ii., p. 134.

own hand. There are numerous anecdotes of the feats performed by him, in his later days, and by the emperors who succeeded him.[1]

There was, however, one faculty somewhat akin to that of physical strength, for which the writers of the *Historia Augusta* profess a guileless admiration —that of being able to drink deep with impunity. This had been a weakness with some of the Antonines; they were, however, imitated and surpassed in this respect. Trajan was a mighty drinker; but the *Historia Augusta* tells us of Bonosus that no man ever drank more than he did. Aurelian once said of him that he " was not born to *live*, but to drink." When the barbarian delegates came to see him, he distrusted them and managed to worm their secrets out of them while they were intoxicated, he himself becoming more and more clear-headed as he drank.[2] I must not translate the exceedingly

---

[1] Vopiscus, *Firmus*, iv., 2 : " *Nervis robustissimus* (Firmus erat) ita ut Tritanum vinceret. . . . Nam *et incudem* superpositam pectori constanter, aliis tundentibus, *pertulit*, cum ipse reclinis ac supinus et curvatus in manus penderet potius quam jaceret " (Firmus was so strong physically that he conquered even Tritanus [a Samnite gladiator]. For on one occasion he supported an anvil on his chest without flinching while it was being struck violently by others, he meanwhile lying on his back supported by his hands, forming as it were an arch with his body). *Cf.* the story related of Pepin by the chronicler of St. Gall, in which we are told that he caused a fight between a lion and a bull to be held in the presence of the nobles who disputed his right to the throne ; he suggested that they should go and separate them, and, on their refusal, himself decapitated both animals.

[2] Vopiscus, *Bonosus*, xiv., 2 ; Peter, ii., p. 230, 2 *et seq.*

realistic detail which his biographer is careful not to
omit.   When, after his defeat by Probus, he went
and hanged himself, it was said that " the body
which hung there was that of an amphora rather
than of a man " (*amphoram pendere, non hominem*).
We must not, however, be too hard on the unfortunate Bonosus; for we read that, at this very
period, the famous Zenobia, who was generally
temperate in her habits, could, when she liked, drink
cup for cup with her officers, sometimes leaving even
Persian and Armenian generals under the table.[1]

In addition to the great Roman patronymics
which it was usual to add as titles after the name of
the new emperor, that of " Alexander " was frequently included along with other prayers and com-
pliments.   ·Indeed, the glory of Alexander the
Great seems to have cast its spell over every one of
the emperors who succeeded to the Palatine, both
good and bad alike.[2]

The Senate, in solemn session, addressed its congratulations to the new emperor in the form of one
of those *adclamationes* of which some curious speci-

---

[1] Vopiscus, *Bonosus*, cap. xxx. (Peter, ii., p. 127, 17).

[2] Alexander Severus honoured him with a special worship ; when
he set out against the Persians he took care to organise a *phalanx* of
30,000 men ; the fact that he bore the same name is more than once
taken advantage of by his biographer for the purpose of comparing
him with his great namesake (v., 1 ; xxxv., 1 ; xxxi., 5).   But even
before him, and for similar reasons, both Caligula (Suetonius, 52)
and Caracalla (Spartianus, ii., 2) had set themselves to copy the same
model.   So, too, after his time, his example was followed by certain
of the Thirty Tyrants, *e.g.*, the *Macriani* (xiv.) and *Quietus* (iv. *et
seq.*), etc.

mens are preserved in the *Historia Augusta*. They frequently terminate with the word "*Omnes*" (all). The remainder of these documents is one long cry of adulation, interspersed with high-sounding titles, protestations of loyalty, and prayers for the emperor's happiness (*di te servent*, etc.).[1] As a contrast, we have the imprecations and maledictions pronounced, in a similar form, against some rival of the emperor's, who is forthwith declared to be an enemy of the State.[2] Doubtless the most amusing shape assumed by these messages is that of a dialogue supposed to take place between the emperor and the Senate.[3] Yet no monarch with any pretensions to common sense was ignorant of the fact that, in time of real need, the Senate was no more to be relied upon for support than the vestals and priests whom Didianus proposed to send with the senators to Severus at Ravenna.[4]

---

[1] Claudius vainly endeavoured to modify the excessive repetition and extravagant language of the *adclamationes* (Dion, lx., 5).

[2] *Cf.* the reference in Peter's index. As instances of *adclamationes* promulgated by the Senate when ratifying the election of an emperor, I may instance those addressed to Gordianus (*Gord.*, ii., 9, and *Maximin.*, xvi., 13), to Claudius of Illyria (*Claud.*, iv., 2), to Maximus and Balbinus (*Max.*, ii., 9). An example of the imprecations will be found in *Comm.*, xviii. 3,. After the death of tyrants like Heliogabalus or Domitian, the new emperor (*e.g.*, Alexander Severus) or the person congratulating him (*Cf.* Pliny, *passim*) never speaks of the deceased monarch except to call him *bellua ista, latro iste* (that monster, that brigand), etc. Others, like Didius Julianus, abstain from mentioning his name.

[3] *E.g.*, *Alex. Sev.*, vi., 3 (Peter, i., p. 251, 16 *et seq.*); *Tacit.*, ii., 3 (P., ii., p. 187,.5 *et seq.*).   [4] vi., 6.

What, then, was the attitude of the senators towards this new power, which seemed to regain its novelty with each new change of rulers, and displayed all the jealousy of an upstart dynasty ? Their attitude was what it had always been from the beginning: the nobles and even the creatures of the fallen dynasty vied with one another in servility, so much so that the emperors were obliged to restrain their indiscreet adulation.   Dion Cassius tells us of a certain tribune, named Sextus Pacuvius,[1] who declared that he had " dedicated " (καθοσιῶσαι) himself to Augustus, after the Spanish fashion, and running up and down through the highways and byways induced all whom he met to imitate his example.   We find the same comedy played even in our own day.   Titles, honours, and congratulations are showered on the living monarch, his flatterers declaring that language fails to express their feelings, and yet he is never satisfied.[2]   Ridicule was thrown on the titles of ancient offices which had now come to be nothing but empty names.[3]   The truth is revealed in certain sayings that went the rounds.   Heliogabalus calls the senators " slaves in

---

[1] liii., 20.

[2] The Senate, after conferring on Aurelian a whole string of traditional surnames (*Gothicus, Sarmaticus, Armeniacus, Parthicus, Adiabenicus*), took it into their heads after his victory over the Carpi to call him *Carpicus*. Aurelian remarked that their next step would probably be to call him *carpisculus* (a kind of shoe) (*Ibid.*, xxx., 5).

[3] Trebellius, *Valer.*, v., 4 ; a decree of the Senate conferring the censorship on Valerian, and an oration of Decius. .

togas " (*mancipia togata*)[1]; while some senators
term Aurelian " the pedagogue of the Senate."[2]

No one, however, was deceived by these shams,
and when the pinch came, the ultimate result never
hung long in the balance. Rebellion in the capital
was quenched with the blood of the Senate[3]; and
when the senators appeared in the triumph accorded
to Aurelian on his return victorious from the frontier,
it was openly said, and they themselves admitted,
that the emperor was " triumphing over the Senate
also."[4]

Each new emperor, once he was safely established on the throne, soon found a means of check-
ing the familiarity of those who had known him in
a humbler sphere, either by a haughty demeanour
or by harsher measures.[5] He was especially dis-
trustful of any who might seek to pose as his
rivals. Those who were known to consult the
soothsayers or Chaldean magicians at once fell
under suspicion and were severely punished.[6] The
emperor was able to spare or strike in turn those
whose support he desired. Those who sought to
flatter him by imitating his likes and dislikes ran
the risk of choosing the wrong moment for the dis-

[1] Lampridius, xx., 1.

[2] Vopiscus, xxxvii., 3.

[3] Vopiscus, *Aur.*, xxi., 6 *et seq.*

[4] *Ibid.*, xxxiv., 4.

[5] Severus caused one of his former compatriots at Leptis to be
beaten with rods (Spartianus, ii., 6).

[6] Spartianus, *Sev.*, iv., 3, and xv., 5. *Cf.* Ammianus Marcellinus,
passim.

play of servility; in such cases their punishment was a terrible one.[1]

The method of repression varied according to circumstances, but it was invariably a cruel one. The heads of defeated rivals in the race for power were carried about on pikes.[2] Their bodies were exposed to public obloquy in front of their houses, or thrown into the Tiber or the *cloaca*[3]; their heads were burnt in the *Campus Martius* amid the jeers of the populace. The citizens of Sicca allowed the body of one of these poor wretches to be devoured by dogs.[4] The "bloodless reigns" of the Antonines[5] had long passed away, and yet all these cruelties proved of no avail, since, as an ancestor of Avidius Cassius wittily expressed it, no monarch, however pitiless he might be, "had ever yet succeeded in checkmating destiny by killing his successor."[6]

[1] Those who were imprudent enough to copy Severus in his hostility towards Plantinianus, were, after their reconciliation, thrown to the beasts (Spartianus, *Sev.*, xiv., 5).

[2] This was the fate inflicted by Severus on Niger (ix., 1), on Clodius Albinus (xi., 6), and by Maximus on Maximinus and his son (*Maxim.*, xxiii., 6, and xxiv., 4).

[3] *Gord.*, xiii., 9. Xiphilinus relates that when the body of Heliogabalus was thrown into the Tiber, the Romans added the name *Tiberinus* to all the high-sounding appellations which he had borne.

[4] Trebellius, *Tyr. trig.*, xxix., 4; Peter, ii., p. 125, 13.

[5] Lampridius, *Alex. Sev.*, lii., 2, "ἀναίματον imperium." Capitolinus, *Anton. Pius*, 13: "solus omnium prope principum prorsus *sine civili sanguine et hostili*, quantum ad se ipsum pertinet, vixit" (He was almost the only one of all the emperors who lived without shedding the blood of any citizen or enemy, for his own private ends).

[6] Vulcatius, *Avid. Cass.*, ii., 2: "*successorem suum nullus occidit.*"

At the beginning of the Empire, its founder, though he fully recognised the solid basis on which the imperial power rested, did not overlook the fact that public opinion had also to be reckoned with, and that it was necessary to conciliate it; we see this clearly in a letter written by Augustus to Livia in regard to Claudius ;[1] he there frankly declares that he cannot afford to have those who surround him made the subject of criticism, mockery, or gossip. The need for such precautions was, however, soon forgotten, as the Empire gradually grew stronger year by year, and it was entirely lost sight of when the supreme power passed into the hands of young men infatuated with their own abilities, like Caligula and Nero, and those who followed in their footsteps. These monarchs affected to despise what stood for public opinion at Rome, and prided themselves on breaking down every barrier.

Indeed, they had but little to learn from those Eastern despots[2] who were regarded by some as their masters in the art of tyranny (τυραννοδιδάσκυλοι). In their eyes, their power knew no limit save their own caprice. They boasted loudly of it. "Remember," said Caracalla to his grandmother, Antonia, "that I have power to do everything and

---

[1] Suetonius, *Claud.*, 4 : "præbenda materia deridendi et illum et nos non est hominibus ; τὰ τοιαῦτα ὃκώπτειν καὶ. μυκτηρίζειν εἰωθόὅιν " (The public must not be given an opportunity of casting ridicule on him [Claudius] and on us ; this in allusion to certain failings which they did not fail to laugh at in private).

[2] Dion, lix., 24, *in.*

6

over everyone." [1]   When someone endeavoured to point out to Nero that the murder of Britannicus might have serious consequences for him, he inquired, " Is there any fear lest the *lex Julia* [2] should be enforced against me ? "   Intoxicated by the impunity enjoyed by his earlier crimes, he affirmed that none of his predecessors " had realised the true extent of their powers." [3]

It will scarcely surprise us to learn that none of the emperors I have named hesitated to gratify their slightest whims, and that each tried to outvie the other in cruel or grotesque devices.   It was regarded as one of " the Emperor's jests " when Caligula compelled a number of senators who had filled high offices to run alongside his chariot in their togas for several miles. [4]   Heliogabalus kept a number of tame lions and leopards which were allowed to come in and lie down beside the guests at the end of a banquet, nearly frightening these latter out of their lives. [5]   His courtiers amused themselves now and then by stifling a parasite under a mass of violets or other flowers. [6]   At another time, when the people were flocking to the games, he set free in the streets of Rome a number of Marsian serpents which he had collected, leaving the multitude to choose between flight and their venomous bites. [7]

[1] Suetonius, 29 : " *Memento, ait, omnia mihi et in omnis licere.*"
[2] Suetonius, 33.
[3] *Ibid.*, 37 : "quemquam principum *scisse quid sibi liceret.*"
[4] Suetonius, 26. Cf. *Galba,* 6.
[5] Lampridius, xxi., 1. *Cf.* xxv., 1.
[6] *Ibid.*, 5.   [7] *Ibid.*, xxiii., 2.

Gradually, and by the force of circumstances, there came into existence on the Palatine a court similar in every respect to those of Eastern potentates. Henceforward everything was decided by a single man [1]; this man, who was accountable to no one, spoke but little, merely enough to express his wishes; indeed, what he said, and what he wished to do, or did, were, as a rule, two very different things. He gave those who fell under his displeasure a short shrift. The *Historia Augusta* shows us that practices which are usually believed to have been peculiar to the petty Italian courts of the sixteenth century existed in full vigour on the Palatine from very early times. We learn from the imperial biographies that from this period onward it became quite a common thing for the emperors to send poison to any person they wanted to get rid of [2]; it was then given out they had died at the hands of robbers.[3] The ears of the emperor, whether on the Palatine, at Constantinople, or elsewhere, though deaf to every moderate or equitable counsel, or to any attempt at justification, " were ever open to the clandestine whispers of cowardly informers." [4] A venal crew of subordinates, freedmen, eunuchs, and others, cleverly contrived to make capital out of the

[1] Dion Cassius, liii., 19.
[2] Spartianus, *Carac.*, iii., 4.
[3] Lampridius, *Comm.*, v., 12 ; Spartianus, *Carac.*, iii.
[4] Ammianus Marcellinus, xv., p. 2, 2 : " ad suscipiendas defensiones æquas et probabiles imperatoris aures *occlusæ patebant* susurris insidiantium clandestinis." And *passim.*

seclusion in which the emperor lived; they posed as indispensable intermediaries (*internuntii*), and traded on the interest which they pretended to possess.   In the reign of Commodus things had reached such a pitch that they openly sold public offices, giving Commodus himself a share of the proceeds.[1]   In the majority of instances, however, they deceived those who had recourse to them, and gave them, as the Romans had it, nothing but " smoke " for their money.   As may be readily imagined, they were objects of general hatred, and the public plaudits rose long and loud when some just emperor visited them with punishment, however cruel.   Alexander Severus, having caught one of these intriguers red-handed, had him tied to a stake, round which a pile of damp straw and green wood had been collected, and then put to death by suffocation, the executioner exclaiming, " He is punished by smoke who sold but smoke " (*fumo punitur qui vendidit fumum*).[2]

Throughout this whole review of the Empire we seem to have found nothing but abuse of power, folly, and cruelty of every description.   But is not this the necessary and logical outcome of all such power as that wielded by these princes—at once un-limited and precarious ?

How came it, then, that such a dynasty was able to exist for so long a period ?   It lasted, apparently, because it secured for the nations of Central Europe an external peace such as they had never before en-

[1] Lampridius, xiv., 4 *et seq.*, and vi., 10.
[2] *Ibid.*, xxxvi., 3.

joyed; because the provinces were, on the whole, well governed and prosperous. Any attempt at rebellion was severely punished and carefully guarded against beforehand. We are told, for instance, that Alexander Severus revived the ancient republican custom, in accordance with which each magistrate on entering office was provided with everything he required at the public expense, viz., with plate, horses, mules, clothing, pocket-money, cooks, muleteers, etc. In short, he was supplied with a regular outfit. At the end of his term of office the magistrate was obliged to return the mules, horses, muleteers, and cooks, but was allowed to retain the rest, provided he had discharged his duties properly; otherwise he had to repay the whole fourfold, apart from his liability to be punished for peculation, and to be proceeded against in the civil courts.[1] This was a system which left nothing to chance!

But one thing was overlooked by those who had organised the vast machinery of the Empire, and this was the fact that even under the best of emperors it was a ruinous affair. I am not speaking now of the personal fortunes of the emperors, which of course shared the common fate[2]; nor do I refer to cases

---

[1] Lampridius, 42.

[2] *Cf.* the speech addressed by Antoninus to his wife which is recorded by Capitolinus (iv., 8): "Cum uxor argueretur quasi parum nescio quid suis largiens: *Stulta*, posteaquam ad imperium transivimus, *et illud, quod habuimus ante*, perdidimus" (When his wife reproached him with being niggardly in his treatment of her relatives, "Fool," he said to her, "can you not see that in attaining the throne we have lost even what we had before that?")

like that of Marcus Aurelius, who caused the rich
plate and jewels of his palace to be sold; the emperors ruined themselves by their bounty to the
people, a bounty which gradually ceased to be
optional.   The amount of money spent in Rome on
spectacles and public doles was in itself stupendous.
Then the treasury was further depleted by the *donativa*, or money gifts, which had to be distributed
among the soldiers, this last being a necessary extravagance.   Thus the two main supports of the
imperial government already referred to, viz., the
army and the revenues of the world, ended by destroying one another; and yet, as Cæsar had said,
each depended on the other for mutual support.   It
was impossible for such a state of things to last.
Day by day the Empire grew poorer and poorer, and
when, at length, the barbarians came to pillage it,
there was nothing left, from a financial point of
view, but mere worthless wreckage.[1]

[1] Cf. *supra*, p. 70, note 1.

CHAPTER IV

THE BATHS AND THE GAMES

THE Romans spent the best part of their lives away from home. Where, then, did they pass their time ? When a Roman of the time of the Empire was not at home, what was the most likely place in which to look for him ? In the comedies of Plautus, when any of the characters leave the stage without entering their own houses, they say that they " are going to the forum." This was a sort of tradition which must have persisted for a long while. Under the Empire, however, the idler preferred to betake himself to the *Campus Martius*, with its countless monuments and porticos. Let us assume that it is still daylight. Then our missing Roman must be at the bath; he is probably lingering at one of the public *thermæ* on which the imperial government lavished such incredible sums. Or, perhaps, there are games being held to-day. In that case no Roman, unless he were either a philosopher or a Juvenal, would willingly absent himself from them. It is, therefore, either at the theatre, the circus, or the amphitheatre that we are most likely to come upon the person of whom we are in search; the hour of the day and our knowledge of his tastes must guide us in our quest.

From our point of view this seems in every respect a bad way of employing one's time. The majority of these amusements were of a demoralising nature. At the bath a terrible promiscuity prevailed. From earliest antiquity philosophers had never wearied of protesting against the hours spent at the circus and against the maddening passions which held sway there; the dangers of the theatre and the horrors of the amphitheatre were also frequently denounced by them; but all their moralising proved ineffectual. In the first place, the political inactivity engendered by the imperial form of government seemed to justify amusements of this kind. One result of placing absolute power in the hands of a single man was to gradually reduce the *plebs* to such a state that they no longer desired anything but " bread and the games " (*panem et circenses*). When Octavius complained of the squabbles between actors and between their partisans, the famous Pylades retorted, " It is to your interest that the minds of the people should be full of our differences." [1] The citizens, freed from all political responsibility, had nothing to occupy them except their pleasures; small wonder, then, that they gave themselves up to these, heart and soul.

Attendance at the baths and the games thus became part of the regular routine of Roman life.

[1] Dion, liv., 19.

The Roman colonist and legionary carried these habits with him under every sky and to every out-post of the ancient world.   On ice-bound plains, in blazing deserts, on the borders of the Sahara or the banks of the Danube, by what sign shall we know that the Romans have passed this way ? By their roads, no doubt; but these roads nearly always lead us to some ruined bath or theatre, or, more often still, to some dismantled amphitheatre; these habits had come to be such an integral part of the life of the Romans that we accept them—strange though they seem in our eyes—as the outward and visible signs of their civilisation.

Numerous ruins of these monuments have come down to us, many of them imposing, some exceed-ingly beautiful.   It is impossible to give a list of them here or to examine them in detail.   It will be sufficient for our purpose to select one or two typi-cal examples which may serve to give us an idea of each kind.   Let us begin with the baths.[1]

I

THE THERMÆ

The bath, which in the time of the Punic Wars had been regarded merely as a matter of personal cleanliness, played an important part in the life of the Romans under the Empire.   To them it was one

[1] For particulars of the baths and *thermæ*, *cf.* the article " Balnea " in Smith's *Dictionary of Greek and Roman Antiquities*, 2 vols., 1890-1.

of their chief objects in life. In the inscription on
the gaming-table discovered at Timgad,[1] the bath
occupies a place between hunting and gambling.
By bathing twice a day the Romans of that epoch
believed that they could make two days out of one,[2]
and thus double the length of their lives. And
since they had no hesitation in taking this second
bath immediately after dinner, we need scarcely
wonder at the serious results which inevitably en-
sued.[3]

The biographers of the *Historia Augusta* are careful to inform us in the case of each emperor how
often he was accustomed to bathe in the day; most
of them took at least two baths every day in the
year, while some took as many as a dozen in sum-
mer-time, with banquets in between, hurrying about
the city from the baths in their palaces to those in
the houses of their friends, and from thence to the
public *thermæ*.[4]

There were baths of every possible description;
some simple and unadorned, others equipped with
every refinement that luxury could devise. In these
latter—apart from the costly decorations—all the
taps were of solid silver and the basins of marble.

[1] "Venari, *lavari*, ludere, ridere occ [*i. e.*, hoc] est vivere" (To
hunt, to bathe, to gamble, to laugh, this indeed is to live).

[2] Petronius, *Sat.*, 72, B., p. 48, 35: "Vero, vero, inquit; *de una
dieduas* facere: nihil malo" (Yes, yes, he says; *to make one day into
two:* nothing could be better).

[3] Juvenal, i., 144: "*Hinc subita mortes atque intestata senectus*"
(Hence sudden death, and old age that dies intestate).

[4] *E.g.*, *Heliogabalus*, xxx., 15 (Peter, ii., p. 242, 15).

For our purpose a convenient classification will be to divide them into public and private baths.

(1) *Private Baths*

The houses at Pompeii supply us with many valuable data in regard to private baths. We know that they consisted, in the main, of a series of rooms or cells, into which air and water were admitted at various temperatures, cold, tepid, or boiling (*frigidarium, tepidarium, calidarium,* or *sudatorium*). There was also the dressing-room (*apodyterium*). The walls were of stucco or marble; the floor in houses of the better class was paved in mosaic. Light was admitted to the rooms by means of windows, or through a circular opening in the centre of the roof which could be closed with a kind of lid.

The heating apparatus was, for reasons of economy, placed in the kitchen, and communicated with the various apartments by means of pipes. Modern visitors are particularly impressed by the method adopted for heating the larger rooms. No doubt braziers were employed, some fine specimens of these having been discovered at Pompeii; but, in addition to these, a number of partitions were built in the basement and side-walls; these were fitted with conduits communicating with the furnaces, and filled with hot air or steam. Montaigne refers to this system of double intermural partitions employed by the ancients for the purpose of heating their baths.   He compares them with the German stove as contrasted with the French fireplace.[1]

Private individuals, especially those who lived in out-of-the-way places, had their baths constructed on a most luxurious scale, with an *atrium*, large bathing-chambers, spacious vaults, swimming-baths, and galleries, not to speak of statues and mosaics. The baths of Pompeianus discovered some twenty years ago on the road from Constantinople to Setif, near the village of Wady-Atmenia, contained no less than twenty-one apartments.[2]

(2) *Public Baths*

Picture to yourselves one of these private baths on a much larger scale, with numerous bathing-chambers, swimming-baths without end, and rooms of every possible description (for all sorts of business were transacted at the baths); you will then have a fairly accurate idea of the *thermæ* or public baths. The two *thermæ* at Pompeii, which are in a fairly good state of preservation, enable us to form some conception of what the public baths in the smaller Italian towns were like.   They are comparatively small, and were consequently all the more easily heated.   A crowded bath was considered an attraction rather than otherwise.[3]   Even in the Pompeian

---

[1] *Essais*, iii., chap. xiii. (Louandre's edition), p. 275.

[2] Boissier, *L'Afrique romaine*, pp. 152 *et seq.*

[3] Epictetus, *Dissert.*, iv., 4, 24: "ἐν τοῖς βαλανείοις ὄχλος· καὶ τίς ἡμῶν οὐ χαίρει τῇ πανηγύρει ταύτῃ, καὶ ὀδυνώμενος αὐτῆς ἀπαλλάσσεται ;" (The bath is crowded ; but who amongst us is not glad to see all this multitude, and who would be so cross-grained as to depart because of it ?)

epoch the baths were sumptuously decorated.   We
have only to imagine an establishment arranged on
a larger scale in every respect, containing rooms for
gymnastic exercises, restaurants, shops for the sale
of perfumes, libraries, picture galleries, porticos,
and peristyles, and we have before us one of the
great *thermæ* of the capital.

Many of these latter, including some of the most
celebrated, such as the baths of Agrippa, Nero, and
Vespasian, have entirely disappeared.   True, we
still possess the superb framework of the baths of
Caracalla; and the *thermæ* of Diocletian, which furnished Christian Rome with the churches of *S.
Bernard* and *S. Maria degli Angeli*, serve to give us
some idea of their internal decoration.

We know for a positive fact that the emperors
were not content with the baths in their own palaces.
Alexander Severus made use of the public *thermæ*.
He was often to be seen returning to the Palatine in
bathing costume, bearing no insignia of his rank
save a purple cloak.[1]   Hadrian had done the same
thing.   The fact is proved by a famous anecdote
which I shall have occasion to quote later on.[2]

The utmost confusion reigned in these establishments, filled as they were by a crowd of the most
motley description, and scandalous scenes might be
witnessed there almost daily.   The noise was simply
deafening; apart from the bathers, who made a
noise either to keep themselves warm or from sheer

[1] Lampridius, xlii. *in.*
[2] *Cf.* Chap. XII., p. 287, note 2.

love of the thing, there was always a gang of philosophers who, like the cynic Theagenes, resorted
daily to the great *thermæ*[1] for the purpose of argument; then there were poets who, like Eumolpus in
the *Satyricon*,[2] insisted on reciting their verses, and
had to be driven away with volleys of stones. Thieves
and pickpockets abounded. Woe to the bather who
failed to set a guard over his clothing! Others came
in search of intrigues. The mere fact that Heliogabalus there made out a list of the citizens suffering
from hernia,[3] or recruited from among the bathers
instruments for his shameless pleasures,[4] may be
allowed to go for nothing, since, in his case, we
could scarcely expect anything else. But the details recorded by Martial and Juvenal, and the decrees issued by the emperors themselves, indicate
that the baths must have been the scene of serious
disorders.

In theory, there were supposed to be independent
establishments for the two sexes.[5] When this was
not the case, the rule was that the bath should be
open at separate hours during the daytime for men
and for women. This rule was, however, persistently
evaded. This is proved by the decrees of Hadrian
and Marcus Aurelius, both of whom forbade pro-
miscuous bathing (*lavacra mixta*).[6] Apparently,

[1] Gallienus, quoted by Friedlaender (French ed.), p. 394, n. 9.
[2] Cap. xc. *in.;* xci., xcii., *et seq.*
[3] Lampridius, xxv., 6.
[4] *Ibid.*, viii., 8, 6.
[5] Martial, vii., 35, 7.
[6] Spartianus, *Hadr.*, xviii., 10; *M. Anton.* xxiii.

however, it was found impossible to suppress the custom, for Alexander Severus ended by legalising it.[1]

We can imagine the scenes which took place among the crowds who filled these vast chambers; all absolutely nude,[2] women, men, slaves, swindlers, and debauchees (*curiosi*); in short, the very dregs of ancient Rome mingling freely with the rest. We find it stated that one of the government departments—that in charge of the revenue—took advantage of the nudity which obtained in the public *thermæ* in order to prevent Jews from evading the poll-tax imposed on them by Domitian. Surely no government can ever have carried its rapacity farther than this, or employed more disgraceful methods.

Montaigne, with his characteristic fondness for piquant anecdote, is careful to inform us that, in his day, a great deal of license prevailed at Rome. He seems, however, to refer to what went on in private houses.[3] Mazois quotes a letter from a papal legate

[1] Lampridius, xxiii. (Peter, i., p. 264, 21). Plutarch, in his life of Cato, tells us that the early Romans were very particular on this score ; Cato "never bathed in the company of his sons ; sons-in-law did not bathe with their fathers-in-law ; they were ashamed to strip before one another. . . . Later on, having learnt from the Greeks the habit of bathing naked before men, they taught these latter in return the custom of bathing naked even with women."

[2] Martial, vii., 35, 5, "*Nuda sub cute.*"

[3] *Essais*, i., chap. xlix., near the end : he remarks that " When ladies were at the bath they made no difficulty about receiving male visitors, and even employed their footmen to massage and anoint them." Elsewhere, in a diary of his travels after his second stay at Rome, he tells us : " I thought I should like to try the Roman baths,

of the sixteenth century, who, when passing through
Baden, saw a number of bathers, including men,
women, and young girls, enter a public swimming-
bath together, in a state of complete nudity.[1] The
legate was much struck by the patriarchal simplicity
of this proceeding, which seemed to be quite free
from any suggestion of evil.   But all this was nothing
to what went on at Rome, and, indeed, in almost
every city of antiquity.

In regard to the luxury displayed in the *thermæ*
of the capital, it may help us to form some idea of
it if we recall the fact that a considerable part of the
best antiques have come from these baths, and that
the *thermæ* of Caracalla have given us the celebrated
Gladiator mosaic, preserved in the Lateran Collection, the Flora, the Farnese Hercules, the Venus
Callipyge, and the Farnese Bull.

II

THE GAMES

The nature of the Roman games varied according
to the kind of entertainment provided and the place
in which they were held.   In the circus there were
chariot-races; in the *stadium*, the games introduced
by the Greeks; at the theatre, tragedies, comedies,
farces, and pantomimes; in the amphitheatre, hunt-

and went to those of S. Mark, which are considered to be the most
fashionable in the city. . . . It is the custom there to bring
your lady friends with you, who are there massaged with you by
the male attendants."

[1] Mazois, iii., p. 73, note.

POMPEIAN PAINTING OF A THEATRE.

ing spectacles or fights with wild beasts (*venationes*) and gladiatorial combats.

The games were regarded by the populace as a sort of debt owed to them by their rulers. They constituted, as it were, an act of government. Suetonius, in his history of the emperors, after giving details of the family, marriage, and official positions occupied by each prince, adds a list of the games and spectacles which he had given.

Throughout the whole history of the Empire, as recorded either by Dion or the writers of the *Historia Augusta*, we find the games mentioned again and again; almost any event was made to serve as an excuse for them—a victory, a death, or an anniversary; occasions were even invented when necessary. The following is an instance of the kind of pretexts employed by the very worst of the emperors. Augustus had induced the Senate to renew his lease of power for ten years, and had instituted the *decennia* in honour of the event. In the absence of any other excuse, any emperor who had reigned for ten years invoked this precedent; even Gallienus, whose father had been defeated by the Persians and remained a prisoner in their hands, celebrated *decennia*, which included a triumph, a hecatomb, and a procession of a very curious kind'; in this the knights, the *plebs*, and the soldiers were dressed in white cloaks, and marched to the Capitol accompanied by women and slaves bearing wax tapers and lamps. The procession also included one hun-

---

¹ *Hist. Aug. Gallienus*, chap. vii.; Peter, ii., p. 86, 15 *et seq.*

dred white oxen, two hundred white sheep, ten elephants, twelve hundred gladiators, two hundred domestic animals of various kinds, and a troupe of mimes and actors of every description.

At the close of each of these state spectacles, whatever their nature might be, a certain number of presents (*munuscula*) were always set apart for the common people.[1] Nero, after the performance of a *togata* by Afranius, allowed the actors to loot the house used as part of the scene, and articles of all sorts were thrown among the people to be scrambled for, such as tickets for the distribution of corn (*tesseræ frumentariæ*), articles of food, birds, money, pearls (the latter probably attached to the *tesseræ*); other objects thus given were pictures, beasts of burden, domestic animals, and even ships, houses, and lands; it was a sort of gigantic lottery.[2] Statius describes in tones of pathetic admiration " the happy day " and " night of intoxication "[3] during which Domitian loaded the people with gifts. We can readily imagine the scenes which took place; and even if we did not possess the testimony of Seneca,[4] we should have no difficulty in picturing the terrible scrambling which occurred on these occasions; many of the articles were either lost, torn to pieces, or stolen; even those who succeeded in getting hold of anything had to pay dearly for it;

---

[1] *Cf.* Chap. V., p. 126, *ff.*

[2] Suetonius, ix.

[3] Statius, *Silvæ*, i., 6, 8 : "diem beatam Læti Cæsaris, *ebriamque noctem.*"

[4] *Ep.*, lxxiv., 7.

prudent men took care to go home before the distribution commenced.

The ordinary spectators at these entertainments, the true *plebs*, were used to the hardships that accompanied them, and thought of nothing but the pleasure. They were easily moved to display a quite unconscious cruelty. This was shown but too clearly in the amphitheatre, but we find the same tendency elsewhere also. An accident having occurred at one of the tight-rope performances, Marcus Aurelius ordered that a net should be used for the future, and the regulation continued in force after his time.[1] Even though we approve of this measure, it astonishes us none the less; from the Roman standpoint it was almost an excess of kindness.

(1) *The Races in the Circus*

Of all the pleasures afforded by the capital, the most popular were the entertainments given in the circus or at the theatres; on certain days " the city lived for nothing but the circus and the stage " (*urbem circo scenæque vacantem*).[2] During the Megalesian games " the whole of Rome flocked to the circus " (*totam hodie Romam circus capit*).[3] The infatuation of the Romans for the races in the circus was so excessive that it survived their Empire. After the sack of Rome by Alaric, the miserable remnant

[1] Capitolinus, xii., 12.
[2] Juvenal, viii., 117.
[3] *Ibid.*, xi., 197.

of the original inhabitants and the peasants who flocked in from the environs to the number of ten thousand loudly demanded games in the circus, which had to be celebrated among the smoking ruins.[1]

The games given in the circus were everywhere much the same, and I do not propose to deal with them here in detail.[2] It will be enough to mention that at Rome, what were known as " the four colours," or in other words four parties, among the spectators were the object of endless contests and struggles in which everyone participated,—upstarts like Trimalchion, slaves, even the emperor himself, in whose eyes the partisans of the opposite colour to his own were little better than rebels.[3] A strange occupation, we moderns are tempted to say (though, indeed, the same remark had been made already by one of the ancients),[4] thus to pass one's time in watching horses and men on chariots racing in this way! Yet thousands took a delight in thus

[1] Orosius, i., 6.

[2] Those who desire further information on this subject are referred to the article *Circus* in Smith, *Dictionary of Greek and Roman Antiquities*, 2 vols., 1890–91.

[3] Thus the Emperor Verus (Capitolinus, *Verus*, vi., 2 ; Peter, i., p. 79, 1) was on the side of the " Greens " ; he had a horse named *Volucer*, in whose honour he had a golden statue erected, an act which drew down on him insults of every kind from the " Blues." Marcus Aurelius (*Medit.*, i., 5) congratulates himself on the fact that, thanks to his tutor, he was never bitten with a passion for either the " Blues " or the " Greens," nor for the *palmularii* nor *scutarii* either. (*Cf.* p. 114.)

[4] Pliny, *Ep.*, ix., 6.

watching them, and never wearied of the sight.   It
was not that they took any interest in the speed of
the horses or the skill of their drivers.   Not so!
With them it was merely a question of a certain
colour and garment.[1]   " Let us assume," says the
author in question, " that the colours were to be
transferred from one side to the other in the course
of a race: the applause of the spectators would at
once be withdrawn from those drivers and horses
whom they have known so long and whose names
they cry, and would follow the morsel of coloured
cloth."

How were ordinary citizens to be expected to restrain themselves when the very emperors set them
such an example of mad folly ?   With the knowledge we possess of these customs, we have no
difficulty in crediting the fact that a successful
charioteer was able to amass a fortune equal to that
of a hundred advocates.[2]   In addition to their regular salaries, the prizes that they won, and the gratuities given them by their backers, they were often
paid large sums for consenting to lose or win a race
in the interest of those who had large sums at
stake.[3]

One charioteer, of Moorish extraction, named
Crescens, who is mentioned in an inscription found
near the places occupied by the " Greens," had
won more than fifteen hundred thousand sesterces

---

[1] Pliny, *ibid.*, " nunc favent *panno, pannum amant.*"
[2] Juvenal, vii., 113.
[3] Saglio quotes the texts ; p. 1196, note 70, *et seq.*

(£12,000) by the time he was twenty-two years old. *Diocles*, who was the most famous charioteer of classical times, left his son more than thirty-five million sesterces (£280,000).   Children's toys and pocket-knives with bone handles have been found, on which are engraved palms and whips, or the names of horses and charioteers, and their portraits.   One small chariot made of lead, evidently intended as a toy for a child of two or three, is apparently a reproduction of some winning chariot, and is inscribed with the names of the horses and charioteers.[1]   The *viridis thorax* mentioned in Juvenal[2] as having been given to a child with a few pence and some nuts, was doubtless the jacket of some charioteer belonging to the " Green " faction. It need not be wondered at that so precocious a passion as this should develop to the full later on.[4]

(2) *The Circus Maximus*

The emperors seem, even the best of them, to have vied with one another in their devotion to the games, for, reign after reign, the circus seems to have

[1] Lanciani, *Anc. Rome*, p. 216.
[2] In the Museum of the Capitol (Lanciani, p. 216).
[3] Juvenal, v., 143.
[4] *Cf.* the well-known passage in one of Tactitus's dialogues (xxix.): " Jam vero propria et pecularia hujus urbis vitia *paene in utero mairis* concipi mihi videntur : histrionalis favor et *gladiatorum equorumque studia*" (Now, however, the characteristic vices peculiar to this city seem to be inherited by the child while he is yet in his mother's womb ; he dotes on actors and is infatuated with gladiatorial combats and horse races).

become ever larger and more splendid; it was em-
phatically declared that this was only in order " to
keep pace with the growth of the Roman people."[1]
Of all this richly decorated edifice, which was enlarged to such an extent that in the end it accom-
modated four hundred thousand spectators, nothing
now is left.   From the top of the Palatine one can
only distinguish the site on which it stood.

If we desire to see a subject which has been
handled by one of our modern painters[2] as it is
represented on an ancient building, viz., the scene
in the circus, where the drivers challenge and defy
one another as they whirl round the course, the
spectators all agog with excitement, one hapless
competitor, his horses thrown and chariot over-
turned, lying prostrate in the dust, while his successful rival sweeps triumphantly up to the goal, we
shall find a rough sketch of it, at any rate, in a
mosaic discovered in 1884 at Gerona, in Spain,
which is reproduced by Lanciani.[3] In this we
can clearly distinguish the starting-point (*carceres*),
the *spina* profusely decorated with trophies, statues,
and an obelisk, four chariots (one of them in the act
of overturning), to each of which four horses are
harnessed abreast, and, underneath, the names of
the drivers and some of the horses.

[1] "Ἐξαρκοῦντα τῷ τῶν Ρωμαίων δήμῳ."   The phrase and
the inscription are due to Trajan (Xiph. Dion, lxviii., 7).

[2] Gérôme.

[3] *Anc. Rome*, p. 215. With this may be compared the drawings
from mosaics discovered at Lyons and Barcelona which are given by
Saglio (figs. 1520 and 1523).

(3) *Greek Games in the Stadium*

The Greek games are too well known to require description. They consisted of foot-races, wrestling-and boxing-matches, etc., and were introduced into Rome by Nero and Domitian. They were held in *stadia*, of moderate size, and in shape something like the earlier Roman circuses, or like those which they built for temporary purposes. We can form a pretty accurate idea of them by examining the Piazza Navone (*Circo agonale*), the earlier *stadium* of Domitian, or from the other *stadium* constructed by the same Emperor on the Palatine, which has just been unearthed through the agency of the *École Française*.[1] This latter must have been lavishly decorated and seems to our eyes very extensive.

(4) *The Theatres*

The theatre has been in all countries and in all ages one of the central points of social life. Inside its walls gentle and simple jostle against one another. It is thither that the stranger must go to observe them if he wishes to discover their habits and tastes.

Nor was it otherwise at Rome. The subjects dealt with or referred to in the Roman plays were identical with those of which the poets sang in pol-

---

[1] *Cf.* the article by M. Deglane in the *Mélanges de l'École de Rome*, 1889, pp. 184 *et seq.* This identification and the proposed reconstruction have since been called in question by Fr. Marx, *Jahrb. K.D. Arch.*, 1895, 3.

ished verse, or which the sculptor sought to reproduce, or the painter and worker in mosaic depicted
on the walls and pavements, such as Achilles, Helen,
and all the other creations of Homer; Bacchus and
his train of Mænads; the luckless Dirce; Hero and
Leander; Paris and the rival goddesses; all these
appear on the walls of Pompeii and in the ancient
mosaics of every country, no less than in the verses
of Ovid. The same subjects are to be found in the
Roman farces and tragedies, and are continually referred to in their comedies. It was at the theatres
and in the banqueting halls that the latest verse of
the day went the rounds.[1] It is to the theatre, no
less than to the public promenades, that Ovid
directs the lover in search of a new flame.

The upper classes cannot indulge their caprices in
matters theatrical unless these caprices are generally
shared by others and harmonise with accepted conventions; it is the taste of the multitude which de-
cides and controls everything. For this reason it
would be extremely interesting could we acquire a
thorough knowledge of the history of the Roman
drama, and ascertain what were the likes and dislikes of the public; we might thus be able to follow
through all its stages that process of evolution which
caused it to sink from the higher ranks of tragedy,

---

[1] Martial, ii., 6, 8 :

> " Hæc sunt . . . quæ sinu ferebas
>   Per convivia cuncta, per *theatra*."

(These are the verses that you carried so carefully concealed in your
bosom, to every banquet, and to all the theatres.)

either translated or imitated from the great masters, and from classical comedy to the coarseness and indecency of farce and pantomime. Unfortunately, the information which we possess in regard to the pieces played in the theatre, the precise elements of which the audience was composed, and the degree of interest they took in the play, is both meagre and vague; so much so, that more than half of what it would be essential for us to know is completely hidden from us.[1]

On the other hand, thanks to Vitruvius, and still more to the numerous ruins which have come down to us, we know pretty clearly what a Roman theatre was like. We have them of all sizes. In so far as external decoration is concerned, the theatre of Marcellus may serve as an example, while the small theatre attached to Hadrian's villa, or those of Herculanum or Pompeii, give an idea of the internal arrangements.

We know that, as a rule, the interior consisted of a sort of semicircle furnished with tiers of seats (*cunei*) in parallel rows (*præcinctiones*), intersected by alleys (*vomitoria*) through which the spectators came in and went out. Facing the seats stood a wall decorated with columns and statues, which served as a background to the stage. There was no roof, though awnings were sometimes used to protect the spectators from the sun. On the outside were por-

[1] We have already seen that Vergilius Romanus, a contemporary of Pliny the Younger, composed with success comedies imitated from Menander. *Ep.*, vi., 21, 2. *Cf.* Bücheler, *Carm. Epigr.*, i., no. 97.

ticos for shelter in case of rain.   These contributed
to make the theatres very imposing buildings.

It will thus be seen that the Roman theatres differed quite as much from ours as did those of the
Greeks, on which they were modelled.   One thing
which strikes us particularly is, that they were almost without exception[1] open to the sky, and that,
though their capacity varied a good deal, the accommodation for spectators was limited.   What they
lacked in size was made up for in better acoustic
properties.   The actors played with masks on, erect
and almost motionless in their *socci* and *cothurni*,
draped in flowing robes and gorgeous cloaks.   We
learn all these details from statues, paintings, and,
above all, from the mosaics, in which masks and
other theatrical " properties " are frequently used
as decorative themes.

At the theatre, as at the circus, the noise was
something deafening.   Horace refers to it in one of
his epistles,[2] and tradition confirms his testimony.[3]

[1] The single exception is the small covered theatre at Pompeii.
In Messrs. Boeswillwald and Cagnat's monograph on *Timgad*, pp.
93 *et seq.*, will be found a description of the theatre of that place,
which held 4000 persons, and a comparison of this building with the
principal theatres of antiquity.

[2] *Ep.*, ii., 1, 202 :
   " *Garganum mugire putes nemus* aut mare Tuscum."
(One might almost imagine one was listening to the rustle of the
Garganian woods, or the thunder of the Etrurian waves.)

[3] *Cf.* Philo, *De Legat. ad Caium*, 45 (M. p. 598 ; P. 1041), where
the story is told how when Caligula received a Jewish deputation at
his country house, " the cries and hooting of those who jeered at us
were so loud, one might almost have thought one was in a theatre "
(ὡς ἐν Θεατρικοῖς μίμοις).

What pieces were played in the theatres under the Empire ? We can scarcely tell, since contemporary writers, when they refer to the subject at all, attach no importance to anything but the demonstrations on the part of the audience or the talents of the actors. Not one of these plays, many of which were probably little more than rough drafts, have come down to us. It seems probable that in addition to revivals of standard works, a good many new pieces were produced: tragedies in which the actor represented the *cantica* by his singing and gestures; next came the classical comedies, the *togatæ* and the *prætextæ*, and last, but not least, farce and pantomime. Neither the subjects of the plays nor the acting of the players were particularly edifying. Indeed, philosophers, and even poets, admitted that the influence of the theatre was a demoralising one.[1]

But, as we have just said, the points which most impressed contemporary Romans, and which have been most carefully recorded by historians, were the topical allusions, which were seized on by the audience and wittily turned against the government. This was a custom which, as we learn from Cicero, was very dear to the hearts of the Roman public. No matter where they were, whether at the circus, the theatre, or the amphitheatre, they never missed an opportunity of making a political demonstration.

[1] Martial, in speaking of an austere man, says (ix., 27, 9): "*Cum theatris* sæculoque rixaris" (You declaim against the license of the theatre and the vices of the day).

Nor can we very well blame them for it, when we find the heads of the government solemnly weighing these plaudits and appraising the importance of every hiss or jeer.[1]   Even the best of the emperors, Marcus Aurelius included, did not succeed in escaping these pin-pricks, and had to put up with them as best they could.   Princes of violent temperament, such as Nero and Caligula, exacted cruel vengeance for them, striking at random.   The theatre was the favourite scene for these spontaneous outbursts; there, demands were loudly advanced, to which even a Tiberius was forced to accede.[2]   The tradition of these demonstrations was jealously guarded by the people of the capital, who set great store by this, the last and only one of their liberties that remained to them.   A modern counterpart of these demonstrations was furnished by the *pasquinades* of papal Rome.   It is needless to add that the popular delight was increased rather than diminished when, as sometimes happened, the emperor failed to catch the drift of one of these outbursts, and those about him did not dare to explain it.[3]

(5) *The Amphitheatre*

The sight of an ancient amphitheatre is calculated to awake in us emotions of a twofold nature:

---

[1] *Cf. Pro Sestio*, lv., 118 *et seq.*; lix., 125 *et seq.*

[2] The Latin word is "*reclamant.*"   The people called upon Tiberius to return a statue by Lysippus, the ἀποξυόμενος (representing a man who has just left the bath and is scraping himself with a *strigil*), originally placed by Agrippa in his *thermæ*, which Tiberius had transferred to his own palace.

[3] *E.g.*, *Hist. Aug.*, *Maximin.*, ix., 3 (Peter, ii., p. 9).

on the one hand, we cannot suppress our admiration for these edifices, which overpower us by their vast size and majestic proportions; on the other hand, the thought of the spectacles which men came here to witness cannot but fill us with horror and astonishment.[1]

An amphitheatre, properly so called, was a double theatre; Curio's two movable theatres when united formed an ordinary amphitheatre. The largest and most splendid of those which have come down to us is the Colosseum; but there are many others of large dimensions and richly decorated. I need but mention those of Pompeii and Verona.[2] We have already commented on the small size of many of the ancient theatres; here, on the contrary, what chiefly impresses us is the extent of the amphitheatres, their imposing bulk, and—in the case of some of them the word is in no way an exaggeration—their immensity.

Everyone knows the purposes for which they were used, and the kind of entertainments that was held in them. Were it otherwise, we should find full details in Martial, not so much in his epigrams —though even these contain frequent allusions to topics of this kind—as in a special book which in most editions of his works is placed before all the others, and known as the *De Spectaculis*.

---

[1] *Cf.* in Saglio the article *Gladiateurs* by M. Lafaye, and the article *Amphitheatrum* by M. Thierry; also Smith, *Dictionary of Greek and Roman Antiquities*, 2 vols., 1890–91.

[2] Friedlaender gives a list of them in the supplement to vol. ii. of the German edition of his *Sittengeschichte*, pp. 502 *et seq.*

(a) *Entertainments in the Amphitheatre, Mythological Subjects, Festivals of Various Kinds*

Stage machinery played an important part in the amphitheatre. The area was so arranged as to permit of its being flooded for naval engagements and then quickly drained again for combats on dry land. By the introduction of scenery and the necessary scaffolding, mythological subjects were represented in a very complete manner. Among the subjects treated in the arena were the Judgment of Paris as described by Apuleius; Leander swimming across the Hellespont; Hercules, Neptune, the Nereids; the earth was made to open, and Orpheus coming forth from it was quickly surrounded by animals. The populace took a particular pleasure in obscene or cruel spectacles; Pasiphæ and the bull, Dædalus torn to pieces by a bear, and Prometheus, played by some unfortunate wretch whose sufferings were painfully real, were, therefore, favourite themes with them. In describing the torments of Laureolus in one of these tableaux, Martial excuses the cruelty of the spectacle, of which he seems to have been dimly conscious, by pleading that the tortured man must be a criminal.[1] Men said of him, as of the hundreds of animals sacrificed in these exhibitions, that it was a loss not worth speaking about (*perdere vile est*).

The other items in the programme at the amphitheatre included gymnastic and rope-walking performances of all kinds, performing animals, etc.

[1] *De Spect.*, 7.

Even in the time of Diocletian we find both the public porticos and those belonging to the emperors' palaces covered with paintings representing the games given by Carus and Carinus, and the feats of the gymnasts and experts who performed before the people on that occasion.[1]

But the greater part of the performances in the amphitheatre consisted of hunting spectacles, wild-beast fights (*venationes*), and gladiatorial combats.

(b) *Hunting Spectacles, Wild-Beast Fights, and Gladiatorial Combats*

The accession of an emperor to the throne, his victories, real or assumed—any of these furnished a good excuse for an entertainment in the amphitheatre. The amount of money laid out on them was enormous, the expenditure of human and animal life appalling. Nothing to approach these spectacles had ever been witnessed in the time of the Republic, although, even in those days, more than one ambitious politician had ruined himself in

[1] Vopiscus, 18 (Peter, ii., p. 244, 4): "Memorabile maxime Cari et Carini et Numeriani hoc habuit imperium, quod ludos populo R. novis ornatos spectaculis dederunt, *quos in Palatio circa porticum stabuli pictos vidimus*" (The reign of Carus, Carinus, and Numerianus was specially memorable by the fact that they provided games for the Roman people into which a number of novel features were introduced, which we have seen painted up on the Palatine round the public porticos). Later on, we find mention made of a *neurobates* (rope-dancer), a *tichobates* (*lit.* mountebank who walks on a wall [τεῖχος], though whether he surmounted obstacles placed on it, or went through some sort of military drill, is not certain), of dancing bears, choruses, actors, fireworks, etc.

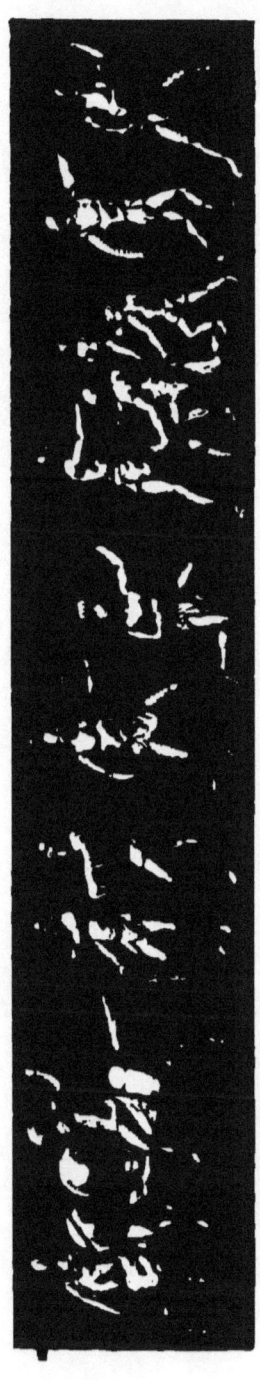
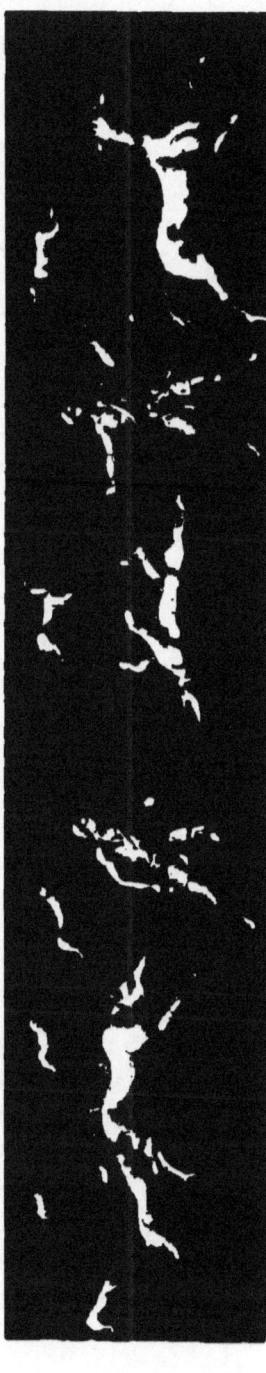

RELIEFS SHOWING FIGHTS OF GLADIATORS AND WILD BEASTS.
(From the Tomb of Umbricius Scaurus at Pompeii.)

the attempt to gain popularity by this means.[1]
When Trajan returned to Rome after his final victory over Decebalus and the Dacians he gave an
entertainment which lasted 123 days, during which
from 1000 to 10,000 animals, both wild and domestic, were killed, and in which as many as 10,000
gladiators took part.[2] The description of a great
hunting spectacle held by Probus in the circus is
given by his biographer.[3] Lions, leopards, and
bears were introduced on this occasion by the hundred; stags, wild boars, and fallow deer by the
thousand, and large trees were brought into the
arena to represent a forest.

In the morning it was the custom to exhibit rare
beasts, such as antelopes and giraffes, in the arena;
then came fights between animals of different species,
such as lions and bears, elephants and wild boars,
rhinoceroses and leopards. Sometimes the proceedings were varied by pitting wild animals against their
tamers. The performance was preceded by processions, including a parade of chariots (*pompa*), this
part of the entertainment being regarded by the
ascetic school with quite as much distaste as the
games in the circus itself.[4] The gladiatorial com-

[1] One of the reasons which led Cassius to kill Cæsar was because
the latter had engaged the lions which Cassius wished to exhibit in
the amphitheatre.

[2] Dion-Xiphilinus, lxviii., 15.

[3] Cap. xix. (P., ii., p. 215, 24 *et seq.*).

[4] It produced a weariness (*tedium pompæ*) quite as great as that
caused by the triumphs. Suetonius, *Vespasian*, 12; Seneca, *Præf.*,
etc.

8

bats took place in the afternoon.   These were not restricted to fencing matches between the participants, fought out to the bitter end; a certain variety was introduced by making the men fight under different rules and with different weapons. The gladiators were followed by the *palmularii* and *scutarii*, the *retiarii*, the Thracians, the Myrmidons, etc.   Some of the actors were dressed up in historical costumes to represent Ajax, Telamon, etc. Combats between dwarfs and women were also much appreciated by the spectators.

No modern can read the accounts of these famous spectacles without giving the first place in his thoughts to the victims.   We can guess but too well what the feelings of the German or barbarian prisoners must have been as they were paraded round in carriages during the " morning spectacle," knowing, as they did, the fate reserved for them in the afternoon.   We can understand why they sought to escape, even when suicide, in its most dreadful forms, was the only alternative.[1]   But the testimony of the Christian Fathers confirms what we find recorded elsewhere, namely, that the sight of these doomed spectators proved an irresistible attraction, even to the more indifferent members of the audience, so easily does the craving for new and violent

[1] Seneca, *Ep.*, lxx., 17, 20, and 22, tells us that one of them choked himself with a filthy sponge, another pretended to drop asleep and fell with his head under the wheel of a chariot, a third plunged the sword which had been given him to fight with during the *naumachia* into his own breast.

emotions lead men to forget the cruelty involved
in their gratification.

We all know what the " Scotland Yard Museum "
of our own time is like, and have heard of detectives
having their pocketbooks bound in the skins of
criminals. The Cæsars, in spite of their frequent
cruelty, indulged in hobbies of a less gruesome
type. When two skilful gladiators killed each
other with simultaneous thrusts, Claudius ordered
a number of small knives to be made for him out of
their sword blades.[1] It was this same Emperor (he
had the reputation of being good-natured but a fool)
who, when a part of the spectacle went wrong
owing to the fault of one of the officials in charge
of the arrangements, ordered the man to be thrown
to the beasts, thus providing the public with an
additional and unexpected sensation.[2]

The craze for going down into the arena and
making exhibition of themselves, either as perform-
ers or as gladiators, had, as we know, infected
even Romans of good family long before the days
of Nero and Commodus. Cæsar allowed himself to
be persuaded into permitting the knights to thus
debase themselves, but he begged that no such
petition should be presented on behalf of the senators. From the time of Augustus onwards there
was scarcely a single spectacle, if Dion may be

[1] Suetonius, 34.
[2] *Ibid.* An *accident* of a similar kind happened to one of his
Nomenclatores (an official whose duty it was to announce visitors),
who was thrown into the arena, toga and all.

credited, in which knights and senators did not thus take part.

In conclusion, I may mention that besides the great mosaic discovered in the baths of Caracalla, which is preserved in the Lateran Collection, copious details in regard to the dress and weapons of the gladiators are to be found in other fine mosaics in the same collection and at the Villa Borghese.   Our knowledge of this phase of ancient life is, therefore, fairly accurate and complete.

CHAPTER V

NEW YEAR'S GIFTS AND PRESENTS UNDER THE EMPIRE

W E now come to a subject which is typically Roman; the practice of making New Year's gifts (*strenæ*) was one peculiarly characteristic of the Latin races. There is, it is true, some controversy as to the derivation of the word. The view which finds most adherents is that it was borrowed from the name of an ancient Sabine goddess, *Strenia*, who bestowed strength and good health on her worshippers. Not long ago, M. Bréal[1] contended that *strenæ* is merely a contraction of *Saturnæ feriæ*. Be this as it may, the custom was essentially a Roman one, which was celebrated on a day dedicated to Janus, an essentially Roman deity. The Greeks, so the Latins assure us, possessed nothing to correspond with him.[2]

[1] *Mémoires de la Société de linguistique*, viii., 1889, p. 29. If this contention be correct, we must treat the word from a Semitic standpoint and disregard everything but the consonants.

[2] Ovid, *Fasti*, i., 89 :
"Te dicam, Jane biformis ;
Nam tibi par nullum Græcia numen habet."
(I will sing of thee, two-headed Janus ; for Greece has no deity like unto thee.)

117

Let us see in what this practice consisted, and what it has to teach us in regard to Roman life and character.   But since the topic is a somewhat limited one and there are numerous gaps in the tradition which surrounds it, I shall not confine myself solely to New Year's gifts, but shall also say a few words in regard to some of the other presents which it was customary to make at Rome on various occasions; these included the presents given during the Saturnalia (*Saturnalium munuscula*), presents to visitors (*Xenia*), and souvenirs distributed by the host at the end of a banquet, which were drawn for by lot and taken away by the guests (*Apophoreta*).

I

THE KALENDS OF JANUARY—NEW YEAR'S GIFTS

The Kalends of January, or New Year's Day, was an important festival at Rome.   To begin with, it was an official holiday.   The emperor, clad in magnificent robes of state, received a deputation of knights and senators who came to present their good wishes.   Indeed, some of the emperors received the whole of the citizens, who filed past in front of them, each of them being presented with a piece of money, in accordance with the general custom.   Moreover, it was a religious festival as well, and was duly observed in every house.   The proceedings began on the family hearth, where the Lares were exposed after they had been decked out in honour of the day.   Then a round of visits was paid at the houses of friends amid general rejoicings.

Let us try to discover the meaning of this festival. What were the benefits demanded from the household gods, and what was the cause of all these real or pretended rejoicings. The reason is not far to seek. This day marked the beginning of the year, and by superstitious minds the beginning of anything is regarded as an omen of its future. The answer which Ovid puts into the mouth of Janus exactly expresses the Roman theory on this point:

" *Omina principiis*, inquit, *inesse* solent." [1]

It was indispensable that the omens should be favourable, and no effort was spared in order to make them so. Desiring, as they did, that this brief space of a few hours might be typical of the days and months that were to succeed it, the Romans regarded a calm and cheerful attitude as a sort of safeguard against the approach of troubles. An obolus received from a friend was made the basis of all sorts of golden hopes, whereas an inopportune or untoward remark gave rise to grave disquietude lest it should " bring misfortune." When Marius and Tiberius, selfish, sceptical, and cruel politicians as they were, declined to postpone even on this first day of the year the execution of their deadly reprisals, their contemporaries did not fail to look upon this as a presage of impending disaster.

The word *strena* was, so we are told, originally

[1] " It is by their beginnings that we can generally tell how things will turn out." *Fasti*, i., 178.

used of the consecrated branch plucked from the sacred grove which encircled the *Streniæ sacellum*. It was, we further learn, a laurel branch, typical of victory. But this connecting link between the festival and the religious ceremony seems to have been relaxed at a very early date.

At first the presents given were of a very simple kind. The poorer classes, who naturally could not afford anything else, declared, later on, that they alone had remained faithful to the ancient tradition. They presented one another with palm branches, figs, honey, or dates, these being occasionally wrapped in a gilded leaf. To these offerings in kind another was added which came in time to be the only one recognised and displaced all others. This was a piece of money (*stips*), at first of brass, afterwards of gold,—in short, a more or less considerable amount,—or some object of either artistic or intrinsic value, which was quickly appraised by the person to whom it was given.

It was usual to attach a symbolical meaning to these gifts. Thus fruit or confectionery foreshadowed a year full of sweetness; gold or silver coins a profitable year. Very often a gift was accompanied by a special inscription expressive of the donor's good wishes; thus a small shield was attached to lamps and candlesticks bearing the words, "*Annum novum faustum felicem*," [1] and on the coins the head of Janus, crowned with laurel, was surrounded by a similar legend.

[1] "A happy and prosperous New Year."

These presents and good wishes became in time a
firmly established national custom, observed by all
ranks of society, and in spite of the trouble and expense which they entailed, the emperors were obliged
both to receive and return them. Although the
practice was more than once suspended, it soon
came into force again. The public liked it, and the
emperor submitted to it for the sake of popularity.
As the natural protector of all the citizens, and
father of his country, it was only right that he
should gratefully accept what was supposed to be a
pledge of affection on the part of his subjects in the
capital; and, naturally, he was expected to return
their offerings three or four times over, a fact which,
as might be expected, did not tend to lessen the
number of his New Year's visitors. Even between
private individuals, the New Year's offering was as
often as not merely a bait, but in the emperor's case
one felt absolutely certain that the fish must rise
to it.

Even if the emperor happened to be absent from
Rome, the ceremony took place all the same.[1] If
he was in Rome, he was obliged to sacrifice himself
and to remain at the Capitol hour after hour, day
after day, and sometimes even month after month,
watching long lines of strange faces file past him,
thanking them for their gifts and rewarding them
with his own hand.[2] We can understand why it was
that Tiberius, after having at first submitted to this

[1] Suetonius, *Aug.*, 57.
[2] *E. g.*, Augustus (Dion, liv., 35).

tedious function, afterwards took care to avoid it whenever he could.[1]   Caligula had only to restore the ancient custom to secure immediate popularity. His enemies alleged that he did so because he loved to handle the piles of coin, and that he even publicly wallowed in the money presented to him.[2]

The practice was continued down to the close of the Western Empire.   Inscriptions still in existence confirm the statement made by Suetonius to the effect that Augustus [3] employed the money received by him from the citizens on the Kalends of January in erecting, on a lavish scale, statues and chapels to various deities, such as Jupiter Tragœdus, Apollo Sandaliarius, etc.[4]

These presents were accompanied by all sorts of good wishes for the welfare of the emperor and his family, and also by oaths of fidelity, so that there was really a kind of double ceremony,—one at the palace, the other in the Senate.   The practice evidently originated during Cæsar's dictatorship, and after his death the triumvirs carried on the tradition as being likely to add to their political stability.   On the first day of the year of the proscriptions they swore, and caused others to swear, that they would ratify all the acts of Cæsar, and, adds Dion,[5] " the

[1] Suetonius, 34.

[2] *Ibid.*, 42.

[3] *Ibid.*, 57.

[4] The formula used in the inscriptions is : " *ex stipe* quam populus Romanus anno novo absenti contulit" (with the money given by the Roman people to the absent emperor on New Year's Day); *e.g*., *C. I. L.*, vi., 457; *cf.* Nos. 456 and 458.

[5] Dion, xlvii., 18.

custom is still observed to this day in the case of all those who succeed to the supreme power, or who have exercised it, so long as they have not been branded with infamy."

II

PRESENTS GIVEN DURING THE SATURNALIA

Shortly before the Kalends of January, on the 17th of December and the following days, which were known as the *Saturnalia*, it was also customary to exchange gifts, which differed in their meaning and nature from the New Year's gifts mainly in this respect, that in January one had to be serious; behind Janus stood Phœbus, Pallas, and the Muses, the newly elected magistrates entered on their functions with much solemnity, and everyone was afraid of doing or saying something which might have a bad effect on the coming year.   During the Saturnalia, on the other hand, all constraint was relaxed; there was no room for anything save smiles and laughter; a temporary madness seemed to pervade everything.[1]   On all sides there was feasting and junketing.   The Romans laid aside their togas and donned an embroidered robe, known as the *synthesis*, with the *pileus* for head-gear.[2]   December was a month of pleasure which they would gladly have

---

[1] *Cf.* Statius, *Silv.*, i., 6, 1.

[2] Properly speaking, the cap given to a slave on his enfranchisement.

made last throughout the year.[1]   Hence the phrase, *libertas Decembris.*

This is not the place in which to speak of the temporary fiction which allowed the slave to do as he liked and eat what he liked, just as though he were free; or of the public rejoicings, marked by gladiatorial combats, farces, acrobatic performances, and doles of food, with which this " best of days "[2] was hailed, once the glad cry of " *Io Saturnalia !* " had resounded.   At present, we are only concerned with the interchange of presents on this occasion.

As in January, they varied greatly both in kind and in value.   Here again it was the poor who took the lead and gave some small gift—the smaller the better—in the hope of receiving a larger offering in return.   The form usually taken by these gifts was either that of wax tapers (*cerei*) or, more frequently, of small coloured casts of figures (*sigilla, sigillaria*). There was such a large demand for them that a sort of market was held for the express purpose of selling them, and one of the streets of Rome—the *Via Sigillaria*—was named after the workmen employed in their manufacture.   These statuettes were generally made in the likeness of some divinity, such as Hercules, Minerva, Apollo Sauroctonus,[3] Victory, or of some celebrated mythological character (Danäe or Hyacinthus); failing this, of some

---

[1] Seneca, *Ep.*, xviii., 1.

[2] Catullus, xiv., 15 : "*optimo dierum.*"

[3] The "lizard-killer"; in a famous statue by Praxiteles a lizard appeared climbing the trunk of the tree by the side of the god.

purely fantastic type, such as an hermaphrodite, or hunchback. These *sigilla* were sometimes made of clay, in which case their worth was but trifling unless the workmanship possessed unusual merit; those made of marble, Corinthian bronze, silver, or gold, were, however, frequently of considerable value.[1] Many people exercised a good deal of ingenuity in the attempt to seem generous at small expense; they made offerings of game, cakes, linen, clothing, or of tablets.[2] The givers, and in some cases the receivers, from motives of vanity, sought to hide the paltry nature of their presents by boasting of their number and size.[3] Thus one of the characters in Martial wittily remarks[4] that as a friendship begins to wear out, the gifts received from one's friends during successive Saturnalia tend to diminish in weight; he is certain of this because he has taken the trouble of weighing them! From good service-able plates and dishes he finds himself cut down to mere spoons. It is the story of Mandrabulus all over again.[5] In place of stanzas written on choice

---

[1] I take these instances from Friedlaender, who quotes them from Martial (xiv., 170–182), though the *sigilla* there mentioned are really presents given at a banquet. But, no doubt, those exchanged during the Saturnalia were of a similar character.

[2] *Cf.* the list given by Statius (*Silv.*, iv., 9, 24 *et seq.*), though this is probably to a large extent imaginative.

[3] Martial, iv., 56, and vii., 53.

[4] *Ibid.*, viii., 71.

[5] Lucian tells the story of a certain Mandrabulus who, having dis-covered a treasure at Samos, offered to Juno a golden sheep in the first year of his discovery; the next year the sheep was of silver; the third year he considered brass quite good enough.

papyrus, with a purple edging and ivory ornaments, the minor poet to his great disgust finds his gift reduced to a battered roll of verses, which prove on examination to be nothing but some antediluvian rhapsody.[1] These were some of the laughable tricks played on one another by friends.

The emperor, however, set an example of generosity in every direction. We read that Hadrian, who was by no means a spendthrift, took advantage of the Saturnalia to send his friends impromptu presents (*Saturnalicia* and *sigillaria*); he repaid to the magistrates appointed by him all their extraordinary expenses, and returned all presents received by him.[2]

The inhabitants of Rome invariably looked forward to some sort of public entertainment at this season. Statius describes in detail[3] a festival given by Domitian in honour of the Saturnalia, "a day of happiness, a night of intoxication," as he calls it. From the top of the amphitheatre (probably the Colosseum) poured down fruit of every possible kind, figs, nuts, cakes, and even cheeses. People of all ranks were invited; the whole body of the citizens sat down to a banquet at which they were the guests of Cæsar himself. Then followed a series of performances; duels between women whose bravery rivalled that of the Amazons; between dwarfs who, with hunched-up backs and legs gath-

[1] Statius, *Silv.*, iv., 9.
[2] Spartianus, xvii., 2.
[3] *Silv.*, i., 6.

ered under them ready to spring at one another, poured out a volley of threats and challenges, to the great amusement of the spectators.   Next came a procession of the various characters who appeared at theatrical performances, women of light character, debauchees—in short, "all the riff-raff of the stage."   A dense flock of birds, including pheasants and guinea-fowl, swooped down from above, and the entertainment terminated with a general illumination.

This description is from the pen of an admirer who only inserts one or two details that bear the impress of realism.   But we need only recall the details of certain popular festivals of modern times to realise that the main programme must have been accompanied by unrehearsed incidents of a kind which appealed strongly to Roman tastes, but which the courtier poet deemed it politic to pass over in silence.   He says nothing of the scramble for gifts, though, from what Seneca [1] tells us, they must frequently have given rise to very disagreeable and even dangerous scenes.

III

OTHER PRESENTS—"XENIA," "APOPHORETA"

Apart from the presents made at the Kalends of January and during the Saturnalia, which recurred at a fixed date every year, there were certain gifts which it was usual to give and receive on other oc-

[1] *Ep.*, lxxiv., 7.

casions, such as the end of a visit or the close of a
banquet.   These were described by Greek words
indicative of their meaning, the former being called
Xenia, the latter *Apophoreta*.   Thanks to the details
given concerning them in the last two books of
Martial, our knowledge of them is fairly complete.

Though the general meaning of these two words
is clear enough, it should be noted that the first of
the two was used in a very wide sense, a fact which
led to occasional ambiguity.   Thus the word *Xenia*
was used of the presents given during the Saturnalia,
these being regarded as really gifts of hospitality, a
man's friends being looked on in the light of visitors;
for the same reason a guest at a banquet was also
regarded as a visitor, and the term *Xenia* was sometimes applied to the presents given to each guest at
its close.   No guest could be allowed to depart
empty-handed; if there was nothing else, he must
at least take away his napkin with him.[1]   In this
case the term *Apophoreta* was used of the presents
made ready beforehand by the host for distribution
at the end of the repast.   The word also came to
be applied to the drawing of lots, because it was
customary to distribute the presents in this way.
A lottery of this kind, with its amusing contrasts
and vicissitudes, was much enjoyed by the Romans,
and, besides, each present was carefully described
(*possumus   .   .   .   pretium dicere muneri*).

In the fantastic code drawn up by Lucian for use

[1] This custom explains the trick played on Catullus by his friends
(xii. and xxv.).

during the Saturnalia[1] it was suggested that each
gift should be accompanied by a note stating what
it was and how much there was of it, so that neither
the sender nor his friends might run the risk of being
defrauded by their slaves. Martial wrote a whole
book of epigrams (xiii.) with a view to supplying his
readers with a sort of complete letter-writer containing mottoes intended to take the place of these
notes.

When a guest came to stay with one, more particularly in the country, it would have shown great
want of respect and civility to allow him to go away
without the usual presents. When Pliny was invited by Trajan to take part in the deliberations of
his council at Centumcellæ,[2] he received the customary *Xenia* on leaving the villa. He does not tell us
what it was that Trajan gave him, but we know
the objects enumerated by Martial in Book xiii.
They consisted almost entirely of fruit, wine, and
food of all kinds included in the *menu* of the ancients, *e.g.*, trout and other fish, including the
muræna and the dory; game, including the dor-
mouse and the peacock; fruit, wine, and, to crown
all, perfumes and wreaths of roses.

We now come to the presents given at the close
of a banquet; these were covered by the word
Apophoreta, used in its primary sense. Presents of

[1] *Cronosolon*, 15.
[2] *Ep.*, vi., 31, 14: "Summo die *abeuntibus nobis* (tam diligens in
Cæsare humanitas) *Xenia sunt missa*" (On the last day, just as we
were on the point of departure, Xenia were sent to us, such is Cæsar's
attentiveness to his guests).

this kind were often made on a large scale.   On one
occasion Caligula, who was a most violent and enthusiastic partisan of the " Greens," presented
Eutychus, one of their most successful charioteers,
with two million sesterces by way of *Apophoreta*[1] at
the end of a state banquet; and Plutarch[2] tells us
that Cleopatra, even after the battle of Actium,
" celebrated Antony's birthday on such a lavish
scale as to surpass all previous limits of sumptuous
magnificence, so much so, that many of the guests
who came to the feast poor men, went away rich."

After the *Xenia* (xiii.) Martial, in another book
(xiv.), describes the *Apophoreta* which were usually
given in his day.   He employs the word in its narrower sense.   These *Apophoreta* were, in part,[3] at
any rate, objects of value, and, moreover, they were
sorted into pairs.   On a previous page we noticed
that in the matter of presents the client always set
his patron an example.   It was probably in memory
of this custom that it became the practice in dis-
tributing the *Apophoreta* to allot first a valuable
present and then a worthless one in regular succession, the real order of things being here inverted,
and the worthless present being, moreover, generally

---

[1] About £16,000 ; the fact is recorded by Suetonius, 55.

[2] *Antony*, xcv.

[3] *E.g.*, the presents of the rich mentioned by Martial.   The tablets of onyx and crystal used by Cleopatra for her love-letters to
Antony (δελτάρια τῶν ἐρωτικῶν ὀνύχινα καὶ κρυστάλλινα),
which the triumvir used to read—to the great indignation of the Romans—as he sat in his tribunal administering justice to kings and
princes, were possibly presents of this class.   (Plutarch, *Ant.*, lxxvi.)

a sort of parody of the valuable one. For instance, one present might be, say, an ivory purse filled with gold; the next on the list would be a wooden purse filled with coppers (xii. and xiii.). A candelabra, statuette, or other object intended to represent a rich man's gift would probably be of some precious metal, gold or Corinthian bronze, while the same thing offered by a poor man would be of some common material such as clay or wood. Naturally, therefore, if chance assigned the same object to two guests in succession, the first alone would be of any value, and the unlucky recipient of the latter would be greeted by the ready jeers of his companions because of his ill luck in having his name drawn too late.

In the case of certain articles, humorous contrasts of this kind were not necessary; the mere fact of a beggar's wallet or a pair of corsets being allotted to a man was in itself sufficiently ludicrous.

From this it was but a step to lotteries in which punning descriptions were attached to the objects raffled for. These were productive of much amusement at the feasts of Trimalchion and at the court of Heliogabalus.[1]

[1] A single example taken from Petronius (56) may be given, the pun in it being a fairly obvious one; the ticket drawn bore the words *muræna et litera* (a muræna and a letter), the present allotted was *murem cum rana fascemque betæ* (a rat and a frog and a bundle of beet). In this the words *murem* and *rana* are a pun on *muræna*, and *beta*, the Latin word for *beet*, is also the name of the Greek letter. As to Heliogabalus, *cf.* his life (cap. xii.) in the *Historia Augusta*. It may be mentioned that the same pastime, or something very like it, was in vogue at the court of Augustus (Suet., 75).

I have already indicated the main principle on which this social pastime was based. The objects given were of the most varied description,—clothing, furniture, musical instruments, books, toilet necessaries, domestic animals, slaves endowed with special accomplishments, etc. The list throws a side-light on many details of Roman manners and customs. The very order in which they are mentioned shows us the relative value attached to each object, material, or work. It is true that the text of this book of Martial seems to be corrupt in more places than one, and it is only by means of emendations and corrections that we are able to arrive at the original order.

Among the presents mentioned by Martial there are some which are of special interest to us. I refer to works of art. The list given by the poet shows us the kind of objects which adorned the tables and sideboards of the rich Romans, and which of them were most in fashion at that date. I shall return to this matter in a subsequent chapter.

If the proverb be true which says, " Tell me what you give and how you give it, and I will tell you what manner of man you are," we ought to be able from these data to draw our own conclusions in regard to some, at any rate, of the characteristics which distinguished the Romans of the Empire.

CHAPTER VI

ROMAN FUNERALS [1]

THE religious beliefs and temperament of a nation
are clearly reflected in its traditions, its usages,
and its institutions; this is specially true in the case
of those observances which accompany the beginning and the close of life.

Many of the customs observed by the Romans at
the birth of a child were either peculiar to themselves, or had been invested by them with a peculiar
form characteristic of the Roman temperament.
The first act of paternal authority at Rome was the
reception or acknowledgment of the child (*suscipere*);
later on he received a name and a *bulla;* he was
now a recognised member of the community; from
the time of Marcus Aurelius onwards his name was
inscribed in the public registers and thenceforward
he ranked as a citizen.

But the ceremonies which surrounded the dead at
Rome were far more characteristic. The child was
merely a type of future hopes and belonged to his
parents. The citizen, on the other hand, after a

[1] For a list of works dealing with this subject, *cf.* the article
Funus, by M. Cuq in Saglio; *cf.* also Smith, *Dictionary of Greek
and Roman Antiquities*, 2 vols., 1890–91.

133

long life spent, as likely as not, in the creation of
his own fame and fortune, did not await the last
fatal moment before taking steps to preserve his
name from oblivion.   He generally chose the site of
his grave beforehand and personally superintended
its construction.[1]   On the death of some member of
a great and famous family everything combined to
ensure his remains being interred with all due ceremonial.   In the first place the deceased had probably made provision for his funeral in his will; then
his relatives were naturally anxious that his obsequies should reflect credit on themselves; and
lastly, the State made a point of showing its gratitude for the services which he had rendered to his
country.   In the funeral ceremonies observed under
the Empire we find a curious medley of conflicting
sentiments; there are traces of the aristocratic pride
of the *gentes*, of the interests of political parties,
more or less cleverly disguised, of the reflex influences of national beliefs, or rather of beliefs which
the nation had once held or passed through, nearly
every one of which had left their mark behind them
on some rite or usage now unexplained and occasionally misunderstood.

The methods adopted by a people in the burial of
their dead show us, first of all, the nature of the
climate in which they lived; and, secondly, the

---

[1] Hence the formula which occurs so frequently in the inscriptions :
V(ivus) F(ecit), or, V(ivus) F(aciendum) C (uravit), or, V(ivus) H(oc)
S(ibi) F(ecit) M(onumentum) ; *i. e.*, so-and-so made this tomb during
his lifetime, or caused it to be made, etc.

resources at their disposal in the country inhabited by them. We may thus contrast an Arab funeral in the desert with the same ceremony as conducted by certain European races, such as the inhabitants of Bohemia in winter-time, or the Lapps at all seasons of the year.[1] Our researches would speedily show us whether the people in question possessed facilities for excavating the soil, whether wood was cheap and easily obtainable, etc. Regarded from this point of view, the Roman funerals present no specially characteristic features for the simple reason that Italy possesses a temperate climate, free from any extremes of heat or cold; its soil lends itself readily to excavation, and wood, without being specially abundant, is not so scarce as in some countries—less scarce, for instance, than in Attica. The Romans, therefore, were free to choose whether they should burn the bodies of their dead or inter them in the ground.

[1] We know that the Arabs cover the bodies of their dead with a shallow layer of sand which speedily desiccates it. In Lapland advantage is taken of the extreme cold; the body is placed in a sort of temporary vault, where it quickly freezes, and it is left there until the advent of summer allows of its being deposited in the regular cemetery. In Bohemia, if a death occurs during the winter, the corpse is placed on a sledge and drawn to the nearest river. There the relatives, in funereal attire, drag or push the sledge along the ice, the invited guests skating alongside. Near Luchon, in the Pyrenees, we are told of a village where burial is impossible owing to the fact that there is no soil, but everywhere solid rock. To carry the body by road would be dangerous. The coffin is therefore let down the face of the cliffs by a rope and transported to the neighbouring lowlands.

In the earlier funerals we might expect to find some usage or other reminiscent of the country originally inhabited by the race prior to its establishment in Italy.   But throughout the whole classical period we come upon no trace of this kind.

On the contrary, in certain rites of recent date we meet with what seems a memorial and in some ways a survival of a bygone creed; thus, in the Roman ceremony of the *os resectum* or *exceptum*,[1] which took place after cremation, and which consisted in removing some small portion of the body, such as the little finger, and burying it in the earth.   What explanation can we offer of this curious custom ? Apparently it was due to the fact that originally all bodies had to be interred, and it was regarded as sacrilege unless the body was duly returned to the earth; in time, this custom was abandoned and the ancient obligation was changed in form, leaving behind it nothing but an empty symbol to preserve its memory.   Similarly it was usual to place food near the body, and the weapons and jewels worn by the deceased, because the early belief was that the dead man would experience in the tomb all the wants and pleasures with which his life had been filled.[2]   These two instances are sufficient to warrant us in examining the funeral customs and the general aspect of the tombs and funeral monuments in the time of the Empire, in order to ascertain what light they have

---

[1] *I. e.*, the bone which has been cut out or set apart.
[2] *Cf.* the recent article by M. Perrot, " La Religion de la Mort" (in Greece), *Revue des Deux Mondes*, 1, Nov., 1895.

to throw on the religious convictions of the Romans and on certain traits in their national character.

I

FUNERALS AT ROME. TRADITIONAL USAGES

Among southern peoples grief is generally demonstrative, and in their funeral ceremonies, as in all other public demonstrations, there is a certain theatrical element mingled with their sorrow, no matter how sincere this may be. At Rome there was something even more than this, and from the close of the Republic onwards, Roman funerals produced a deep impression on strangers; we know this from the vivid effect they had on an author whom we are about to take as our guide, and who was, moreover, a southerner himself, an educated and unprejudiced Greek. I refer to Polybius, who took the trouble to describe them in detail.[1]

Leaving details on one side, let us consider the two most usual forms of sepulture, viz., those in which the body was buried in the earth or cremated (*humare*, *urere*, and *cremare*); let us next distinguish between the periods at which these two customs were observed simultaneously, and those during which one of the two was practised to the almost complete exclusion of the other; we will finally deal with ritual forms, similar to that mentioned above, in which a purely symbolical act marked the transition from one usage to another.

[1] Polybius, vi., 52, 11–54.

I shall here confine myself to a general review of
the subject from a strictly historical point of view.

The usual procedure at a Roman funeral was as
follows:

On the death of a Roman the citizens were sum-
moned to the house in which the dead man was
lying; the funeral couch, placed in the atrium, was
carried by the pall-bearers on their shoulders; the
procession was marshalled into order, the *imagines*
being placed at its head. The dead body was
clothed in the national dress, the toga. If the deceased had been a magistrate, he wore the *prætexta ;*
if he had been awarded a triumph, the triumphal
robe: in any case, he was invariably arrayed in the
richest dress he had ever been privileged to wear on
the most solemn occasions during his lifetime. Near
to the deceased stood his relatives in clothing of a
sombre hue; it was only under the Empire, or, to
be more accurate, after the time of Augustus, that
women took to wearing white as a mourning colour.[1]
The relatives were surrounded by female mourners,
who sang their dirges (*næniæ*) to the accompaniment
of the flute and made the welkin ring with their
cries. Incense and perfumes were burnt on every
side. In the case of citizens who had either made
or inherited a great name, the procession halted in

---

[1] This change had not yet been introduced in the time of Augustus,
for we read in Tibullus, iii., 2, 18, in reference to Neæra and her
mother:

"   .   .   . ossa
Incinctæ *nigra* candida veste legant."
(They collect my white bones, clad in black garments.)

the forum, where the next of kin pronounced a panegyric of the deceased; from thence the procession moved on to the place of burial, where the body was to be either interred (*situs est*) or cremated. Near the grave, or in the neighbourhood of the funeral pyre, domestic animals beloved by the deceased were sometimes immolated, and objects on which he had set a value, such as weapons, etc., were either placed by his side or burnt with him.[1] When the body was cremated, the bones were collected (*ossilegium*) and placed in an urn (*ossa componere*), which was then crowned with flowers.

Great families, desirous of doing honour to the memory of one of their members, either distributed sums of money or gave a public banquet, or, more often than not, celebrated the occasion by means of games. Both at Rome and throughout Italy these latter were originally held in the forum, and consisted, as a rule, of wild-beast fights (*venationes*) or gladiatorial combats. No noble family could afford to disregard the custom without loss of prestige. Some of them, indeed, were not satisfied even with the notoriety conferred on them by funeral orations and games; they either wrote a biography of their dead kinsman or had one written for them, which was read before a vast concourse, copies of it being circulated throughout Italy and the

[1] Regulus did so with the pet ponies, dogs, and birds of his son (Pliny, *Ep.*, iv., 2, 3). In the will of the Gallic Lingon (Bruns, *Fontes juris*, p. 297, 17) directions are given that all his hunting weapons are to be burnt with him.

provinces, with a request addressed to the decurions that they would appoint the best elocutionist in the district to read it to the inhabitants.[1]

Immediately after the funeral the house was purified, and nine days later a funeral banquet (*novemdialia* or *feriæ novemdiales*) took place; the family of the deceased also underwent purification (*feriæ denicales*). Finally, those who treasured his memory celebrated a special festival after the 21st of February in each year, which lasted for several days. This was known as the *feralia placandis manibus*, or funeral festival held in order to appease the *manes*.

The above is a general outline of the procedure adopted, and it remained unchanged. But with the gradual increase in aristocratic pride and the general introduction of luxurious habits, the traditional ceremonial became more and more elaborate. At the funerals of nobles, the processions were organised on an enormous scale; boundless extravagance was displayed in the entertainments given to the people, in the draperies and garments used, in the precious woods used for the funeral pyre, the gold that was scattered broadcast, and, above all, in the costly perfumes burnt on the occasion. In every one of the *Silvæ* addressed to those of his patrons who had suffered some bereavement, Statius devotes long passages to the enumeration of the various products of Arabia and the East

---

[1] We are told that Regulus did this on the death of his son (Pliny, *Ep.*, iv., 7, 2).

which had been burnt round the funeral pyre. It was in this somewhat ostentatious manner that the survivors endeavoured to display their respect for the departed.

Even before the days when their funerals bid fair to outdo the pyramids and mausoleums of the East in magnificence, the Romans had seen two statues of cinnamon and myrrh, prepared by the hands of Roman ladies, and intended to represent Sylla the Fortunate,[1] borne in a funeral procession : on another occasion the features of Pompey the Great were reproduced in a mask of precious pearls.[2] Tacitus must surely have had his own countrymen in view when he makes favourable mention of the fact that the Germans displayed little or no magnificence at their funerals.[3]   .

The expense varied according to the place and time, the fortune of the deceased, and the conditions under which he was buried, ranging from a few hundred or thousand sesterces to hundreds of thousands, or even millions. As might be expected, it reached its maximum in the case of an imperial funeral. Herodian has described one of

---

[1] Plutarch, *Sylla*.

[2] Pliny, xxxvii., 6.

[3] *Germ.*, 27 : "Funerum *nulla ambitio;* id solum observatur ut corpora clarorum virorum certis lignis crementur. Struem rogi *nec vestibus nec odoribus cumulant*" (They do not attempt to outvie one another in the splendour of their funerals ; the only observance to which they attach importance consists in cremating distinguished men with wood of certain kinds. They do not heap up clothing and perfumes on the funeral pyre).

these in a well-known passage.[1] A funeral pyre
was erected in the *Campus Martius* in the shape of
a pyramid, and several stories high, each one of
them being ornamented with gold embroideries,
ivory carvings, and pictures representing the leading
incidents in the life of the sovereign who was about
to undergo apotheosis. On top of all was placed
the coffin, and at the critical moment, when the
flames began to consume all this magnificence, an
eagle, taking wing from the tabernacle which surmounted the highest story of the pyre, rose into the
empyrean, a fitting type of the new god who was
now quitting the earth on his way to Olympus.[2] Of
course there was always some senator or other who
was prepared to swear that he had seen the dead
emperor ascend to heaven and take his place among
the gods; the person who volunteered this statement
was careful to invoke a curse on the heads of himself and of his children if he spoke false. An oath
of this kind was generally worth from two hundred
to two hundred and fifty thousand drachmæ to the
man who burdened his conscience with it.[3]

It was a piece of make-believe which deceived
nobody, but which was nevertheless regularly repeated at the end of each reign. The funerals of
the earlier emperors had given rise to demonstra-

---

[1] Herodian, iv., 2.

[2] This happened even at the funeral of Augustus (Dion, lvi., 42).

[3] The drachma was worth about 9d. *Cf.* the conduct of Numerius
Atticus at the funeral of Augustus (Dion Cassius, lvi., 46) and of
Livius Geminus at that of Drusilla (*ibid.*, lix., 11).

tions of a more sincere and, occasionally, of a really pathetic character. The inaugural ceremony during the obsequies of Augustus at Rome is a case in point. The knights had gone as far as Bovillæ, some ten miles in advance of the procession. They travelled by night because of the season of the year; and while the crowd awaited them at the Capena Gate, the escort advanced to meet them by the light of thousands of torches.

The funeral of Julius Cæsar, which took place in the midst of a political crisis, gave rise to many scenes of passionate regret and despair.[1] Antony had just pronounced the funeral oration; the funeral couch, inlaid with gold and ivory, and hung with draperies of brightest purple, stood before the *rostra* in the forum. No one knew where the body was to be burnt, whether in the Capitol or in the *Curia Pompeiana*, when all at once two armed men carrying torches began to collect everything they could lay their hands on,—leafy branches, seats, and funeral offerings. Flute-players and actors cast their gala robes on this improvised pyre; veterans threw their arms on it, and matrons their jewels and even the *bullæ* and *prætextæ* of their children, the whole scene culminating in a violent outburst of popular grief.

Effigies of the Deceased

It was usual at every funeral to place a lay figure with a head of wax on the funeral couch instead of

[1] Suetonius, lxxxiv.

the real corpse.   We learn that there were three of these images in the procession at the funeral of Augustus.   One of them started from the Palatine; the second, which was of gold, from the *Curia;* while the third was borne in great pomp on a chariot.[1]   A still more extraordinary feature of these Roman funerals was the representation of the dead by a living person; his bearing and gestures were faithfully reproduced by a masked actor, who stood upright on the funeral car.   This fictitious presentment of the dead was considered indispensable, and accepted as a matter of course; the same idea, in a slightly altered form, is to be found in the Egyptian mummies, which were usually provided with masks.   We find the same thing among the Etruscans, the dead man in their funeral processions being represented either by an effigy or by an actor.   To the Romans such a representation must have seemed the most natural thing in the world, since they had daily before their eyes a whole series of these images ranged round the atrium in their houses.   Nor must we forget that it was a very common thing to parade them on other occasions, such as triumphal processions.   Dion[2] tells us that in the triumph granted to Octavius after his victories in Egypt, an image of Cleopatra reclining on a couch in the very attitude in which she met her death, was carried in the procession, in order that she also might be seen in the company of the other

[1] Dion, lvi., 34 *in.*
[2] li., 21.

captives and of her own children, and thus add a lustre to the spectacle. The same writer, in his next chapter, adds that a golden image of Cleopatra was to be seen in the temple of Venus.

The Romans were a people who had, for centuries, been passionately fond of farce, and who, before this kind of theatrical entertainment was introduced among them, had always, even on the occasion of the most solemn and serious festivals, instinctively looked for some kind of mimic element to relieve the monotony of the long processions. In the provinces this farcical element was supplied by a character named *Petreia*, who represented a drunken old woman, while in Rome itself the groundlings were always ready to applaud the glutton *Manducus*, whose humour consisted in opening and shutting his huge mouth with much loud snapping of teeth. No triumph was complete unless it included some such grotesque personage as this, preferably of a pronounced patriotic type, who gesticulated violently and taunted the captives beside him; at funerals the grotesque element was provided by a gossiping old woman known as *Citeria*, who carried on a humorous dialogue with the bystanders. Characters of a similar type figure in Flemish processions to this day.

The usages which chiefly differentiate Roman funerals from those of other countries, and more particularly from those of Greece, are, however, of a different kind. It is only in Rome that we find the procession of the *images* and the funeral panegyric (*laudatio*) forming a feature in the obsequies of citizens of high rank.

(1) *The Imagines*

The images in question constituted a broad line of demarcation between ordinary citizens and those who had been called upon to fill some high office which entitled them to share in the *jus imaginum*. As is nearly always the case in countries where the aristocracy has long been a dominant factor, the common people took a perfect delight in this exhibition dictated by the vanity of the great families. In the atrium of every noble house hung a series of masks reproducing the features of the family ancestors, their names and a list of the honours each had achieved being appended on a long *stemma*, or family tree. The images of ancestors who had made themselves specially famous were reproduced on medals struck by their descendants. The common people prided themselves on being able to identify these images, and eagerly looked forward to seeing them carried past in the funeral processions. On these occasions they were removed from their places in the atrium.[1]

A spectacle of this kind produced a deep impression on foreigners, as the narrative of Polybius

---

[1] *Pro Sulla*, 88 : "*Aperientur* majorum imagines" (The ancestral images will be uncovered). Polybius, vi., 53, 4 : "εἰς τὸν ἐπιφανέστατον τόπον τῆς οἰκίας ξύλινα ναΐδια περιτιθέντες· . . . ταύτας δὴ τὰς εἰκόνας ἀνοίγοντες" (In the most prominent part of the house, small wooden *lararia* are exposed . . . on these occasions the images are disclosed).

clearly shows.   Nor was their effect on the Romans themselves much less marked, on certain occasions. Thus, at the funeral of Drusus, the son of Tiberius, there appeared the images of the Claudii, from Attus Clausus, the founder of the family, downwards, and those of the Julii, going right back to Æneas, behind whom came the kings of Alba, and last of all thè founder of Rome himself.[1]   Then again, at the funeral of Junia, sister of M. Brutus and wife of Cassius, the images of the Manlii, the Quinctii, and of a score of other illustrious families, were included in the procession.   " But," says Tacitus,[2] " Cassius and Brutus outshone them, from the very fact that their portraits did not appear "; a sentence which breathes the true subversive spirit to be found in every capital.

So, too, with the remainder of the ceremony, we are made to feel that the scene is not laid in Greece. There the great nobles prided themselves on collecting and producing works of art, jewels, statues, or statuettes; the Romans, though not averse to making a show of their wealth on occasion, were also, and more particularly, concerned to prove that they were neither *homines novi* (upstarts) nor *sine imaginibus* (without ancestral images).   Even if we no longer possess any real power, it is something to be able to say that we are descended from men who once took their turn at the helm of state.

I use the word " men " designedly; for once a

[1] Tacitus, *Ann.*, iv., 9.

[2] *Ann.*, iii., 76.

dead emperor had been transformed by the fictitious
process of apotheosis,—which, frequent at first, afterwards came to be regarded as a regular institution
in the imperial houses,—once he had been thus transformed from an ancestor into a god, he no longer
figured among the other images.   His mere presence
in a funeral procession would have been a desecra-
tion.   Henceforth he was supposed to dwell on the
heights of Olympus, from which he never again descended.   His very absence was one of the outward
signs of his apotheosis.[1]

(2) *The Laudatio*

And now, what do we understand by the term
laudatio?   On its arrival in the forum, the dead
body was carried on a funeral couch and generally
placed standing on its feet.[2]   The family of the deceased had just shown by the magnificence of the
funeral and the procession of ancestral images, the
place it occupied or once had occupied in the State.
In order to prove all this still more clearly, it now
had recourse to words.   This panegyric on the dead,

[1] The triumvirs, anxious to do honour to Cæsar, ordered that no
image of him should ever appear in the funeral processions of his
relations (Dion, xlvii., 19).   So, too, at the funerals of the emperors,
none of their predecessors who had undergone apotheosis were ever
represented by images ; the image of Cæsar did not appear at the
funeral of Augustus (Dion, lvi., 34) and the Senate ordered that the
image of Augustus was never to be paraded at any subsequent funeral.

[2] Polybius, vi., 53, 1 : " ποτὲ μὲν ἑστῶς ἐναργής, ὁπανίως δὲ
κατακεκλιμένος."

pronounced by his next of kin, was in reality little else but a vindication of the family to which he had belonged, pronounced by one of its own members; a vindication, moreover, which was neither particularly scrupulous nor particularly modest. On more than one occasion those who listened must have smiled on hearing the speaker refer in glowing terms to consulships and triumphs which had never existed outside his own imagination. No one dared protest against anything that might be said in praise of the dead; the speakers at funerals had, therefore, a free hand. But the consequence was that by dint of constant repetition, these vainglorious fictions made a place for themselves in tradition, and crept into the annals in the guise of actual historic facts. It will, moreover, be clearly seen from the foregoing that these panegyrics differed essentially from the funeral orations occasionally pronounced by the Greeks in honour of their dead; in Greece, it was a public discourse addressed to the whole people, whereas the Roman *laudatio* was a purely private and individual affair.

At an early date these panegyrics came to be employed by the Romans in the case of women; and the very interesting eulogies of *Turia* and *Murdia* which have come down to us in the form of inscriptions, give us a fairly accurate idea of this branch of eloquence, being probably simpler and more true to life than the *epicedia* interpolated among the *Silvæ* of Statius. It is somewhat amusing, by the way, to read in the second of these *laudationes*—that on

Murdia—reflections on orations of the very type to which it belongs, deploring the monotony which it was so difficult to avoid in them.[1]

TOMB OF NEVOLEIA TYCHE AT POMPEII.

II

THE TOMBS

We will suppose that the dead body has now been reduced to ashes, or, perhaps, laid in the earth,

---

[1] "Quum omnium bonarum feminarum simplex *similisque* esse laudatio soleat, quod naturalia bona, propria custodia servata, *varietates verborum* non desiderent," etc. (Since in the case of good women the panegyric must necessarily be simple and of the same character, seeing that good qualities, carefully preserved, do not need to be described in varied phrases).

though this was the less usual course. The funeral ceremonies and rites of purification have been duly observed. The next question to be dealt with concerns the nature of the monument which is to preserve the memory of him who is no more.

Here, again, I do not propose to enter into details. I shall not describe all the various forms of tombs, or how they varied at different periods and in different places. Full information on these points will be found in archæological handbooks, or in the work to which I have referred the reader at the beginning of this chapter.

It will be sufficient for my purpose to recall the fact that a number of imposing buildings may still be seen at Rome, which were originally intended to serve as tombs for the emperors or for members of their families: to this class belong the mausoleums of Hadrian (*Castello S. Angelo*) and of Agrippa (*Pantheon*); and that we come upon the tombs of famous Romans in the environs of Rome, in its suburbs and museums, and—though this is the exception—in some of its streets. These latter include the Pyramid of Cestius and the tombs of Metella, of the Scipios, of the Plautii, and of Bibulus. At Pompeii the avenue of tombs which was excavated and carefully examined at the end of the last century and the beginning of this,[1] serves to give us an idea of the kind of graves that rich provincials residing in a small town were accustomed to provide for themselves.

[1] *Cf.* especially Mazois's book.

Though, it is true, a great many of these tombs still exist, an even larger number of them have disappeared, and that, too, at a very early date. Martial draws a striking picture of the state of neglect into which the family graves of Messala had fallen.[1]

The amount expended on these tombs (which was frequently fixed by will)[2] varied frequently in the case of different persons, periods, and places. From the information at our disposal, the amount seems to have ranged from a couple of pounds to as much as £800. Members of great families looked on it as a duty to devote a considerable sum to these memorials of themselves or of their relatives. Thus Cato of Utica spent nearly £2000 on the grave of his half-brother.

The form adopted shows great diversity. In accordance with a characteristic Italian custom, every effort was made to render the appearance of these monuments as cheerful as possible, by surrounding them with gardens, orchards, vineyards, and even with ponds (*silvæ, pomaria, topiaria, lacus*). A few words will suffice to describe the general form of the tombs; they were usually hollowed out of the rock, with arched roofs, and whitewashed, or—better still —decorated with paintings in the Etruscan fashion. The famous tombs at Corneto are well known. Sometimes the tombs were built above ground;

---

[1] viii., 3, 5, and x., 2, 8.

[2] *Cf.* the interesting inscriptions and texts quoted by Friedlaender, *Mœurs romaines* (French ed.), iii., p. 271. Similar cases have been noted even in the most distant provinces, such as Gaul and Spain.

they were square in shape and surmounted by a
pyramid or tower.   Occasionally there was an adjoining chamber with one or more *exedræ*, or meeting-
rooms (*cella memoriæ*), or even a *triclinium* (one of
these has been found at Pompeii), for the banquets
given in memory of the dead.   During the excavations undertaken near Rome on the Appian Way,[1]
Count Tyskiewicz discovered a tomb, on the first
floor of which was a room intended for meetings
between the relatives and friends of the deceased.
In the centre of this room was a mosaic, in a perfect state of preservation, representing a skeleton
lying on a couch, with the legend γνῶθι σεαυτόν written beneath it.[2]

In Africa it was usual to place near the graves
funerary tables with dishes and *pateræ* hollowed out,
in order that the relatives of the dead man might
come on certain fixed days and place food in them.
From this we get the term *mensa*, frequently applied to African graves even by Christians.

Nor must we forget to mention the inscriptions
intended to attract and retain the attention of passers-by; many of them are very neatly turned.[3]

[1] *Revue archéologique*, 1896, p. 135.

[2] This mosaic is now in the new museum near the *Thermæ*.

[3] Propertius, iv., 7, 84.   Cynthia asks the poet :

"Hic *carmen* media, dignum me, scribe columna,
 Sed breve, quod currens vector ab urbe legat."

(Place here, in the middle, an inscription in verse worthy of me on
a column ; but let it be short, in order that even the traveller hurrying from the city may find time to read it.)   Friedlaender, *Mœurs
rom.* (French ed.), i., pp. 409 *et seq.* ; iv., pp. 448 *et seq.*, 464 *et seq.*,
quotes some most interesting inscriptions.

Those who wished to be out of the common run, treated the dead man to an inscription in verse; these were generally taken bodily from collections of epitaphs, a practice which occasionally led to curious blunders.[1] Very much the same thing was done in the case of statues, and—not to wander from the subject—more especially in the case of seated figures, intended for the decoration of graves. Here we find endless reproductions of a single type, which seems to have been selected in the first instance as suitable for the purpose, and then repeated time after time.

A few words more in regard to the paintings and bas-reliefs found on the tombs. Some of these depict the ceremonies which we have just described a few pages earlier[2]; reproductions of these will be found in dictionaries and manuals of archæology. The most famous of them all is, undoubtedly, the bas-relief preserved in the Lateran Collection.[3] In this we see the dead woman with her *pugillares* (or tablets) lying at her feet; by her side are two female mourners (*præficæ*) and an embalmer (*pollinctor*); to the right and left are candelabra and lamps; on the left a female flute-player; on the right sit three women wearing the *pileus* (or cap of liberty pre-

---

[1] *Cf.* Bücheler, *Carmina Latina Epigr.*, i., at the end of Nos. 475 and 476 and *passim*.

[2] Similarly, in the Dipylon at Athens, vases have been found on which funeral ceremonies, the lying in state, procession to the cemetery, etc., are depicted.

[3] Saglio, *Funus*, fig. 3360.

sented to slaves on their liberation; these are probably slave girls set free by will); in the foreground
are the relatives and a number of vases, in which
perfumes are being burnt.

Some of the other bas-reliefs, and certain paintings as well, are interesting from the fact that we
frequently find represented, or at any rate suggested
in them, the ideas of the ancients in regard to the
life to come. Almost all civilised communities
have employed this method of symbolising their
religious convictions: the Etruscans in their subter-
ranean tombs; the early Christians in the catacombs
and in the sarcophagi preserved in the Lateran Collection; the Middle Ages in the curious paintings
to be seen in the Campo Santo at Pisa (*e. g.*, the
Triumph of Death and the *Last Judgment*), and in
the carvings on some cathedral fronts.

Whether it was due to lack of inspiration, vague-
ness of dogma, or simply to want of skill on the part
of the artists, we cannot say, but the fact remains
that Roman antiquity is relatively barren in this
respect, the details of their creed on this point being
much less precise than in the case of other civilised
communities. No sooner do they attempt to tackle
this subject, than the Roman artists, like their
brethren at Pompeii, at once take refuge in mythology. The descent of Orpheus into Hades in the
Lateran Collection, which was taken from a tomb,
only interests us by the realistic treatment observable in some of the details.

The Gemoniæ and Puticuli [1]

And now we come to an uglier side of Roman antiquity.   So far, we have been concerned with the official splendours of the state funerals, and with the monuments intended to perpetuate the memory of grandees or emperors.   We must now say a word or two of those who were forgotten and vilified, or whose memory it was desired to hand down to infamy.

There was, perhaps, some excuse in the case of shipwrecked politicians.   They were seldom offered any alternative between apotheosis or semi-apotheosis, and the *Gemoniæ* with their dreaded stairway (*scalæ*) and the hooks which served to drag the bodies of the dead down to the Tiber.   How many nobles and even emperors do we read of in Suetonius and in the *Historia Augusta* who met with this fate, or whose heads were paraded about on the points of spears!

But there is no such element of poetic justice to temper the horror inspired in us by those hideous *puticuli* into which paupers and abandoned slaves—in short, all those who had failed to provide a last resting-place for themselves, or who had no relations, friends, or burial clubs to secure them proper interment, were thrown by thousands and by tens of thousands, tò rot in the company of dogs and cattle. Until recently it was thought that these *puticuli* must have been somewhere in the environs of

[1] Literally, a place where bodies are placed to *rot*.

Rome, or, at any rate, no nearer than the base of the rampart of Servius. In spite of the direct testimony of Horace,[1] it is difficult to believe[2] that the Romans could have tolerated so many and such terrible hotbeds of infection within the city walls. Imagination failed to suggest anything half so hideous as the state of things revealed by M. Lanciani's excavations.[3] The bearers of the dead had but one object, that was to get rid of the body they were carrying at the earliest possible opportunity.

Thus a series of ghastly charnel-houses, each one more hideous than the other, each one open continually to the vault of heaven, came to be established in Rome, and particularly on the Esquiline. Little wonder, therefore, that epidemics were of frequent occurrence, and that the city was so often visited by the plague.

[1] *Sat.*, I., viii., 14.

[2] It is true that Gibbon did not allow this difficulty to escape him.

[3] *Ancient Rome*, chap. iii., or *cf.* the article by M. Cagnat in the *Revue Critique*, June 10, 1889.

CHAPTER VII

WILLS

THE number of deaths in Rome was not much higher than in other towns, but far more people made their wills, and wills were the object of a much more general interest there than elsewhere. On the one hand, testators were anxious to indicate clearly what property they were leaving, and to whom; while, on the other, a host of potential legatees was still more anxious to secure by fair means or foul either the whole or a part of some one's else heritage; in other words, to attain some sudden and unlooked-for stroke of good fortune. Thus hare and hounds, alike eagerly bent on escape or capture, expended every effort of their intelligence and all that remained to them of life to secure their objects. When fair means seemed likely to be unsuccessful, resort was had to more questionable methods, flattery, cajolery, trickery, and intrigue being employed in turn. The man who sought to force the hand of fortune in this way had need of all his ingenuity. In case of success the end was held to justify the means; while in case of failure it was always something to have given the world a cause for laughter!

The legacy-hunter we have ever with us. He belongs to all nationalities and all ages, but never did he find fuller scope for his energies than in Rome during the first century of our era. When all other methods failed him, he did not shrink from forgery, and often managed to commit it with impunity.

The literature of the period abounds in satirical descriptions of these pests of Roman society under the Empire. We find numberless portraits of the legacy-hunter, and of those whom he duped or by whom he was duped. The subject formed part of the satirist's regular stock-in-trade, and the details of this aspect of Roman life furnished by lawyers, moralists, and historians are supplemented in the happiest manner by the works of poets and romancers.

I

WILLS FROM THE LEGAL POINT OF VIEW

Let us first of all briefly review the usages and legal enactments by which probate proceedings at Rome were governed, taking care to confine our attention to strictly essential details.

In all ages there has been a certain strain of rigid and punctilious formalism observable in the Roman character. It need not surprise us, therefore, that when this natural predisposition came to be intensified by motives of self-interest, a positive delight was taken from the very earliest times in a form of transmission of property which was generally— though not always—attested by a written deed.

The making of a will was surrounded by all sorts of minute regulations, the authority vested under Roman law in the head of the family being exercised—at any rate, in early times—without any sort of limitation.

At Rome it was the exception for a man to die intestate; indeed, it was generally regarded as one of the most serious misfortunes that could befall him.   It was even considered unlucky to die without leaving a will of recent date; in such a case, the chances and changes of life rendered it only too probable that a man might leave his latest friends unprovided for, and benefit those for whom he no longer cherished any affection.[1]

Anxiety to transmit to others their family gods and *sacra* may have been a prevailing influence with the devout; in the majority of instances, however, the Romans regarded the making of their wills as the exercise of a privilege which was not accorded to travellers or men of Latin blood (*factio testamenti*).[2]   It was a privilege which they jealously guarded.   Those who fought the battles of Rome, in the legions, had early claimed this special right for themselves, and had secured exemption from many of the legal conditions imposed on other citi-

---

[1] Pliny, *Ep.*, v., 5, 2: "Decessit *veteri testamento*; omisit *quos maxime diligebat*; prosecutus est *quibus offensior erat*" (He died leaving an early will behind him, in which those whom he most loved were not mentioned, while those with whom he had become unfriendly were benefited).

[2] It was not until later that the validity of a will made by a traveller in accordance with the laws of his country was recognised.

zens; it was recognised that these men had no taste for legal subtleties and that they were often pressed for time at critical moments; in the case of soldiers, therefore, the *testamentum in procinctu*,[1] which was nothing more than a verbal expression of their last wishes, was held to be sufficient. As we shall see later on, special privileges were accorded to soldiers on active service.

When an army began to think of will-making and was continually busied with testamentary dispositions, it was a sure sign that the soldiers were infected with some anxiety, or even fear, which nothing would have induced them to betray in any other way. Thus Cæsar at the beginning of his Gallic campaign was able to gauge the apprehension felt by his legions at the approach of Ariovistus and his German troops, from the fact that " wills were being signed, on all sides, throughout the camp."[2] Thus, even on the banks of the Rhine, the view of the moralists who declared that wills were " the mirror of manners "[3] and that they contained " the only true statement ever made by a Roman in the whole course of his life, for the simple reason that this was the only occasion on which plain-speaking could be indulged in without evil consequences,"[4] was amply confirmed.

From the foregoing we can readily imagine the

[1] *I.e.*, a will made at the moment of girding one's self up for the fray.

[2] *B. G.*, i., 39, 5: " *vulgo* in castris *testamenta* obsignabantur."

[3] Pliny, *Ep.*, viii., 18, 1: " *speculum* morum."

[4] Lucian, *Nigr.*, 30.

enormous number of these documents which must have been drawn up, and what a flood of light they would throw on the private life of the Romans. Unfortunately the great majority, if not all of them, have been lost, leaving little or nothing behind. This may be accounted for, firstly, by the custom of making verbal wills,[1] and secondly, by the fact that even where a will was reduced to writing, the papyrus or tablets on which it was written was very fragile and perishable.   We possess, however, a few extracts from wills[2] which occur in sepulchral inscriptions, especially in those intended to commemorate gifts, legacies, or endowments.   The following are a few of the formulæ: " *Ex testamento licet* . . . *Kaput ex testamento* . . .; *exemplum epistulæ* . . .; *reliquit ex testamento* . . .; *legatis ex testamento.*"[3]

The best means of obtaining a more precise idea of their form will be to refer to the works of authors who have either quoted or parodied them.

But in order to render what follows quite clear, it will be well to state briefly the usual form adopted in making a will, and the conditions required in order to make it legally binding.

Originally, the citizens were in the habit of declaring their wishes in regard to their property at special meetings assembled for the purpose (*comitiis calatis*).

---

[1] *Inst.*, ii., 10, 14.
[2] *Cf.* Bruns-Mommsen, *Fontes Juris*, chap. xiv.
[3] "It is permitted by the will . . . clause of the will . . . copy of the letter . . . he left by will," etc.

But before long the making of a will became a private act which was thrown into the form of a deed of sale, *per æs et libram.*[1] The heir, or other interested party, was supposed, by a legal fiction, to buy the goods of the testator. In addition to the two principals concerned, there were, as in regular sales, the official who held the balance (*libripens*), and five witnesses. The *lex venditionis*, or contract showing the conditions under which the sale had been effected, which, in the present instance, constituted the principal act, was entered on the tablets, to which the witnesses then attached their seals. The testator then declared, "*ita ut in his tabulis cerisque scripta sunt, ita do, ita lego, ita testor*" (I hereby give, bequeath, and appoint in accordance with what is written on these waxen tablets). In this way he disposed of all his property in such manner as seemed good to him; this was the object in view.

The tablets were sometimes double, triple, or even quadruple, and were distinguished by being paged in numerical order (*cera prima, secunda, tertia*). They were fastened together by a cord passed through holes bored at their edge or centre and sealed with the testator's seal. The possibility of the person appointed as heir being unable to administer was not overlooked, and a second or third beneficiary was frequently named. If there were several heirs under the will, their individual shares in the estate were estimated in *unciæ*, or twelfths of the whole, the *uncia* being a twelfth part of the *as*.

---

[1] Literally, "by means of brass [*i.e.*, money] and the balance."

The reading of the will (*resignare*) usually took place in the forum or the basilica, if possible in the presence of the witnesses who had sealed it; it was then copied and deposited in the archives.[1]   Prior to the death of the testator, no other person had any right to break the seals.   The penalty applied to anyone who did so was the same as that awarded in cases of forgery.[2]

This did not, however, prevent Octavius from reading the will of Antony in public, in order to stir up the hatred of the Romans against him.[3] When we read of a man publishing the contents of his own will, we may safely infer that there must have been some political or other motive at work. He must either have desired to prove his devotion to the republic or the emperor, or to get into some-one's good graces.[4]

At first the head of the family had absolute power to devise his property as he chose; it was not until later that laws were passed, in the public interest, imposing restrictions in regard to legacies to women (*lex Voconia*), to bachelors, or married persons with-out children (*lex Julia* and *lex Papia Poppæa*).   Nor was it until later that the head of the family became liable to have his will amended by the courts if he

[1] Paul, *Sent.*, iv., 6.

[2] *Dig.*, xlviii., 10, 1, 5.   [3] Dion, l., 3.

[4] Dion tells us that Augustus laid his will before the Senate (liii., 31); that Tiberius opened his before his mother and Augustus (liv., 9); C. Germinius Rufus having fallen under suspicion after the over-throw of Sejanus, brought forward his will to prove his innocence (lviii., 4).

failed to leave less than a fourth of his property to his child or children.[1]

We have already seen that the legal requirements necessary to the validity of wills made by civilians, more especially those which referred to the number of the witnesses and the terms employed, etc., were either modified or suppressed in the case of military wills (*testamenta in procinctu*). Another privilege accorded was that a son, even though still under the tutelage of his father, might, if he were a soldier, dispose freely of his private property (*peculium*).

Roman society differed from that of our day not only in the extraordinary number of wills that were made, but also by the fact that legacies and inheritances were regarded as forming a legitimate road to the rapid acquisition of wealth. A very common method of showing one's gratitude to one's lawyer or patron was to leave him a legacy. Insignificant people took a sort of pride in bequeathing legacies to important personages, and the latter had no scruples about accepting them. It gives us rather a shock to learn that on the day before the murder committed by Milo, Clodius and Cicero had met at the deathbed of one Cyrus, a Greek architect, who left both of them a share of his estate, and had asked them to affix their seals to his will.[2] The tone in which Cicero refers to this circumstance shows that this was a sort of everyday occurrence, at which no one need feel surprise. Among the multifarious occupations which went to fill up the Roman day,

[1] *Inst.*, iv., 18. [2] *Pro Mil.*, xviii., 48.

Pliny mentions the signing of one's friends' wills (*signare* or *obsignare testamentum*).[1]   Atticus increased his large fortune by the aid of numerous legacies left him by his friends and clients.   Cicero prided himself[2] on having received over twenty millions of sesterces (£160,000) in bequests.   And finally, Augustus, in his will, admitted having received four milliards of sesterces (£32,000,000) in this way.   There is nothing in the usages of modern society which can compare with this.

In our "probate duties," however, we have reproduced, in another form, the famous *vicesima* devised by Augustus.   In the year 6 A.D. Augustus conceived the idea of levying a tax on this characteristic institution of Roman life.   On every bequest or testamentary legacy of 100,000 sesterces (£800) or over, bequeathed to any but a near relative, the State levied a tax of five per cent.   This duty, always a very productive one, was jealously guarded by the emperors.

II

"CAPTATIO," OR LEGACY-HUNTING

In all ages the state of the wealthy bachelor has not been without its advantages; Periplectomenes, the old bachelor in the *Miles*[3] of Plautus, fully realised this, and he takes a malicious pleasure in describing the attentions with which his friends and relations overwhelm him from the moment he gets

---

[1] *Ep.*, i., 9, 2.   [2] *Phil.*, ii., 16.   [3] iii., 1, 112 (705).

up in the morning. The only change, in this respect, which took place between the time of the
Punic wars and that of the Empire, was that legacy-
hunting was reduced to a regular system. It was
no longer a question of making the best of a given
relationship or intimacy. Under cover of assiduous
attentions paid to the rich, the thing really resolved
itself into a regular chase, with the usual incidents
of the chase; the prizes secured were few, and the
numerous reverses sustained by the competitors
furnished matter for general amusement.

Legacy-hunting was such a recognised industry
at Rome that it came to be looked upon as one of
the characteristic features of life in the capital. At
least, this was the opinion of officers stationed on
the frontier: " The inhabitants of the new Rome,"
they declared, " have no regard for anything born
outside the *pomœrium*,[1] unless it be for rich bachelors
without near relatives; the indefatigable and obse-
quious court paid to childless men is almost incon-
ceivable." [2] This very explicit testimony, though
it belongs to a period two centuries later, only serves
to show how enormously the evil had grown in the
interval. Numberless quotations might be adduced
to prove how universal it had become from the beginning of the Empire onwards.

One of the things which most favourably impressed Tacitus about Germany was that, there,
children inherited the property of their parents, that
no wills were made, and that old men enjoyed credit

---

[1] The sacred enclosure.   [2] Ammianus, xiv., 6, 22.

in proportion to the number of near relatives and
connections they possessed; in a word, that but little
value was attached to a state of gilded solitude
(*orbitas*).[1] In Rome every " house without children," and every house where the children were all
girls, was simply besieged by fortune-hunters.
Catullus describes how a flock of these vultures who
had already begun to hover greedily round the
hoary head of a wealthy old man, were at once put
to flight by the birth of a grandson.[2] No legacy-
hunter who understood his business ever thought of
wasting his time in a house where a budding Æneas
(*parvulus Æneas*) or even a little girl was to be found
playing in the courtyard.[3] Patrons thought little
of their clients unless they happened to be childless.
What had they to gain by the death of the others ?

Seneca protests in scathing terms against the self-
ishness of those old men who used their isolation as
a decoy duck or pretended to hate their children,
in order that they might be courted [4]; he describes
the crew who surrounded them: " these anglers
whose sole occupation consists in throwing out a
bait in the hope of hooking either a part or the
whole of an inheritance; these birds of prey who
keep a watchful eye on the dying man and hover
round his corpse."[5] Seneca's enemies, however,
declared that he spoke from personal experience of
the practices he denounced, and that while with one

---

[1] *Germ.*, xx.   [2] Catullus, lxviii., 123 (or lxxviii*b*, 79).
[3] Juvenal, v., 140.   [4] *Ad Marciam*, xix., 2.
                    [5] *Benef.*, vi., 20, 3.

hand he drained Italy and the provinces [1] dry with his usury, with the other he had contrived to sweep into his net a goodly haul of legacies and childless old men (*orbos*) at Rome.

The favourite dream of every ambitious young man or aspiring woman, and the unfailing prediction of the Chaldean soothsayers whom they went to consult, was a fine fat legacy which would make them the heirs of some rich old man (*divitis orbi testamentum ingens*).[2]

Augustus endeavoured by various enactments to discourage celibacy and promote fruitful marriages. With a view to repressing the selfish instinct which prevented a man from taking a wife and bringing up a family, he sought to defeat the object aimed at by such conduct; he reduced the amount of the legacies which could be legally devised to any person having less than three children. In a frivolous and sceptical society such as that which existed under the Empire, enactments of this kind were nearly always evaded. The emperors themselves contributed to make them a dead letter; by granting the *jus trium liberorum*,[3] and other special dispensations to their favourites, they helped to defeat the object which these laws were intended to bring about.

On the other hand, the persons interested did not fail to entrench themselves behind the privileges guaranteed to them under other laws. If the worst

---

[1] Tacitus, *Ann.*, xiii., 42.   [2] Juvenal, vi., 548.

[3] *I. e.*, the rights and privileges granted by law to those who had three children.

came to the worst, there were plenty of perfectly
legal and convenient methods of getting out of these
compulsory marriages; nothing was easier.   The
new law stipulated that preference should be given
at elections to candidates who were married and
had children.   In order to evade the legal disability
thus imposed on them, celibate candidates con-
tracted marriages before the polling, and promptly
obtained a divorce as soon as the election was over;
in like manner, they adopted children, whom they
no less promptly discarded once they had obtained
the prætorships or governments to which they
aspired.   Tacitus[1] records the protests of married
Romans with families who had been tricked in this
way by unscrupulous rivals.   It is true that the
Senate, on the receipt of these protests, decreed
that, for the future, these fraudulent adoptions
should count for nothing.   But decrees of this kind
must have furnished but cold comfort to candidates
with children.

By the middle of the first century the art of
fortune-hunting had been reduced to a system with
recognised rules.   Seneca[2] mentions the names of
two persons of his own time in connection with this
subject, though he does not make it quite clear
whether they had actually practised the art themselves or had been cynical enough to lay down rules
for the guidance of those who did.

[1] *Ann.*, xv., 19.
[2] *De Ben.*, vi.. 38, 4 : " Arruntius et Haterius et *ceteri qui captan-
dorum testamentorum artem professi sunt*" (Arruntius and Haterius,
and others who professed the art of legacy-hunting).

The great secret lay in refusing to allow oneself
to be disheartened by a temporary reverse; if one
fish refused to bite, all one had to do was to bait
one's hook and try for another.[1] Unfortunately,
legacy-hunting, whether practised as an art or as a
profession, was subject to all sorts of risks. The
main thing was to know how to set about conciliat-
ing the old man or old woman whose fortune it was
wished to secure, and to find out what foibles and
weaknesses of theirs were likely to give one an
opening. If their weak point was gluttony, then
the finest fish and all the delicacies of the season
must be secured as gifts for them. " The very
markets have turned fortune-hunters," [2] as Juvenal
wittily expressed it. Possibly the rich old man was
more of a miser than a glutton. In that case he
probably turned the presents you gave him into
hard cash.[3] But what difference did it make, provided he gave you credit for your liberality ? Or
perhaps he had other vices. It mattered not how
shameless or repugnant they might be, you must
try and turn them to your own advantage. Under
the guise of presents, it was really a form of organ-

---

[1] This is the advice given by Horace, *Sat.*, ii., 5, 24 :

> " Neu si vafer unus et alter
> Insidiatorem *præroso* fugerit *hamo*,
> . . . *Artem* illusus omittas."

(Nor must you give way to despair and renounce what is really an
art, simply because one or two clever men after nibbling at your
hook have got clear away); but see the whole of this satire and *cf.*
Cicero, *Parad.*, v., ii., 39.

[2] Juvenal, vi., 40. [3] *Ibid.*, v., 97.

ised pursuit, which Ovid himself compares[1] with the
ruses employed by a lover in order to secure his
mistress's favour.

III

FORGED WILLS

Everyone knows that the evolution of Roman
law was largely due to the prætors, who, by refusing
its protection save under certain conditions, were
able to extend the letter of the law by rulings in
harmony with its spirit, and to interpret and even
modify it by artifices of legal procedure; in short,
they wielded an influence which reacted against the
spirit of formalism ingrained in the Roman character and inclined the balance on the side of equity.
In all cases where private individuals disputed the
provisions of a will, they did so, as may be readily
imagined, entirely from interested motives, and took
care to appeal, as far as possible, to the actual word-
ing of the will itself.   The prætor did his best to
respect the wishes of the testator, and to set aside
the pettifogging interpretations and legal subtleties
employed with a view to defeating them; in a word,
he invariably tried to defend the interests of the
family and of society at large.

The above is merely meant to show the general
tendency in this matter; the actual progress in this
evolution was slow, and was for a long time much
retarded by the audacity of forgers, who, certainly

[1] *Ars. Am.*, ii., 271.

more criminal than the legacy-hunters, were nearly as numerous and quite as audacious as they.

The crime of forgery has been prevalent in all ages and countries. But in a community where so many wills were made and so much importance attached to them, it must have been exceptionally frequent or, at any rate, have seemed to be so. Once wealth had become the sole object of life, and the sole source of power at Rome, the temptation to employ some such means of carrying fortune by storm, must have been well-nigh irresistible; and those who once yielded to it became henceforward capable of anything. On the other hand, those who had been disappointed in their expectations were a numerous body, and they seldom hesitated to accuse their more successful rivals of theft, or even worse crimes. Add to this, that the facilities for detecting forgeries, and convicting the guilty, were far less numerous and less accurate than those which chemistry and the progress of science have placed at the disposal of modern experts.

The satirists may have exaggerated matters; but even after making due allowance for this, it is evident that a great many forgeries were committed in Rome, and that many of them were committed with impunity. No wonder, then, that these mushroom fortunes due to crime led to a revulsion of public opinion. Juvenal merely gives voice to the universal feeling when he expresses his indignation at meeting " a forger who has achieved wealth and luxury by means of small tablets and a wet signet ring (*exiguis tabulis et gemma* . . . *uda*), lolling at his ease in a litter borne by six slaves, and giving himself the airs of a Mæcenas in the face of all men."[1]

We can scarcely read Regnard's *Légataire Univer-sel* through without feeling that in this brilliant comedy—and more especially in the famous will scene—the imagination of the poet has pushed mat-ters to the very verge of improbability. And yet there is a passage in the *Historia Augusta*[2] which clearly proves that, if the Roman gossips are to be believed, an almost exactly similar scene was played on the Palatine for no less a stake than the empire of the world.[3]

It may be objected that in a community like this, which was just on the point of creating a written code of laws, there must have been magistrates and machinery for the repression of crime. No doubt this was so. But those who had run the risk in-volved in putting forward a forged will, employed ingenious methods of avoiding punishment which must very often have proved successful. In the deed thus manufactured at leisure, they were care-ful to insert the names of leading politicians or well-known orators as legatees. Nothing could be easier,

---

[1] *Sat.*, i., 64, *et seq.*

[2] Spartianus, *Hadr.*, iv., 10.

[3] "Nec desunt qui . . ., *mortuo jam Trajano*, Hadrianum in adoptionem adscitum esse prodiderint, *supposito qui pro Trajano fessa voce loqueretur*" (There are some who aver that Hadrian was not adopted until after Trajan had died, a man who spoke in a faltering voice being made to take his place).

and in doing so they merely conformed to what was, as we have seen, a regular custom of the period. What was the result ? When the will was read the improvised legatees were in no way surprised at receiving a considerable bequest even from a person who was unknown to them; in case the will was disputed, their support and that of their party and their friends were assured beforehand. In a case of this kind it often happened that the persons defrauded, even though they possessed ample evidence of the forgery, abandoned, in despair, an action which they felt was foredoomed to failure; the forger, after handing over to his defenders the percentage which he had assigned them, as a sort of insurance premium, entered into possession of the inheritance which he had wrongfully usurped.[1] We frequently find it stated that there were a number of persons at Rome who lived entirely on the proceeds obtained from the bearing of false witness[2]; and we need scarcely wonder if now and then by the exercise of a little ingenuity they sought to turn their capacity for lying to a still more profitable purpose.

[1] When we find men like Hortensius and Crassus (cf. Cicero in the De Off., iii., 18, 73, and Parad., v., 43 and 46) mixed up in shady affairs and intrigues of this nature, we have no difficulty in gauging the actions of the others. The fable of " The Countryman who Made his Way into Paradise by Pleading the Will of the Ass" seems to have had its counterpart in ancient times. Nor must we forget that Claudius was mixed up in a fraudulent will case before he became emperor. (Cf. Suet., 9.)

[2] Juvenal, xvi., 32.

IV

LEGACY-HUNTING IN ROMAN LITERATURE

The subject we are now considering has always been a favourite theme with the satirists, dramatists,[1] and novelists of almost every age and country. It was a subject which yielded an almost inexhaustible fund of material. The Romans of the Empire, who were daily witnesses of the practice in its most bare-faced form, could hardly fail to introduce some mention of it in their works of fiction.

In art we have bas-reliefs intended to represent a *collocatio* in·which tablets (*pugillares*) appear either at the feet or in the hands of the dead man or woman, so inseparably associated were the ideas of death and will-making.[2]

In Roman literature, or rather in that part of it which has come down to us, there are two famous passages, of which we shall have something more to say later on (viz., one of the satires of Horace and the end of the *Satyricon* of Petronius), in which childless old men, or those who give themselves out to be such, are brought on the scene surrounded by a train of greedy flatterers. On the stage there must have been many plays and scenes based on the same theme. The new school of comedy in Greece may perhaps have thought them beneath its dignity, though it is by no means certain that this was so;

---

[1] *Cf.* Ben Jonson's *Volpone*.

[2] Saglio, *Funus*, fig. 3360; *cf.* Chap. VI., p. 154, of the present work.

but it seems very improbable that the writers of more characteristically Roman pieces such as farces and *togatæ*, which were of a more decidedly realistic type, should have failed to draw on a vein of comedy which was certain to please their audiences. St. Jerome tells us that the young folks at school were in the habit of acting a piece which evoked roars of laughter, entitled " The Pig's Will," or " The Little Pig's Will " (*Grunnius Coroccotta*)[1]; it is possible that this was a relic of some popular tradition, which may have been used more or less frequently on the regular stage, and thus came to be adopted by young scholars as a form of literary pastime.

Juvenal,[2] Epictetus,[3] and Lucian,[4] also, frequently refer to the practice of will-hunting, but only in passing allusions or in rapidly sketched portraits. It suggested the satire of Horace mentioned above, and supplied material for the closing scenes of Petronius's romance.

Horace's satire (ii., 5) is a somewhat exaggerated burlesque in a style which rather surprises us, but seems to have hit the Roman taste. Tiresias, the celebrated soothsayer of the Νεκυία,[5] is consulted

---

[1] *Apol. cont. Ruf.*, i., 17 ; *Comm. Is.*, xii., 1.

[2] Juvenal, i., 37 :

> " qui *testamenta merentur*
> *Noctibus*, in cælum quos evehit optima summi
> Nunc via processus, *vetulæ vesica beatæ?* " etc.

(those who earn their legacies by night [or rather in many nights] and seek advancement by what is the best road to it nowadays, viz., by gaining the love of some rich old woman).

[3] *Dissert.*, vi., 1.   [4] *Timon*, 21 *et seq.*

[5] *Odyssey*, xi., where the descent of Ulysses into hell is described.

once again by Ulysses who is anxious to enrich
himself; the hero has just been thrown shipwrecked
on the coast of Ithaca, and it is very important that
he should be able quickly to repair his broken fortunes.   Tiresias seriously advises him to take to
legacy-hunting; he points out to him what dangers
to avoid (he must never show his hand or allow
himself to be disheartened) and describes the wiles
which have been successful in the past and never
fail to attract fish to the bait and to fill the angler's
fish-pond; he must make small presents of fish and
game, must decline to read the will if offered to
him, while at the same time assuring himself of its
contents by a rapid glance; he must show every
possible attention to his aged friend in the streets
or in the forum, must volunteer to defend him in
his lawsuits, and if he cannot hope to rank as principal legatee, must do his best to secure the second
place, etc.   The curt and serious answers of Ulysses
offer a capital foil to the cynicism of Tiresias.   The
ancient epic thus transplanted into the midst of the
Roman life of that period here degenerates into
sheer burlesque, the most piquant trait being the
rôle reserved for Penelope by her husband and his
adviser.[1]

The final episode in our *Satyricon* (by " our " I
mean the romance of Petronius in the fragmentary
state in which it has come down to us) is nothing
but one prolonged satire on legacy-hunters.   Cro-
tona, the town in which the scene is laid, is a sort

[1] 76 *et seq.*

of travesty of Rome, where the sole business of life consists of a race for bequests. In this case the will-hunters are completely taken in.[1] The aged poet Eumolpus, with the help of his friends, organises an elaborate piece of mystification.[2] He gives himself out to be an elderly nabob from Africa, of immense wealth, who has just been shipwrecked on the coast and is greatly afflicted by the death of a beloved son. He coughs, continually complains of his aches and pains, jumbles up the names of his slaves and estates (he has such an enormous number of them), and, last but not least, is continually making fresh wills.[3] The fish rise greedily to the bait. Then follows a series of episodes as obscene as they are laughable, intermingled with others in which the fooling becomes more cold-blooded and methodical and assumes a logical shape. The old nabob (here again we come upon one of the traditional features of the subject) imposes on his future

[1] This is merely a further development of what Horace had already hinted at in line 57 ("*Captatorque dabit risus* . . ."). The joke seems to have been one of old standing.

[2] 117, B., p. 83, 13: "Quid ergo, inquit Eumolpus, *cessamus mimum componere?*" (Why, then, says Eumolpus, do we delay the arrangement of our farce?)

[3] *Ibid.*, 30 and 34. In the text we have: "Sedeat præterea quotidie ad rationes, *tabulasque testamenti* omnibus . . . *renovet*" (The companions of Eumolpus arrange the plan of action to be followed; it is settled that he is to "sit all day adding up his accounts and renewing the tablets of his will every . . ."). There is a word missing after *omnibus;* some commentators restore it as *mensibus* (months); others as *diebus* (days); others again as *horis* (hours);—it is a sort of Dutch auction!

heirs and legatees a condition which is to put their devotion to the test [1]; in the present instance the condition is somewhat original; only those who shall have dined off his corpse are to be eligible for legacies. With an inexhaustible verbosity acquired in the schools, and only too freely employed by him, Eumolpus manages to lead the conversation on to this subject again and again; he points out to his hearers with many a sarcastic sally and more or less obscure allusions, all the historical and other grounds which ought to induce them to accept this condition.

But, we may ask, how long did this farce continue? Carthage, the city from which the adventurers hailed, was not far from Italy, and it would have been a very simple matter to ascertain the truth of their story. Eumolpus argues out the pros and cons of the situation with his friends and reassures them on this score. He admits that all their objections are perfectly just, but then those who covet the goods of others (*i. e.*, in this instance the legacy-hunters) are obliged to make the first advances, and in so doing they are playing what is really a very hazardous game for themselves; for it is inevitable and only right that they should lose their money. They are certain to do so in the present case. How would it be possible for people with brains (*e. g.*, Eumolpus and his friends) to make a living if it

[1] Horace, ii., 5, 84: "Anus . . . *ex testamento* sic est elata," etc. The old lady, finding that she never could get rid of her heir during her lifetime, stipulated that he should carry her body rubbed with oil on his naked shoulders, thus hoping that he might at last be obliged to let her go.

were not for the stupidity of those who allow themselves to be taken in by their artifices ?[1] Thus argues Eumolpus, and the reader does not feel any
great regret at the success of the double deception
whereby the flock of vultures for once in a way is
made to feed, clothe, and amuse the living corpse
whom they had come to devour.

[1] Cap. 140.

CHAPTER VIII

COUNTRY LIFE

I

THE COUNTRY FROM THE ROMAN POINT OF VIEW

THE Romans were fond of the country, but it was after a fashion of their own. Their writers praise the peacefulness, the solid pleasures, the true joys of a rustic life; it was there, in some cool and shady nook, that Tibullus and Propertius loved to place the scenes of their elegies. Historians commend the virile Sabine race (*Sabella pubes*) which filtered ceaselessly Romewards, and contributed the pick of their soldiers to her legions; the Sabine women and children were tall and strong and no less bronzed by the sun than were the men. It was in the country, between the stilts of the plough, that tradition loved to place the bearers of some of the most illustrious names in early Roman history, such as Cincinnatus, Fabricius, Dentatus. On the other hand, in the Roman theatres no opportunity was lost of contrasting the amusements and comforts of town life with the dulness and disadvantages of a residence in the country.

In comedies, nearly all the loutish, coarse, and brutal young fellows come from the country (*rustici, truculentı*); they are flouted by the courtesans or by their waiting-maids, who promptly set to work to relieve them of some of their rusticity: similarly, in these plays the paterfamilias is generally represented as harsh and stingy [1]; it was part of the stage tradition that some unpleasant surprise or other should always await him on his return home. In no other literature do we find the two characters represented by the words *rusticus* and *urbanus* so violently contrasted with one another as in the Roman. Horace [2] has even carried the contrast so far as to apply it to the very rats.

In what, then, did the Roman liking for rustic life—which they saw clearly enough in its true colours—consist ? On what was it based ? What changes did it undergo in the course of time ? In how far was it deficient in that sympathy with nature which the moderns are ready enough to deny to the Romans ? We are now about to consider one aspect of Roman life from the modern standpoint, and we shall find that the reputation of the Romans does not suffer under the test.

At no period of their history did the native Roman race attempt to conceal their contempt for the inhabitants of the city (*urbani*). It was a sort of tradition with them that the slaves of the capital were useless creatures, and that those citizens who never left it were not much better. At each succeeding census, politicians with an anxious eye to the future

[1] Suetonius, *Galba*, 13: "venit Onesimus (Galba), *a villa*" (a hit against a parsimonious old man, whom the public quickly identified with Galba). [2] *Sat.*, ii., 6, 80.

contrived to get together numbers of shady recruits in the four tribal divisions of the city, from the ranks of the freedmen, a class who gradually reinforced and ended by swamping the lower ranks of the free-born citizens; this was the material from which the *plebs* of the Empire was eventually produced.   The real *populus Romanus* despised it from the outset. The real Roman was a countryman, and it was from the ranks of countrymen like himself that he re-cruited the soldiers in whom he trusted, and, on occasion, leaders worthy of Rome as well; upright, disinterested men, full of quiet courage, and steeped in pure and healthy traditions.   This was the true old Roman spirit, only one side of which appears occasionally in their literature, but which may be found in all its purity in their works on agriculture (*scriptores rei rusticæ*).   In these a wholesome con-tempt for the town is regarded as the beginning of wisdom.   This is an article of faith which every writer of this school places at the beginning of his books as a sort of necessary introduction.

The Greeks had written largely on this subject. Varro [1] mentions no less than fifty Greek works on agriculture.   A number of specialists at Carthage, chief among whom was Mago, had noted all that the experience of their contemporaries and predecessors had taught them, and the Romans, true to the policy which led them to introduce into their own country everything which they saw to be useful amongst others, it mattered not whether they were friends or

[1] *Pref.*, 7.

enemies, lost no time in combining this double importation from a foreign soil with their national traditions. This led to the production of Cato's *De Agricultura* and of the three books of Varro (*Rerum Rusticarum Libri Tres*); the first of these treats of agriculture proper, the second, of the rearing of flocks (*pecuaria*), the third, of the special produce of the farm, such as honey, poultry, etc. (*pastio villatica*). The twelve books of Columella and the works of Palladius were also due to the same cause.

We may dismiss the last-named writer as being post-classical; he owed the success enjoyed by him in mediæval times to his ingenious idea in classifying the various operations of husbandry according to the months in which they had to be performed. The three other writers are fairly representative of the ideas which obtained during the republican epoch and the first century of our era. Let us try to discover what their conception of an ideal farm was like (we shall afterwards have occasion to speak of country-houses, which were quite another matter); what, according to their view, were the conditions essential in a well-ordered agricultural holding ? This was a subject in which the Romans took a great interest, and their opinions in regard to it are well worth listening to.

II

FARMS, "VILLÆ RUSTICÆ"

The *villa rustica*, or *rus*, was a house in the country kept up by its owner for the sake of the

profit obtained from it, or, in other words, a
" farm." The Roman country-houses, on the other
hand, variously described as *villæ, deversoria, præ-
toria, prædiola*, etc., roughly correspond with our
country-seats, castles, halls, domains, etc. In these
latter the chief objects sought for were a fine view
(*species*), absolute quiet, and pleasant surroundings.
In the case of a farm, on the other hand, the main
desideratum was that it should bring in a large
revenue (*utilitas, fructus*); " before all things it is
necessary that the gross produce should show a
profit after deducting expenses." [1] To persist in
working an estate at a loss " is not husbandry, but
sheer folly." [2] In this initial axiom we recognise
the sound common sense of the Roman race.

Roman writers on agriculture do not fail to add,
with what seems to be unquestionable sincerity, that
no country is more fertile than Italy. It is true that
there, as elsewhere, ignorance and incapacity meant
ruin for the farmer. The first care of the landed
proprietor must be to choose a farm in a suitable
position. He must satisfy himself of the healthful-
ness of the soil, the air, and the water, these being
the three main sources of disease. Ease of communication was another important point, and the farm
must therefore be near the public highway—not
actually bordering on it, since this has its disadvantages, yet not too far away from it. The experience

[1] Varro, *R. R.*, i., 53: "summa spectanda ne in ea re *sumptus
fructum superet.*"

[2] Varro, *R. R.*, Pref., i., 6: "*frustratio est, non cultura.*"

of neighbouring farmers may prove a useful guide.
What are their farms like ?   Do they look thriving ?
Are the people of the country robust, with bright
and straightforward eyes,[1] perfect hearing, and clear,
sonorous voices ?   Do the properties in the neighbourhood often change hands ?   Do their owners
appear to be prosperous ? Avoid marshy land and
be careful not to settle down too near a river or the
sea, if you would be free from insect pests, serpents,
and unhealthy vapours of all kinds.

The position of the farm once decided on, the
next point is to see that its general arrangement is
satisfactory; the farm buildings must be of a suitable size in proportion to the extent of the holding,
and well adapted for their different purposes.   Columella gives a number of detailed precepts in regard
to their arrangement: the dwelling of the owner
should be in the centre, flanked on either side by
the lodgings for the slaves, the stables, cow-houses,
and poultry-yard; next in order come the store-
houses, granaries, barns, and cellars.   The Romans
insisted on the same order and system which prevailed in the camp being maintained on the farm
as well.   The next point to receive attention was
superintendence of the farming operations.   A suitable *villicus*[2] must be chosen; he must be industri-
ous, sober, and a good disciplinarian.   A reasonable
amount of authority should be placed in his hands,
but correct and detailed accounts should be required

[1] Palladius, i., 2 : "*inoffensum lumen oculorum.*"
[2] The *villicus* was a sort of steward, generally a slave.

of him.   Careful supervision is nowhere more necessary than on a farm; every person employed should feel that he is under the master's eye. "The presence of the master is the soul of progress."[1]

It surprises us to find a good many superstitious ideas intermingled with all this sound advice. Cato's marvellous cabbage which was supposed to cure all diseases is bad enough, but what shall we say when we find our good friend Varro solemnly declaring that, as seeds grow older, they change their species, and that you may sow rape-seed and get a crop of cabbages; that wood and moss should be cut after the full moon, but that on no account ought men or beasts to be shaved or shorn at this critical period.   Respect for tradition, which—here, perhaps, more than anywhere else—lies at the bottom of these precepts, occasionally degenerates into absurd superstitions of this kind.

But only for a space; the writers on agriculture soon return to the dictates of common sense, and it is not without a spice of malice that they refer to some of the absurdities practised by their contemporaries.   They can scarcely find words to express their contempt for those who built pretentious dining-rooms, picture-galleries, and libraries on their farmhouses, even encroaching on their fruit-lofts (*oporothecæ*) for the purpose.   The gentleman-farmer, doubtful whether his home-grown fruit is likely to do him credit when he invites his friends to dinner,[2]

[1] Palladius, i., 6: "*Præsentia domini provectus est agri.*"
[2] Varro, *R. R.*, i,, 59, 2.

orders a stock from Rome, with which he makes a brave show. Carry out a system like this to its logical conclusion, and your farm becomes as great a sham as that of Martial's Bassus,[1] with its turrets and towers and painted chambers, its plane-trees, laurels, and myrtles, where everything, corn and vegetables, fruit and cheese, and even eggs, had to be obtained from the town!

The old Roman farms may not have been pretty to look at; the writers on agriculture do not pretend that they were; they represented the real country, wild and unadorned (*rus verum barbarumque*); but their poultry-yards were well filled, those who dwelt there had fine, healthy appetites, everyone worked hard, including even the slaves whom the master had brought with him from town, and who had to work during their stay in the country. These genuine farms were worth a dozen country-seats, though, thanks to Metellus and Lucullus, they were gradually being displaced by these latter, a change which, Varro declared,[2] would result in incalculable loss to the State. Even in his time people had begun to neglect their barns and cellars and to turn their whole attention to the decoration of their dining-rooms. This luxury was the thin end of the wedge which was eventually to bring about the ruin of the landed proprietor.

Cato was the first to take the field against this new order of things, and Varro is scarcely less vehement in his denunciation of it, while the works

[1] iii., 58.   [2] ii., 13.

of Columella continue the tale. True, the evil increased as time ran on; in spite of the protests of moralists and the fruitless efforts of politicians, the country steadily became more and more depopulated; the small landed proprietor gradually disappeared; until at last *latifundia*,[1] that pest which undermined the Empire,—its ravages being still further increased by the universal moral decadence, —became the general rule.

III

COUNTRY-HOUSES

As we have seen,[2] the Romans had a number of different names for the country-houses to which they went in search of repose. By a natural reaction common enough in the inhabitants of large towns, they desired, in these houses, to breathe a purer air, and to feel that they were far removed from the dust and din of Rome; on the other hand, since distance and economy of time were important objects, in order that they might be able to visit them frequently it was necessary that their country-houses should be within easy reach, and as near the capital as possible; they must be some little way out, yet not too far; suburban, yet right out in the country. A fine view was also a desideratum.

When the Romans were resting, they liked to do

[1] Large estates occupied by a single tenant, or belonging to a single owner, badly cultivated and often allowed to lie fallow.
[2] *Cf.* p. 186.

so with a fine landscape before their eyes.[1]   Their
taste in such matters was fairly eclectic; thus, they
greatly admired the mouth of the Euxine and the
Straits of Gades,[2] and pointed them out to other
people as objects of admiration.   In this case their
choice was not a bad one.

In Italy there were, and are, two kinds of fine
views obtainable.   One may settle down inland
within view of the mountains, and, if possible, not
far from forests and lakes; or one may take advantage of the admirable coast scenery, which is one of
Italy's great attractions, and charms the traveller by
the infinite variety of its effects.   There the waves
which lap upon its sands change with every hour,
now lost in a golden halo, now flecked with silver
spangles, the embodiment of liquid motion and
sparkling radiance; that distant strip of blue sea
which is the first thing that catches the eye after we
have crossed the Alps, and which we never seem to
weary of watching.

The ancients fell under its charm as readily as we
do; they knew and revelled in the delights of the
Bay of Naples.   But no matter where it was, no
villa seemed quite satisfactory unless it enabled its
inhabitants to obtain a glimpse of the sea.   From
one of the smaller dining-rooms (*cenatio*) in Pliny's
villa at Laurentum, he not only commanded a view
of the beautiful villas near it, but also obtained a

---

[1] Cicero, *Tusc.*, i., 44: "quod nunc facimus, cum laxati curis
sumus, ut *spectare aliquid* velimus."

[2] Cicero, *Tusc.*, xx., *in.*, 45.

distant prospect of the sea and of a long strip of the coast-line.[1]   In another *triclinium* he could hear the beat of the surf even though but very faintly: still, it was enough to invest this part of the villa with an additional attraction. A third dining-room possessed this advantage in Pliny's eyes, that when a gale was blowing off the African coast, the breakers dashed against the walls and fell in spray at the foot of the building.   As there were large doors and windows on every side of this room, the guests, as they sat at dinner, obtained a view of the sea in three different directions,[2] or " of three seas," as Pliny expresses it with pardonable emphasis.   On the fourth side one saw the inner courts and entrance portico, with a glimpse of forest and mountain beyond. Pliny adds, as a final touch, that in the baths at his villa, " even swimmers in the *piscina* could look on the sea."[3]

It was, therefore, within sight of the mountains or of the sea that the Romans were wont to seek repose for their tired eyes and bodies. They longed, so they declared, to escape, for a space, from the boredom and worry of the capital; with some of them the longing was a sincere one, and they were able to satisfy it. According to Pliny, the great charm of life in the country lay in the fact that there a man was his own master; he could wake up, or go to sleep, as he pleased; the day was his own

---

[1] Pliny, ii., 17, 12 : "quae *latissimum mare, longissimum litus, amœnissimas* villas prospicit."   [2] Pliny, ii., 13.
[3] ii., 11 : "piscina . . . *ex qua natantes mare aspiciunt.*"

to do what he liked with.¹ " Farewell! *calcei* and holiday *toga*." ² Life in the country was the only " true life." ³ It was there that Pliny found the readiest inspiration. " O sea, O beach, secret haunt of the Muses, how many ideas you suggest, how many you dictate to me!"

No doubt Pliny spoke as he felt; but in many cases the methods adopted to secure isolation were, to say the least of them, peculiar. A spirit of contradiction, not without parallel in our own time, impelled the Romans when they wished to get away from Rome, to hasten off to places like Puteoli, Sorrento, or—favourite resort of all—Baiæ, there to meet the whole of Roman society crowded into a still narrower circle. Baiæ was the Roman ideal of a holiday resort. Our good friend Pliny himself⁴ built two villas at Como, one close to the lake, the other commanding a view of the lake from the mountains; both of these, he tells us, were constructed " in the Baian fashion." ⁵

Although the ostensible reason put forward by the Romans for taking refuge in the country was that they might live a more simple life there, the luxury of their town houses soon made its way into their country residences. From the close of the republic onwards, enormous sums were lavished on the appointments of these villas. Marbles, statues, mosaics—nothing was considered too splendid for their

---

¹ *Ep.*, vii., 3, 2. ² "*Calcei* nusquam, *toga feriata*."
³ i., 9, 6: "o rectam *sinceramque vitam*."
⁴ Pliny, ix., 7, 1. ⁵ ". . . *more Baiano*."

13

adornment.¹ When—as sometimes happens—some
miserly individual decided on spending part of his
hoard with a view to making a show in the world,
he bought huge gardens, adorned them with monu-
mental porticos, and encircled them with a fringe
of statuary.² The provincials were not slow to follow the example thus set them by the people of the
town. Pliny, in describing an inundation of the
Tiber,³ tells us how costly furniture and richly carved
gable-ends were swept away in a confused mass with
agricultural implements and cattle. The incident is
eminently typical of the heterogeneous condition of
society at that date, when the only point of general
agreement was the determination to give oneself up
to the enjoyment of the passing hour.

Great pride was taken in the possession of a villa
which had formerly been the home of some famous
man, such as those that had belonged to Cicero, Hortensius, or Lucullus. In one of his letters Pliny⁴
congratulates a friend on being able to revel in the
joys of country life, in a villa which had formerly
been the favourite residence of one who afterwards
attained the highest honours. As he omits to mention the name of this illustrious personage, we cannot tell who it is that he refers to.

Of all these villas few, if any, now remain. The
most we can hope for is to recognise the sites they

---

¹ Cicero, *Ad Att.*, xvi., 3 and 6 : " prædiolis nostris *et belle ædificatis
et satis amœnis ; ocellos Italiae,* villulas nostris " (our little country-
houses beautifully built and pleasant as they are ; beauty spots of
Italy).   ² *E.g.*, Regulus, see Pliny, iv., 2, 5.
³ *Ep.* viii., 17, 4.   ⁴ Pliny, v., 18.

occupied from the mountains that surrounded them,
or from their position near some lake or sea. Most
of these pleasure and health resorts have since become hotbeds of pestilence. The ravages of time
have been aided by the depredations of ancients and
moderns alike, and the work of destruction has been
all the more rapid because the villas being isolated,
and thus more exposed to spoliation, offered less
resistance than many other edifices. As a natural
consequence, we are obliged to fall back on the
testimony and descriptions of the ancients in order to
form an idea of what their country-houses were like.

The imperial villas, built and decorated in accordance with the tastes of the monarch who inhabited
them, may be placed in a class by themselves. Antoninus had one of these at Lorium, which was his
favourite place of residence. There, everything was
in harmony with the severe and sober tastes of its
owner. The only festivals held there were those in
celebration of the harvest and vintage. Walking
and riding were the ordinary amusements there, the
alarm caused among the shepherds by the sudden
approach of young Marcus Aurelius as he careered
about the neighbourhood on horseback furnishing
quite an exciting incident in an otherwise eventless
existence.[1]

The sumptuous villa which Hadrian had built for
him at the foot of hills near Tibur was of quite a
different type. I have already referred to it.[2] Even
now the ruins help us to form some idea of its vast

[1] *Ad Front.*, ii., 12, 1.   [2] Preface, p. viii. *et seq.*

extent and of the imposing appearance it must have presented.   The entertainments given in its two theatres and its stadium alternated with solemn assemblies held in the Lyceum and the Academy, or in the Pœcile.   On quitting these, the Emperor and his train would go on to the Tempe or Canopus, thus, as it were, transported in an instant to the easternmost confines of the Empire.

Villas of this kind were, of course, the exception; and we must look elsewhere for descriptions of the average country-house.   Even then, however, we shall find that the Roman villas were much larger and more elaborately decorated than those of our own day.   They abounded in statues,[1] in mosaics, and in peristyles; they contained dining-rooms of every possible kind and for every season of the year; if there was no lake, its place was supplied by an euripus,[2] or a leafy grove of plane-trees; then there were porticos and cryptoporticos, whither the owner was carried in a litter to take the air (*gestationes*), so that even the smallest villa covered a great deal of ground—so much so, that they presented the appearance of so many towns.[3]   We are able to

[1] The statues occasionally included some which belonged to the State, and others which had been consecrated, or something like it; the owner made little or no distinction between them (Cicero, *De Leg.*, iii., 13, 30).   *Cf.* in the same passage an anecdote in regard to the magnificent villa of Lucullus at Tusculum.

[2] So called in memory of the channel which separates the island of Eubœa from Greece; they were long trenches embellished by waterfalls and bridges, and sometimes surrounded by porticos and statues.

[3] Pliny the Younger, ii., 17, 27: "præstant *multarum urbium faciem.*"   *Cf.* Tacitus, *Ann.*, iii., 53: "villarum *infinita spatia*" (the limitless expanse of our villas).

form some sort of idea of the character of the average country-house, first of all from what Pliny tells us of the two villas belonging to him, and, secondly, from the descriptions given by Statius of the country-houses of his wealthy patrons.

The *Silvæ* of Statius on the villas of Manilius Vopiscus at Tibur,[1] and of Pollius Felix[2] at Sorrento, abound in the mythological details of which the poet was so fond. He deals out flattery with an unsparing hand. To hear him speak, one would think that nature and art had striven which should do most to beautify these delightful residences. No doubt the poet had drawn largely on his imagination, but there was an element of truth underlying his inventions.

He tells us that in these two villas the first care of the architect has been to take full advantage of the sites. In the villa of Vopiscus at Tibur, the Anio, passing through the midst of marble porticos whose pillars were reflected in its waters, gave forth coolness and verdure all around. A view of the neighbouring woods gave promise of absolute quiet ; countless works of art, statues, and mosaics helped to rest the eye in whichever direction one looked. At Sorrento the view of the gulf and of the neighbouring islands furnished an admirable setting, the beauties of which were not lost on the ancients, though their appreciation of them seems to have been less keen than ours. For we find that even with this marvellous seascape before their eyes they

[1] Statius, i., 3.   [2] ii., 2.

are every whit as loud in their praise of the view landwards,[1] where they were attracted by the silence and the pleasing aspect of the vines.[2] Here too there were numberless antique waxen masks and brazen statues.

Pliny possessed numerous villas in Tusculum, at Tibur, and at Præneste. He has left us a detailed description of his villa at Laurentum,[3] and of the one which he preferred to all the rest, that at Tifernum in Tuscany.[4] Indeed, the details he supplies are so minute, that Canina and others have tried to reconstruct these two country-houses for us.

In describing the different parts of these houses, Pliny uses a good many Greek words, in this, no doubt, conforming with the practice of the architects, who were mostly Greeks.[5] This is not surprising; nor, from what we know of Roman usages, need it astonish us to learn that at Laurentum he had baths with all the usual accessory chambers, tennis-courts, porticos, open and closed (*cryptoporticus*), where one could either walk on foot or take the air in a litter (*gestatio*), etc. But we are scarcely prepared to find that, in addition to two large dining-rooms (*triclinia*), he also had four smaller ones (*coenationes*) as well. And but for the fact that we are aware of the good man's literary habits, we

---

[1] Statius, v., 45.   [2] v., 99.   [3] Pliny, ii., 17.

[4] v., 6. In order to complete our knowledge in regard to Pliny, it will be well to add to the description I am now about to give, the letter (i., 3) in which he speaks in high praise of the charms of a country-house belonging to his mother-in-law.

[5] *Procoeton, zotheca, heliocaminos,* etc.

should find it difficult to explain why, in addition to the various towers and *zotheca*, he found it necessary to have as many as eight studies (*dietæ*).[1] But in Pliny's eyes a villa was rather a place where he could work in quiet than a country retreat.

The general arrangement and distribution of the various rooms were very much the same at his villa in Tuscany, which formed part of his ancestral estate, and which Pliny had taken the utmost delight in altering and embellishing. The air there was very healthful, and people were so long-lived, and there were so many generations of a single family in existence at the same time, that one almost felt, on coming amongst them, as though one had been transported into another century.[2] In view of the summer heats, fountains with basins were laid on in the rooms underneath frescos of rivers and woods. But it strikes us as a curious way of praising a house to compare it with a picture,[3] and we find it difficult to sympathise with the taste of a man who cut his boxwood into shapes resembling fruit

[1] In the other villa there were no less than thirteen *dietæ* and one *zothecula*.

[2] See § 6. *Cf.* what we learn from the inscriptions as to the longevity of the country people in Africa ; Boissier, *L'Afrique romaine*, pp. 142 *et. seq.*

[3] So, too, the President de Brosses (at the end of Letter xii.) after dilating on the beauty of the country between Vicenza and Padua, which he greatly admires, is so ill-advised as to add, " The whole road is bordered with trees planted in squares or quincunxes ; even the scenery at the opera is not more beautiful or more ornate than such a country as this." [An excellent translation of these letters has recently been made by Lord Ronald Gower.—TRANSLATOR.]

and trees, or even the letters of the owner's or gardener's name. This custom seems to have come originally from the East, and has, alas! been religiously preserved even down to our own day.[1]

I purposely omit any mention of other villas, such as that known as the villa of Diomedes at Pompeii; this latter is rather a suburban residence than a genuine country-house. Similarly I abstain from discussing the villas of Cicero, of which we know scarcely anything but their names; it is true we are told that Atticus bought a number of fine statues for their adornment, but nothing now remains of them, and, unlike Pliny, Cicero has not left us a description of them. He did not avail himself of themes of this kind to fill his letters, or as a convenient means of displaying the niceties of his literary style.

IV

DID THE ROMANS POSSESS ANY FEELING FOR THE PICTURESQUE IN NATURE?

We have seen how the Roman ideal of a country-place became gradually modified. At first they looked upon it as a source of profit; later on it was considered enough that it should be agreeable and restful. Now comes the turn of the poets; Tibullus transfers to some ideal country spot the scenes in

---

[1] Later on, at Florence, in a castello belonging to the Grand Duke, Montaigne saw a room built in among the branches of a growing tree, and also the Duke's crest surmounting a porch, "excellently formed of the branches of a growing tree."

which he may dream of his love for Delia without fear of rivalry.   But we readily leave such poetic dreams on one side, as quite foreign to historic reality, and, returning to sober fact, put to ourselves the following questions.

The Romans in general—for here we need not concern ourselves with exceptional types—saw and loved nature in a manner quite different from ours. What, then, is the difference between their perfectly genuine love for a country life and our own ?   In ancient art we are certain to find a reflection of some part, at any rate, of their feelings.   What has it to teach us on this subject, and, to be more precise, what place are we to assign to landscape in the history of Roman art ?   To put the whole matter in a nutshell, in how far did the Romans possess what we call a feeling for the picturesque in nature ?[1]

This last question has been much discussed by people who overlooked the fact that in an inquiry of this kind, modern students run great risk of being led on to the wrong track and thus rendered incapable of arriving at any definite conclusion.   In the

[1] In regard to the feeling for the picturesque among the ancients, the reader may with advantage consult Friedlaender, *Mœurs romaines*, towards the end of the second volume of the French translation ; it should be pointed out, however, that the latest German edition contains many extensive additions.   One of the best works on the place occupied by landscape in ancient art is that of M. Woerman, *Die Landschaft in der Kunst der alten Völker*, 1876 ; and *Ueber den landschaftlicher Natursinn der Griechen und Römer*, by the same author.   An excellent analysis of the first of these two books, with a number of original observations, appeared in an article by M. Michel in the *Revue des Deux Mondes*, June 15, 1884, pp. 896 *et seq.*

first place, we have lost many important witnesses among the monuments of Roman art and literature which no amount of inductive reasoning can replace; and on the other hand, it is quite possible that the Romans may have possessed sentiments, and very keen ones too, of which no trace survives in their literary or artistic productions. We often find that the sincerest feelings are those which defy analysis and refuse to lend themselves to artistic expression. No sane person imagines that the taste for beautiful landscapes was non-existent in Flanders prior to the rise of the Flemish school of painting. Let us turn our attention, however, to facts which seem to me to be outside the region of controversy.

(1) *The View of Nature Held by the Romans as a Whole*

All Romans, whatever their station in life, were passionately fond of their native country. They were great travellers and great conquerors, but none of them ever quitted Italy without some intention of eventually returning to it. It was to them the fairest region on the earth; and in spite of its fever-stricken marshes and the manifest decline of its agriculture, they were always ready to maintain that it might also be made the most fertile; according to their view, all the failures in this direction were due to the ignorance or laziness of the rustic population.

As for the world of nature, they enjoyed its good gifts and its beauty in an unthinking fashion, taking

them as part of the inalienable heritage of mankind.
No doubt there were a few choice spirits who possessed a deeper and loftier insight.   In the works of
Virgil we can detect a natural sympathy with the
labours, the inhabitants, and the deities of the
country.   Lucretius, too, seems to have been alive
to the more exalted, austere, and occasionally rugged
aspects of wild nature.   But the remainder of the
Romans, even the more cultured of them, even such
men as Horace or Cicero, when they sought refuge
in the country had little appreciation of anything
beyond its bracing air, which helped to restore their
energies, its material comforts and pleasures, and
the absolute repose which it afforded to their minds.[1]
The Alps and Apennines with their snowy peaks,
which are so attractive and imposing to our eyes,
made them feel melancholy and uncomfortable.   At
the great crises of their lives they could not endure
the crowded city; their sole desire was for solitude.
They were ready to call on the forests and mountains to witness the unmerited ill-fortune that had
befallen them.   Once the crisis had passed, however, the longing for action soon took hold of them
again.   In their darkest hours of sorrow they seemed
to find distraction and consolation, not in some wild
and rugged landscape, such as the modern mind
would naturally fly to in similar circumstances, but
rather in some beautiful view with the sunlit sea

[1] *Cf.* the dictum of Socrates in the *Phædo* of Plato; he refuses to
go for a walk "because neither the woods nor the country have anything to teach him."

shining in the distance.   Their love was not so
much for the country in general as for some favourite and charming spot.   They were not naturally
contemplative, and, in spite of their elegiac poetry,
they had, unless I am mistaken, little or no taste
for the idyllic.   Their desire was for the charms of
Baiæ and its environs.   What they were in the habit
of describing as " the beauty spots of Italy " (*ocelli
Italiæ*), possessed few of the qualities which attract
us.

(2) *Landscape in Roman Art.   Descriptions of Landscapes in Roman Literature*

From what has already been said, the reader will
have no difficulty in understanding why it was that
landscape did not occupy such an important place in
Roman art as it does in that of our own day.   Unlike the Greeks, in whose paintings the landscape
merely served as a sort of setting for the rest of the
picture, the Roman artist loved it and painted it for
itself alone.   The charming fresco of an aviary (*ad
Gallinas*) in the house of Livia on the Flaminian
Way,[1] proves that the landscape was not always and
in every instance regarded as a mere accessory.
This fresco and the drawings in the Vatican manu-
scripts representing scenes taken from the Odyssey,
show that the ancient landscape painters could,
when they liked, produce works full of genuine and
poetic feeling.

[1] *Cf.* M. Michel in the *Revue des Deux Mondes*, June 15, 1884,
p. 883.

It cannot be denied, however, that instances of such work are rare; just as their compositions in the grand style remind us but distantly of the master-pieces of Greek art, so here, too, the painter is more often than not a mere decorator; he makes no claim to be anything more, and his landscapes are purely decorative. He appeals to the eye rather than to the mind. The Romans had not yet found out for themselves that landscape painting is '' nature seen through a temperament.'' Nowadays the artist must make his landscape live, breathe, and palpitate; the Romans were less exacting in their demands on painters or writers who introduced descriptions of scenery into their narratives.

Precision of any sort was avoided here, though the ancients were by no means averse to it elsewhere; the painter was quite content with a few very scanty, vague, and general indications, and writers and their readers were no less easily satisfied. In proof of this, I may quote the closing scenes of the *Satyricon*, in which the love affairs of Polyænus and Circe are described.[1] The first meeting between them takes place in a laurel grove (*daphnon*) near a pro-menade.[2] On two separate occasions, the author, though as a rule by no means squeamish, finds it necessary to leave his characters to themselves, and, for lack of anything else to say, falls back upon the beauties of the spot in which they found themselves.[3] He describes the green turf which serves as a couch

[1] Cap. cxxvi. *et seq.*
[2] Cap. cxxvii.
[3] Cap. cxxvii. and cxxxi.

for the lovers, and tell us it was strewn with flowers which turn to love the thoughts of those whose secret passion Venus favours: " roses, violets, and tender catkins." These are the only details he gives us.   At their next meeting the lovers come together under the shade of a clump of trees among which are plane-trees, laurels, cypresses, and pines. Through its midst flows " a foaming river, its waters plashing on the pebbles, while around the green turf and tender violets flit the nightingale of the woods and the town-bred swallow." From the standpoint of the ancients this description was doubtless full enough, but to our minds it seems very meagre.   The picture has no definite setting; the scene is not laid in any particular place or at any particular time—or rather it belongs to all ages and all countries.   It is an artificial and empty composition which smells of the lamp, and is absolutely deficient in any sort of realism.

So, too, though in a somewhat different manner, in most of the paintings at Pompeii the artist has given his imagination free scope.   Fantasy reigns supreme in the decoration and intentional complexity of the nooks and corners of the great houses which generally served as a background to these pictures, in the numberless caricatures, many of which are very amusing, and above all in those graceful conventions of ancient art, the centaurs and *Chimaerae*, the Cupids, storks and pygmies, satyrs or nymphs, and all the motley train of Bacchus. Add to these the paintings in which we find traces

of those exotic influences which appealed so strongly
to the ancients, more particularly those Egyptian
landscapes, in which the ibis and other larger birds
of the East disport themselves among lotus- and
palm-trees, while crocodiles slumber on the banks

SPECIMEN OF ROMAN ANIMAL PAINTING, POMPEII.

of the stream. Nor must we forget the representations of crowded thoroughfares, streets, houses,
balconies, and staircases, with figures of slaves or
maid-servants looking out either from the top of the
stairs or from a window; in short, all the various
optical illusions so dear to the Italian taste.

I have already had occasion to quote [1] an interesting passage from Pliny in regard to the frescos

[1] *Cf.* Chapter I., p. 24.

which were brought into fashion by a painter of the time of Augustus, named S. Tadius. We here recognise a large number of his favourite subjects; gardens (*topiaria*) are represented by the aviary found in the house of Livia (*ad Gallinas*); at Pompeii we find pictures representing "the sea, harbours, and villas; people fishing, sailing, or gathering the vintage." Elsewhere there are woodland views. It is true that we have not yet come upon some of the realistic and picturesque subjects mentioned by Pliny; we have not found " people riding on donkeys," or that curious picture representing " men who have gone into a swamp anxiously carrying women on their backs, whom they are taking to a villa, the road to which runs through marshy ground."

It cannot be said that any of these subjects denote a very high or refined standard of taste; but we shall be well advised if, in examining these pictures, we dismiss from our minds all thought of sentiment, poetry, and innate truth. Our wisest course will be to show what indulgence we can to this amiable, easy-going, unpretentious, and frequently humorous side of ancient life, and, above all, to bear in mind the large element of hypothesis on which the foregoing remarks are based, that the monuments representing this branch of ancient art are meagre, scanty, and liable to rapid deterioration, and that even when we have laboriously collected all available information in regard to it, the data at our disposal are, after all, inadequate and incomplete.

CHAPTER IX

SCHOOLS AND BOOKS

I

SCHOOLS

OF all the institutions and usages of the ancient world, there was, perhaps, none which exercised a more marked influence on the development of literature, or which was more characteristic of the imperial epoch, than the Roman school. It is, however, an institution which we are apt to lose sight of, and which it is well, now and then, to bring under the notice of modern readers.

If a good fairy, such as we read of in fairy-tales, were to offer us the choice of some one aspect of ancient life, which she would reveal to us by her magic power and flood with the broad light of day, I am not sure but that we should be wise to give the preference to this one. Speaking generally, we know pretty well how the Romans taught. But, in the first place, where did they teach ? How interesting it would be if someone were to show us one of the successors, or, better still, one of the predecessors of the famous grammarians of this period, such as Aulus Gellius, Donatus, or Servius. We can scarcely suppose that they wore college caps and gowns; but would dearly like to know what their outer man was like. How did they wear their own togas, these men who laid down rules as to how orators should wear theirs ? What costume did they put on when about to deliver their lectures on rhetoric ? It is much to be regretted that we do not find a single authentic portrait of a grammarian in any of the frescos, or in any of those mosaics in which the names of the figures are given underneath.[1]

But let us leave the schoolmaster and his dress, and inquire as to the arrangement of the places in which the pedagogues of antiquity taught, the memory of which was treasured by their pupils with so much gratitude and veneration.[2] Unfortunately, the word school in Latin (*schola*), like many other

---

[1] A mosaic in the hall of Pompeianus, near Constantina, bears the inscription *filosophi locus* (Boissier, *L'Afrique romaine*, p. 161). But here the reference is to a *philosophus*, and no matter what the precise meaning attached to this word may have been (a subject on which there is some difference of opinion), this particular *philosophus* is presented to us in a somewhat ridiculous light. He is a young man placed near an elegantly attired lady with a fan in her hand, who holds a little dog on a leash, while, with the other hand, he shelters the lady with a sunshade.

[2] Cicero, *Pro Plancio*, xxx., 81 : "Cui non *locus ipse mutus ille*, ubi alitus aut doctus est, cum grata recordatione in mente versetur?" (Who does not remember with a feeling of gratitude that silent place in which one was educated and instructed?) The word "silent" is used in contrast to the voice of the master.

words, such as *philosophus*, *Academia*,[1] etc., came to
be applied to so many other places and to so many
other groups of ideas that, even in ancient times,
its original meaning had gradually disappeared.
From buildings in which instruction was actually
given, with an occasional oration interspersed now
and then (*scholæ philosophorum*, *rhetorum*, *grammat-
icorum*), the word came to be applied to the addresses and lectures of the masters,[2] and then to the
various callings in which discipline and training were
required. Thus we read of *schools* of gladiators, and
schools of wild-beast fighters. It was also applied to
certain associations (thus in military phraseology,
scholæ speculatorum),[3] and to the buildings belonging
to guilds or corporations (*e.g.*, *scholæ medicorum*).
It was used of galleries for the exhibition of works
of art, such as the *schola Octavia* at Rome. A
favourite resort of the wits in Martial's[4] time was
known as the *schola poetarum*. Finally the word
came to be employed as a designation of the offices
of scribes or notaries (such as the *schola Xantha* in
the forum near the *tabularium*),[5] or to the place

---

[1] Montesquieu, in some notes on his travels recently published
(*Italie*, p. 88), tells us that at Verona he found both an Academy of
Letters and a riding academy in the same building, which struck him
as a curious hotch-potch.

[2] Cicero himself (*Tusc.*, I, 4, 8) describes his *Disputationes Tusculanæ* as "quinque dierum *scholas*." Cf. *ibid.*, iii., 81.

[3] *Cf.* cap. xi., p. 284.   [4] iii., 20, 8, and iv., 61, 3.

[5] The *schola Xantha* of the *scribæ librarii ædilium curulium*, discovered in the sixteenth century on the *Via Sacra* near the *rostra*, was
a small but sumptuous edifice constructed entirely of marble, and
adorned with seats of bronze and statuettes of silver.

where people waited their turn to go down into the *piscina* in the public baths (*schola labri* or *labrorum*),[1] and toward the close of the final era of antiquity, *schola* was often used, together with the words *thermæ* and *palatium*, to designate any ancient ruin. It will thus be seen that the term suffered a gradual but undoubted degradation as it fell from one meaning to another.

The same process of degradation acted, though in a less marked degree, upon its derivatives. According to the circumstances and context in which it is used, *scholasticus* may either mean a student, a pedant, a member of " that race which smells of greasy oil,"[2] or an educated man of the world with a knack for turning verses, who, unless fortune was specially unkind to him, and especially if one of his pupils was raised to the throne, had every chance of becoming *vir clarissimus et spectabilis*.[3]

Archæologists have little or nothing to tell us of the internal arrangements of the schools; nor is this to be greatly wondered at. The rhetoricians, whose aim it was to acquire eloquence, an art which can be practised in any surroundings or any situation, prided themselves on being everywhere prepared for practice, and that any sort of shelter sufficed them. They declaimed their speeches in the *exedræ* and in the *palæstræ* (indeed, Vitruvius made special provision for them in planning his

---

[1] Vitruvius, v., 10.

[2] Virgil, *Catalecta*, vii., 4 : " *scholasticorum* natio madens pingui."

[3] *Cf.* in the *Anthologia*, R. I., 286, " Symphosius *scholasticus*."

exedræ)[1]. They declaimed in the public baths, under the porticos, and even in the open air, in the broad sunlight, which unkind critics never lost an opportunity of contrasting with the gloom of the schools. Almost any room or any place, therefore, contented both masters and pupils for teaching of this kind.[2] In the provinces, travelling sophists and professors of rhetoric were accustomed to collect their audiences in the largest buildings available, preferably in some basilica or theatre.

The small schools, presided over by the grammarians (*viles ludi*)[3], being of a very unpretentious character, were equipped in a totally different manner. It was necessary that they should be established at a fixed abode.   If the master enjoyed the favour of the city authorities, he sometimes obtained the use of a room in some public building, or in some corner of the forum.   Failing this, he was obliged to install himself, at his own expense, in some shop (*taberna*), or, if needs be, in some garret (*pergula*) under the roof.[4]

[1] v., 11 : "exedræ spatiosæ habentes sedes in quibus philosophi, *rhetores*, reliquique qui studiis delectantur, sedentes disputare possint" (spacious *exedræ* with seats in which philosophers, *rhetoricians*, and all those who love study may sit and debate).

[2] S. Augustine (*Conf.*, vi., 9) tells us of his friend and pupil Alypius: "cum . . . medio die *cogitaret in foro* quod recitaturus erat, *sicut exerceri scholastici solent*" (when in the middle of the day he prepared what he intended to recite in the forum, as the pupils of the rhetoricians are wont to do).   [3] Horace, *Sat.*, 1, 10, 75.

[4] In the story of Virginia (Livy, iii., 44, 6) we read : "Virginj venienti *in forum*, ibi namque *in tabernaculis litterarum ludi erant*" (As the young girl came into the forum, for it was there, in the small shops, that the schools were held).   In the *Historia Augusta* (*Pesc. Niger*, 11) mention is made of the *pergulæ magistrales* of the capital.

The life led by these *grammatici* or *litteratores* was a hard one.   A great deal was expected of them, and they were miserably paid.   It was no uncommon thing for some wretched master to be beaten by his pupils.[1]   It is true that many of the rhetoricians were treated every bit as badly.   S. Augustine[2] has a good deal to say about the young rowdies (*eversores*) whose escapades, both at Rome and at Carthage, nearly always took the form of some sorry trick played on their masters.

The scenes from school-life, which are numerous enough among the frescos at Pompeii and Herculanum, apart from the fact that they are probably idealised, tell us little that we could not have imagined for ourselves without their help.   They include the figures of children holding a scroll or single or double tablets; some of them are writing, or preparing to write, with the stylus in their mouths; others are engaged in sketching or reciting; lastly, in a framework formed by pillars connected overhead by vine-branches, we have the famous fresco of the whipped child.[3]

The paucity of archæological details on which I have commented above, is scarcely surprising when we remember that, so far, no trace has been found

---

[1] Juvenal, vii., 213: "Sed Rufum atque alios *cædit sua quæque juventus*" (But Rufus and others were beaten, each by his own pupils).   [2] *Conf.*, iii., 3, and v., 8.

[3] This has been reproduced over and over again.   *Cf.* Duruy, *Histoire romaine*, v., 245; Saglio, under *Educatio*, fig. 2614; Rich, under *Ludus*, etc.; Smith, *Dictionary of Greek and Roman Antiquities*, 2 vols., 1890–91.

of any of the numerous public and private libraries which must have existed at Rome.[1]   We are, therefore, again obliged to fall back upon imagination. But in order to prevent it from going astray, we must try to keep steadily before our minds some of the differences—whether due to material causes or not, it matters little—which distinguished the schools of antiquity from those of our own day.   Let us briefly recapitulate what ancient writers have to tell us on this point.

(1) *Primary Schools*

In the Roman system of education there were two main periods through which each pupil passed in succession.   Of the first of these, which was spent under the ferule of the grammarian, there is little to be said.   The rudiments of education are everywhere pretty much the same.   The instruction given was of a very modest description, the teachers belonged to a very humble class.   The subject is such a hackneyed one that I shall confine myself to quoting two inscriptions, one of which records the good qualities of a schoolmaster, the other the accomplishments of a promising boy.   We are told of

---

[1] I use the words "at Rome" in a general sense, for we are no longer entirely dependent on the texts of classical authors or on the library discovered at Herculanum (in 1753); the excavations undertaken since 1876 at Pergamus, at Pompeii, and at Rome, have placed the whole question on an entirely new footing.   *Cf.* Lanciani, *Ancient Rome*, pp. 178 *et seq.*   In regard to the discoveries made by him at Rome in 1883, *cf.* pp. 191 *et seq.*

the master, Philocalus[1] by name, that " he was a man of the highest character, and that he wrote wills very honestly and never refused to render this service to any who asked him."[2]   In regard to the boy, who died at the age of ten years and some months,[3] we are assured that he knew " the dogmas of Pythagoras and the teaching and books of the learned "[4]; in other words, he knew a number of " golden rules " off by heart.   He had read Homer and had studied Euclid, tablets in hand.   Here we have clearly indicated the three elements—reading, arithmetic, and the training of the memory.

By reading the works of standard authors with a running comment, the pupils were enabled from childhood upwards to lay up a store of quotations from the early poets and historians which they dragged in at every opportunity.   Even the writers of the *Historia Augusta* are not above making a pedantic display of the knowledge thus acquired.[5] It was largely owing to this early influence that

---

[1] Bücheler, *Carm. Lat. Epigraph.*, i., No. 91.

[2] " Summa cum castitate in discipulos suos
    Idemque testamēnta scripsit cum fide
    Nec quoiquam pernegavit."
Cf. *C. I. N.*, 4699, and *C. I. L.*, vol. ii., 1734.

[3] Bücheler, i., No. 434, vv. 5 *et seq.*

[4] " Dogmata Pythagoræ sensi studiumque sophorum
    Et libros legi."

[5] See Peter's *Index*.   The authors are Virgil, Cicero, Ennius, Sallust, and Cato.   Severus, when confined to his bed, sent to his eldest son " *divinam Sallustii orationem qua Micipsa filios ad pacem hortatur* . . . idque frustra* " (Spartianus, *Severus*, xxi., 10); the last two words are delicious !

Virgil came to occupy and retain such a considerable place in the intellectual and moral existence of the Romans. From the second century onwards, the *Æneid* was regarded by them as something more than a mere national epic; it was looked upon as a general compendium of learning, a history of gods and men. There was scarcely anything to which some verse in it could not be made to apply, and readers accepted the application, no matter how forced it might be.[1] The poem was held to be an oracle which revealed,[2] or was supposed to reveal, their future destiny to emperors and to those who aspired to imperial honours.

I said just now that the grammarians were a very humble class. It should be noted, however, that during the confusion which prevailed in the third and fourth centuries, some of them succeeded in attaining very exalted positions. Thus Timolaus, the brother of Odenatus, who began life as a grammarian, and afterwards became a celebrated teacher of rhetoric (*summus Latinorum rhetor*), ended by becoming one of the Thirty Tyrants.[3] Similarly, at Laodicea, the rhetorician Polemon was raised to royal rank by Antony and Augustus.

[1] *Cf.* the embarrassment which Vopiscus (*Numerianus*, 13, 3; Peter, ii., p. 240, 10) seems to feel in recording a supposed remark of Diocletian made as he killed Aper, the father-in-law of Numerianus, with his own hand.

[2] The Emperor Claudius of Illyria learned the lofty destiny of his race from a verse in Virgil (Trebellius Pollio, 10, 4; Peter, ii., p. 140).

[3] Trebellius Pollio, *Tyr. Trig.*, 28 (Peter, ii., p. 124).

(2) *Schools of Rhetoric*

So far, however, we have discovered more points of resemblance than of difference between our modern primary schools and those of the ancients. The discrepancy is much greater when we come to what constituted the second stage of Roman education, viz., to the teaching of the rhetoricians.

Here the pupil had more chance of showing what he was capable of, and was clearly given to understand that he was now about to lay the foundation of his future career.   In order to develop his natural gifts, he had to narrate, discourse, argue, declaim, and, above all, he was taught to condense a whole line of argument or chain of ideas into a single flowing period (*sententia*).[1]   His hearers were generally wearied and bored and there was no other method of arousing their attention; unfortunately, it was a method which frequently necessitated the sacrifice of sense to mere sound.   Even the " jargon of the schools " in the Middle Ages[2] was probably more intelligible than the lucubrations of these young chatterboxes, who began to retail their extravagant eloquence at the age of eighteen or earlier.[3]

These purple patches (*purpurei panni*) were afterwards introduced into subjects which were little better worth listening to.   We know from what Seneca and Quintilian have to tell us that the most

---

[1] Juvenal, viii., 125 : "quod modo proposui, non *est sententia*."

[2] Montaigne, *Ess.*, i., 36.

[3] Spartianus, *Sev.*, l., 4 (Peter, i., p. 123, 13) : "*octavo decimo anno* publice declamavit."

extraordinary and out-of-the-way situations were accepted as a matter of course in these imaginary lawsuits; cases of abduction by pirates, of the exposure of young maidens, of seduction with the alternative of either death or marriage for the seducer. The moderns have made merry over these themes, and even the ancients recognised that they were ridiculous. But those that put them forward pointed out that there was a tacit agreement between the rhetors and their audiences to regard them merely as a framework on which to build a superstructure of argument, and that, in themselves, they possessed no importance. They were little more than stalking-horses. In our modern schools the same conventional element is not entirely absent from our methods of teaching.

A good deal of ridicule has been cast on the teachers of rhetoric, as well as on their pupils, and it cannot be denied that the rhetorician in the *Satyricon*, the pompous Agamemnon, is a most amusing figure. He is a great braggart, ready to roll forth a sonorous period or turn a couplet at a moment's notice, and in confidential chat he out-Herods Herod in his strictures on his pupils and on the art he teaches; he is, moreover, very fond of good living, and when he finds himself in comfortable quarters generally contrives to get invited a second time. We must not forget, however, that this is only a part of the picture, and that if we wish to get a complete view of the facts we ought to remember that there were other masters besides the hero of Petronius's romance, many of whom achieved great reputations, some of them even taking their place among the Fathers of the Church. Ambrose, Augustine, and Lactantius had all started in life as brilliant rhetoricians.

In such an atmosphere as this, it is not surprising to find a goodly crop of strange ideas springing up. Gordianus, who became emperor in the third century, took it into his head to rewrite the early poems of Cicero (*Marius, Aratea*, etc.), in order to prove how much they stood in need of being brought up to date.[1] One amusement consisted in performing extraordinary feats of memory. Hortensius had been the first to set the fashion in the days of Cicero, and the tradition[2] was perpetuated by Porcius Latro and Seneca the Elder. Another favourite pastime was the writing of quaint or eccentric verses, an occupation to which both the Greek and Roman decadents were much addicted. Poems were composed in which the lines were arranged in the shape of an egg or hatchet, or in which all the words began or ended with the same letter, or where each word contained a certain number of letters or syllables, or where the number of syllables in each succeeding word increased in a fixed ratio (1, 2, 3, 4, 5).[3] Montaigne[4] rightly compares dexterity of this kind to that of a man who used to give exhibitions, in his day, of his skill in passing a grain of

---

[1] Capitolinus, *Gord.*, iii., 2.
[2] *Controv.*, i., Præf., 2, 3, and 18, 19 (M., pp. 2 and 11).
[3] *Cf.* Porphyrius and the *Anthologia Latina*.   [4] *Essais*, i., 44.

millet seed through the eye of a needle with his left hand, a feat in which he was never known to fail.

Eloquence was a sort of national gift at Rome, having flourished there long before Greek influence had made itself felt. The Romans were, therefore, unable to conceive of a statesman who lacked eloquence, even in the days when eloquence had ceased to be a power in the State. Everything else might change, the Empire might be assailed and shaken on its base, this national prejudice, strengthened as it was by the acquired prejudice of education, still remained intact. That this was so, is clearly shown by certain anecdotes preserved in the works of the historians of the Empire and in the *Historia Augusta*. The youthful Cæsars declaimed and recited their verses in public.[1] Every one of the emperors laid claim to eloquence as a sort of official quality. In the reign of Caligula, Domitius, the most celebrated orator of the day, only saved himself from the jealous rancour of the despot by pretending that he was nonplussed by the Emperor's arguments and by publicly admitting himself vanquished.[2] Numerianus, son of the Emperor Carus, having delivered an admirable speech in the Senate, it was agreed that a statue should be erected in his honour in the Ulpian Library; this statue was dedicated to him not in his capacity as Cæsar, but as a *rhetor*, and bore the - legend, " To Numerianus Cæsar, the ablest orator of his time."[3]

[1] *E.g.*, *Numerianus*, xi., 1 (Peter, ii., p. 238, 16); *cf.* what Suetonius says in regard to Nero's speeches and poems (*Nero*, 10).

[2] Dion, lix., 19.   [3] *Numerianus*, cap. xi. (Peter, ii., p. 239, 5).

It has long been a matter of common remark that
the influence exercised by these schools of rhetoric on
the literature of the Empire was both powerful and
disastrous.   That poets who declaimed like Lucan
and Juvenal, and prose-writers who moralised without ceasing like Valerius Maximus, or whose works
consisted of one long peroration like those of Florus,
must have owed a part of their defects to the bad
taste of their contemporaries, is a very old story.
But is is only in quite recent years that traces of this
influence have been clearly recognised even in some
of the masterpieces of the silver age, such as the
Annales and *Historiæ* of Tacitus.[1]   When we find
that authors of the highest originality, including
such a masterly writer as Tacitus, were infected by
the general failing, we can readily imagine how it
must have fared with the lesser men, what an inexhaustible mine rhetoric must have been to them,
and what countless themes it must have furnished
them with.   Great men whose glory was marred by
an untoward death,[2] great men whose very bodies
were denied burial, Pompey and his sons, Cato and
Marius, these were some of the trite and hackneyed
commonplaces which issued in a bounteous stream
from the schools of rhetoric, and which we come
upon at every turn throughout the whole of the

[1] M. Cas Morawski, *De rhetoribus Latinis observ.*, 1892 ; *Zeitschr.
f. d. osterr Gymn.*, 1893 ; *Zur Rhetorik bei den röm. Historikern ;*
Eos, ii., 1, Leopoli, 1895 ; *De sermone scriptorum Latin, æt. arg.*
Cf. *Revue Critique*, 1893, ii., p. 155, and 1895, ii., p. 443.
[2] *Cf.* Morawski, *Philologus*, liv., 1.

Latin literature of the Empire, in verse and prose alike. There are numerous other subjects stamped with the same trade-mark. All of them are products of the same gigantic factory—the schools of rhetoric.

It was quite as much owing to their influence as to the example of the Greeks that the practice of re-writing speeches which had been actually delivered in a different form, became so general. Since the orator had a free hand and could alter as he liked, it was quite possible, and, indeed, often happened, that the published speech did not contain a single line of what had originally been delivered. This practice was followed even in classical times by Cicero and Pliny the Younger. We all know the story of how Milo, after he had been exiled at Marseilles, ridiculed Cicero because, though he could not find a single word to say in his defence at the critical moment, yet he had afterwards taken great pains in preparing useless speeches (ἀκάρπους λόγους), and had sent them to his exiled client, as though they could then be of the slightest advantage to him![1]

The traditional curriculum included exercises in panegyric and invective. As a matter of prudence some historical personage was always selected as a

---

[1] Dion Cassius, xl., 54. Elsewhere the same writer (xlvi., 7) makes Calenus remark to Cicero : " Don't you know that everyone is aware that you never delivered one of the speeches which you have published, and that they were all written after the event, just as men fashion dashing generals and cavalry officers out of wax ? "

subject for the latter. Eulogies, on the contrary, were invariably addressed to some prominent man of the day. The author of the paneygric seldom went unrewarded, the case of Pliny furnishing an example which found many followers. True, it happened now and then that some cross-grained emperor of the blunt, soldierly type kicked against this fulsome adulation. When Pescennius Niger made his way to the throne by sheer force of courage, one of the fashionable orators of the day offered to pronounce a panegyric in his honour. His reply was characteristic:

"Write, rather, in praise of Marius or Hannibal (a subject that had already been done to death), or of some great general of the good old days ; tell of what he did, in order that we may imitate him. It is absurd to praise the living, especially if they be emperors, who are the source of all favours, who are feared, who have the power to give presents, to put men to death, or to proscribe them." [1]

In reality, however, more than one of these up-start Cæsars regretted their oratorical deficiencies and the lack of the faculty which was regarded as an indispensable qualification of every wearer of the toga. They made up for it by retaining the services of some able man, whose duty it was to compose all their orations. The authors of the *Historia Augusta* are careful to inform us whether any given oration

[1] Spartianus, *Pescennius Niger*, xi., (P. i., p. 156, 16).

was really the work of the emperor to whom it is ascribed. Their silence in regard to the others is significant.[1]

The above were some of the defects and weaknesses of the Roman schools. And yet by a revulsion of feeling, common enough in maturer years, men who had made a name by merits acquired elsewhere, often remembered their masters with gratitude. It was a sort of idealisation of their young days. Historians, infected by the same respect for the schools, collected details concerning them with pious care; in the case of more than one emperor they give a list of the grammarians, rhetoricians, and provincial or metropolitan philosophers who took part in his education.[2]

---

[1] Trebellius Pollio, *Claudius*, 7, 2 (P. ii., p. 127, 21), after quoting from one of his speeches, remarks : " Hanc autem *ipse dictasse* perhibetur ; ego *verba magistri memoriæ* non requiro " (We are told, however, that he dictated this speech himself ; the productions of a master whose duty it is to compose orations for another do not interest me). Vopiscus, *Tacitus*, 6, 5 (P. ii., p. 189, 12) : " Di avertant principes pueros . . . quibus ad suscribendum *magistri litterarii* manus teneant " (Heaven preserve us from boy emperors whose hands have to be guided by a writing-master when they sign their names). *Ibid.*, *Saturninus*, 10, 4 (P. ii., p. 227, 12) : " M. Salvidienus hanc *ipsius* orationem *vere fuisse* dicit, et fuit re vera non parum litteratus. Nam et in Africa rhetoricæ operam dederat, Romæ frequentaverat pergulas magistrales " (M. Salvidienus tells us that this speech was really his own [Saturninus's]. Indeed, he was fairly well educated. In Africa he attended the classes of a rhetorician, and at Rome he had frequented the garrets of the schoolmasters).

[2] Lampridius, *Alex. Sev.*, iii., 3 ; *cf.* the end of note 1.

15

II

BOOKS

In order to render our conception of the intellectual life of the ancients a little less incomplete, we may with advantage place what may be termed school accessories side by side with the pupils and their masters. Books, libraries, methods of publication, all these were very different among the ancient Romans from what they are with us, and the differences have even left their impress in the form of their literary productions.

The first thing to be noticed is that books, in spite of the fragile material on which they were written (I refer of course to the papyrus), were much more plentiful than might be supposed. Though the number of volumes contained in private libraries rarely exceeded one or two thousand, yet we hear now and then of others which were much more extensive. A physician of the third century, named Serenus Sammonicus, a friend of Gordianus the Elder, possessed, we are told, as many as sixty-two thousand.[1] This is a respectable figure even when compared with the four hundred thousand volumes which were burnt at Alexandria.[2] So far from there being any scarcity of books, we find references, even at this date, to certain would-be scholars whose

[1] Capitolinus, *Gord.*, xviii., 2.

[2] Seneca, *Tranquill.*, 9, 4. Josephus estimates the number at 500,000, Aulus Gellius at 700,000. The discrepancy between these figures may, perhaps, be explained by the fact that the same work might be divided into a different number of rolls or *fascicula*.

brains were buried under a pile of dusty tomes, and
to rich bibliophiles who collected books as a matter
of mere empty vanity.[1]

The peculiar arrangement of the rolls (*libri*) necessitated a different form of building and library furniture from that now in use, and one which at first
sight seems less convenient than ours.[2]   The incon-
venience may, however, exist only in our imagination.   The rolls were placed in cupboards (*armaria*).
On the door, or on top of each cupboard, a portrait
of the author whose works were contained in it was
fixed in a sort of frame or medallion, in accordance
with a custom which dated back to the time of Varro or Pollio.[3]   In the library itself were placed
statues, bearing on their pedestals either summarised catalogues or biographical notices or portraits[4];
if the latter, care was taken to secure good likenesses, copies being made either at Rome or in the
author's native country.[5]   Then there were mosaics
(*lapelli*), *terra cotta* statuettes, pastels (*ceræ dis-
colores*), representing poets and orators.   In the

---

[1] Seneca, *De tranq. animi*, ix., 4 *et seq.*

[2] I have already drawn attention to an arrangement of this kind
in the library of the Palatine (*cf.* Chap. III., p. 65).

[3] Lanciani, in 1883, was thus enabled to recognise the existence of
a library in one of the rooms in a house situated between the Esquiline and the *Suburra* by coming on a frame which bore the inscription, "Apollonius Thyan. . . ." (*Anc. Rome*, p. 194).

[4] Cicero, *Litteræ ad Atticum*, i., asks his friend to buy him some
good Greek statuary for his libraries ; he does not want Bacchantes
such as Atticus had bought for himself, at first, byt Muses and
Apollos.   [5] Pliny, *Ep.*, vi., 28, 1.

great libraries there were separate divisions for Greek and Latin literature. The works were further subdivided according to subject: law, medicine, geography, philosophy, theology, etc.

The fine editions of books were written with greater care and on better material, carefully glazed. In the Ulpian Library there were books written on sheets of ivory (*libri elephantini*). As a rule (with the exception of the *umbilicus*),[1] only the outside was decorated. The decoration generally took the form of ivory clasps and handles, a rich, embroidered case, with an elegant signet or label. It was at one time the fashion to condense the whole of a long work, such as the *Æneid*, the *Metamorphoses*, or a poem of Homer's, into a book of small size.

The Christians early became infected with the pagan love for books.[2] In the churches or basilicas the place of honour contained, we are told,[3] three compartments. The middle one was reserved for the bishop or officiating priest, the objects used in the ritual on the right, and the sacred books on the left. The Christian libraries included, in addition to the Old and New Testaments and the various commentaries thereon, their correspondence with the sister churches (*epistolæ salutatoriæ*), the *gesta martyrum*, and the *matriculæ pauperum*. Persecutors never let slip an opportunity of rifling and emptying the Christian archives. In order to pro-

---

[1] This was the name given to the central cylinder round which the papyrus leaves were rolled.

[2] Lanciani, p. 196.   [3] *Ibid.*, p. 187.

Schools and Books 229

tect themselves, the latter were in the habit of hiding their precious writings and putting in their places heretical books or works, the destruction of which would be a benefit rather than a loss. An example of a great Christian library is that founded by Pope Damasus in the basilica of S. Lorenzo *in Prasina* (*i. e.*, on the site of the huts of the *factio prasina*, the " greens " of the circus). The arrangement adopted here was almost exactly similar to that which obtained at the public libraries of Rome.

These latter perished at a very early date, before the end of the classical age, not from pillage, but by fire. The *bibliotheca Octavia* was burnt in A.D. 8, in the reign of Titus; that which Tiberius had collected in his palace (*bibliotheca Tiberiana*), in A.D. 191, in the reign of Commodus; that of the Palatine in the great conflagration of A.D. 363, recorded by Ammianus Marcellinus.[1]

In the foregoing I have briefly summarised all that we know of ancient libraries. In our modern collections we have scattered here and there the remains of some very fine editions of Latin authors in the form of complete works (as in the case of Cicero); the earliest of these date, for the most part, from the reign of Charlemagne. Apart from palimpsests and the *Papyri of Herculanum*, we have nothing earlier than the uncial MSS. of the fourth and fifth centuries, among which may be mentioned Cardinal Bembo's *Terence* and the *Virgil* in the Vatican, which is illustrated by numerous miniatures.

[1] xxiii., 3, 3.

We now come to the booksellers and their usages.
The influence of these on the writing of books is
much greater than might be supposed. Although
a literary work may be in itself a purely ideal creation, once it comes to be clothed in a material shape
it becomes dependent on its environment, as the
scientists put it; when the material form changes,
the literary substance changes with it. To take an
example from our own day, the substitution of
novels in a single volume at a popular price for the
costly three-volume editions which were formerly
universal, is already beginning to make its influence
felt on modern fiction.[1] Similarly certain material
forms, the arrangement and price of the rolls, were
imposed on the Roman public, partly by habit,
partly by fashion, and no matter how independent
the character of an author might be, he was obliged
to comply with these conditions whether he liked
them or not.

The size of the book and the method of publication varied with the nature of the work. In the
case of occasional verse, it was published in booklets
containing from two hundred to three hundred or
four hundred verses each. The price was only a few
pence. It was generally good policy for the author
to read either the whole or a part of his works in
public before they were published. Otherwise any
purchaser, or even purchasers, of the work, were not
unlikely to affix their names to it in a most shame-

[1] [I have taken the liberty of slightly altering M. Thomas's illustration here, so as to render it more readily intelligible to the English
reader.—TRANSLATOR.]

less manner and give it out to be the product of their own brains, and this, too, it would seem, with a fair chance of finding people ready to believe them.[1] It is true that the risks run at a public reading were almost as great. There was always the possibility that some member of the audience with exceptional powers of memory might get the poems by heart and pass them off as his own. For some time past, though not a very long time either, the property of modern artists and authors in their works has been recognised and safeguarded by various laws and treaties. In ancient times there was scarcely any right so generally disregarded as that of the author's copyright in his works. They received payment from no one, and found themselves robbed on all sides with impunity.

In the case of books of any considerable length, the work was divided up into successive parts and brought out volume by volume, or in sets of five, ten, or fifteen books, etc. The author issued these publications separately and wrote a special preface and conclusion for each. If he understood his business, he did his best to make each of these parts begin and end with some interesting episode in the history he was narrating.[2]

[1] Martial, i., 66. *Cf.* 65 and 72.

[2] Apparently it was not always possible to do this, and even among classical writers we find several who end their books in the same negligent manner as that adopted by Lactantius in the first book of his *Institutions :* "Restant adhuc aliqua : sed jam *finem facere libro decrevi ne modum excedat*" (There are still several points I should like to deal with, but I have decided to end this book here to prevent it from running to too great length).

It was in the writing of his book, however, that the ancient author laboured under the greatest disadvantage, as compared with the moderns. Of the valuable aid to be derived from chronological tables, indexes, dictionaries, and atlases he knew absolutely nothing. He had to extract his facts as best he could from cumbrous rolls, clumsy to handle and entirely innocent of headings or divisions of any kind. Even the taking of notes was a far from simple matter on the ancient tablets. As to the verification of original authorities on the actual spot, a precaution entirely neglected, to our great regret, by both Tacitus and Livy, we must remember that it was not usual in their day, and that the means of doing so were far less convenient than they are now. Apart from postal communication, printing, photography, and easy methods of transport, writers of the present day have at their disposal large collections of archives and numerous admirable museums. The Roman writer who wished to produce a work of the same kind was obliged to do everything for himself, and even then frequently met with failure.

On the other hand, we are burdened with a number of scruples which were quite unknown in classical or mediæval times. For one thing, we do our utmost to escape even the suspicion of plagiarism.

Froissart was not content simply with borrowing from the chronicle of his predecessor Jean le Bel; he appropriated it bodily, and calmly proceeded to incorporate it into his own work. This was the system adopted by all the ancient historians. They generally took the work of some previous writer which had been successful in its day, as a groundwork, and brought it up to date, modernising the language and borrowing not only its narrative but also its judgment on men and things, and even its phrases as well. They scarcely ever did more than graft on to this main source the results of a few other authors, which were used to check the statements of the writer who furnished the groundwork, and which they generally followed throughout. No doubt in some cases the historian profited by experience gained in the course of the work, and either changed his method or even abandoned his original main source and followed another instead, without any intimation to his readers. This constitutes one of the chief difficulties which modern critics have to contend with when they endeavour by a careful examination of the writings of ancient historians, to distinguish the sources on which they are based and the kind of treatment to which these sources have been subjected. .

CHAPTER X

THE PLACE OCCUPIED BY ART IN THE LIFE OF THE ROMANS [1]

TO the denizens of the modern world Rome is the mother-country of the arts; institutes of every nationality are grouped round her museums, and hither flock intelligent young people from every quarter of the earth in search of inspiration at the fountainhead. Ancient Rome possessed very nearly the same advantages; with this important difference, it is true, that though large numbers of her works of art were to be found in the capital, they were not all concentrated there, and the taste for art extending as it did to the very confines of the Empire, gained in area what it lost in depth.

In so far as art is concerned, we can readily gauge the distance which separates us from antiquity. The very expression " antiques," which has been used ever since the Renaissance to indicate works which serve as models for the whole civilised world, is in itself deeply significant.

[1] For further information on the subject here treated I must refer the reader to Friedlaender's *Mœurs romaines*, where the chapter on the fine arts has been written with masterly care ; *cf.* more especially vol. iii., pp. 207 *et seq.* in the French translation.

It may be urged that in a comparison such as that which we are about to institute, masterpieces ought not to be taken into account on either side.   A perfectly fair answer to this objection would be that perfection is the sole object of the artist, and that it is only the genius and his work that count.   But let that pass.   Let us agree to this limitation and voluntarily confine ourselves to productions of average merit; even there in the ordinary channels of everyday intercourse, we cannot but admit that the ancients enjoyed a manifest superiority over the moderns.

I

THE MULTITUDE OF WORKS OF ART

The first thing that strikes us is that works of art were employed much more extensively among the Romans.   In the imperial epoch we need but cite the case of Tullus, a friend of Pliny the Younger,[1] who had such a vast quantity of valuable objects stored away in his lumber-rooms that he was able to adorn some large gardens which he had purchased, on the very day on which he acquired them, with countless statues, both of recent and ancient date.

The reader may, perhaps, object that this was an exceptional case, and is mentioned on account of its singularity.   There is, however, other evidence at hand.   From what is left of the public and private monuments of antiquity, from the testimony of

[1] x., 18, 11.

authors and historians, it can be readily shown that, in spite of their obvious defects of taste and want of critical discernment, the Romans of the first century lived in more cultivated surroundings, amid refinement which was something higher than mere luxury—in short, in an artistic atmosphere which no longer exists in modern times.

Let us first of all examine the public monuments. It is extremely doubtful whether any civilised people of the present day can hope to transmit to posterity nearly as many memorials of themselves as the Romans have done. They were a race of builders. Yet they also knew how to embellish and decorate their edifices, and useful and imperishable as are their roads, there are countless monuments scattered over the four quarters of Europe, and even Africa and the East, such as arches, baths, theatres, and amphitheatres, which are not merely useful and well built, but beautiful and often marvellous as well. It almost seems as if they could not do without these things. No matter where they went, they would have felt like barbarians, or like shipwrecked mariners, had they failed to construct some such surroundings as these about them. The true barbarians came after them. They looted and pillaged everything that the magistrates sent from the capital had not previously seized and carried off, or that had not perished in great upheavals of nature, such as eruptions and earthquakes. And yet we find monuments like Hadrian's villa at Tivoli—no regular palace, but a mere suburban residence—which are almost inex-

STATUE OF THE FAUN.
(From the House of the Faun at Pompeii.)

haustible mines of wealth to the archæologist.   The palaces and museums of Rome and Naples are decked with its spoils.   The following remark has already been made more than once, but it will bear repetition.   No modern mind can conceive even by the utmost effort of imagination, all that has been taken from this single villa in the way of bas-reliefs, statues, mosaics, silver ornaments, and other objects of value.   The list is such a long one, that even the author of the most recent catalogue of them that has been drawn up, is obliged to admit that it is a very incomplete one.[1]   Let us imagine, for a moment, even a part of these splendours restored to their original places.   Could we then conceive any residence more worthy of admiration ?   If this be a fair specimen of their suburban villas, what must the great palaces of the capital, and especially those on the Palatine, have been like ?

If we go to the opposite pole of the ancient world, a similar impression awaits us.   We have but to turn our thoughts to Pompeii and the tiny houses of that tiny town.   It is useless to deny that its inhabitants display a certain narrowness of taste. There is something artificial, something obviously immature and conventional, in the decoration of their houses and in the subjects and handling of their paintings.   Yet in this paltry provincial town,

[1] Winnefeld, *Die Villa des Hadrian, Suppl. Jahrb., K. D., Arch. Inst.*, Berlin, Reimer, 1895.   *Cf.* also Friedlaender, *Mœurs romaines* (French ed.), vol. iii., pp. 208 *et seq.;* and Geffroy, *Revue des Deux Mondes*, Jan. 15, 1896, pp. 441 and 445 *et seq.*

of which a Roman grandee would hardly have deigned to pronounce the name, far less dream of paying it even the briefest visit, there have been found bronzes which we regard as masterpieces, not to mention paintings and mosaics which furnish all the information we possess in regard to this department of ancient art.   We need but go to Pompeii itself and wander through its famous houses with their marvellous frescos—preferably one of those recently unearthed in which all the decorations have been left in their places, in accordance with a recent and most felicitous decision; we need but visit one of the modern Italian museums, in which, as was formerly the case at Rome, the works of art unfortunately lose half their charm through overcrowding,[1] or walk through the galleries of the museum at Naples, whither, until quite recently, were transported all the jewels, utensils, and various implements discovered in the course of the excavations; it will not be necessary to examine in detail each chain, brooch, or necklet, each gem, bronze, or ivory carving, though there are many such that we could hardly tire of looking at ; we have but to regard them as a whole and consider the enormous number of them, at once to admit that in no country of the present day can we hope to find a community capable of displaying, under similar conditions, such a highly developed taste and appreciation for things artistic.   Every department of art, from the veriest

[1] *Cf.* the saying of Pliny in regard to Rome (xxxvi., 27): " Romæ quidem *multitudo operum etiam oblitteratio est.*"

THE SKULL AND WHEEL MOSAIC, FROM POMPEII.

knickknacks which are found in such infinite variety, up to the great masterpieces of high art, is reflected in the existence of this little provincial city, and yet there is nothing to indicate that it was either wealthier or more favoured by artists than any of the other towns in the vicinity of Naples.

The collection of antique plate discovered at Bosco Reale last year, and presented to the Louvre by Baron E. de Rothschild, has been fully described in the press, and may now be seen in the galleries in Paris. The silver tablets and vases of which it consists were evidently the property of some rich Roman, and it is evident that, in addition to being rich, he was a man of taste as well. The wild-boars, hares, geese, pomegranates, grapes, and other fruit represented on the bodies of these vases remind us of Pompeian paintings which have been reproduced over and over again. The artist, who, from his signature, seems to have been a certain Sabaïnos, was evidently a clever fellow. The idea of using skeletons representing the famous poets and philosophers of Greece in the decoration of a goblet is quite in harmony with the style of the mosaics at Naples, where we find death's heads,[1] skeletons, and other grisly objects. The collection includes a *patera* with an African

---

[1] In writing the above I had in my mind a curious mosaic in the Naples Museum, where a skull surmounting a wheel is shown under a square, from the extremities of which various objects are suspended. A reproduction of this is given by Lanciani (*Anc. Rome*, p. 165). Another mosaic in the same museum represents an entire skeleton. *Cf.* what I have said in Chapter VI., p. 153, in reference to a mosaic discovered on a tomb by Count Tyskiewicz.

bust in the centre, in addition to a second *patera* and two *canthari.* The whole constitutes a remarkable find, valuable alike for its workmanship and the precious material of which it is composed, and we can readily understand the anxiety of the proprietor to keep it for himself.' Although these objects possess far more than average merit, they prove clearly, if indirectly, how high this average must have been, even in the small Italian towns.

But though this convincing evidence has come into our hands by pure chance, it would be unreasonable to conclude that a taste so widely diffused was confined within the narrow limits of Pompeji.   Recent excavations undertaken far away from Italian soil, such as those lately carried out in Africa, tend to convey the same impression as that suggested by the Pompeian monuments.   We cannot forget that we are only acquainted with a very small portion of the ancient world; it is quite possible that future discoveries have surprises in store for our descendants similar to those which have been experienced by scholars on more than one occasion during the last century and a half; we must therefore try to rid ourselves of the false ideas formerly current in regard to ancient life and art during the imperial epoch, if we would avoid having our theories again upset by stubborn facts.   The passion for works of art was felt even at a distance

---

¹ In regard to the discovery at Bosco Reale, see the articles by MM. Héron de Villefosse and E. Bonnaffé in the *Gazette des beaux-arts*, August, 1895, and February, 1896.

ROMAN MYTHOLOGICAL PICTURE.
(Possibly representing Orpheus killed by the Bacchantes, from Pompeii.)

from the Italian capital and among the lower ranks of the military hierarchy. Art was not an exclusive privilege of the wealthy classes, of the aristocracy, or of any limited body of cultured people; it was a general necessary of life. In the Augustan era, the masterpieces of Greek painting were to be found in every temple, forum, and portico.[1] Private houses vied with public buildings in this respect. At that period the whole community possessed the feeling for art in some degree or other. The vices of that time are only too well known; every care has been taken that we should not lose sight of them. In common fairness, therefore, let us give equal prominence to that admiration for the beautiful which was possessed by all, and that refinement of taste which is all the more surprising at a period during which original creation is generally supposed to have entirely ceased.

II

INDIRECT EVIDENCE

As a rule, we are somewhat slow to admit merits of this kind in the case of past generations. It seems difficult, however, to refuse it in the case of the Romans of imperial times; even apart from the evidence of the monuments and the testimony of historians, there are other indirect proofs which are, to my mind, scarcely less convincing.

The influence exercised on poetry by the graphic

---

[1] *Cf.* the list given by Girard, *La Peinture antique*, p. 317.

16

arts of the imperial epoch is well known.   In their
descriptions the poets of the first century—especially
Ovid—very often have some famous work of art in
their minds and try to recall it to the minds of their
readers.   Now the subjects of these paintings or
groups of statuary were nearly always taken from
the Greek mythology.   Among all the paintings at
Pompeii only one deals with an incident in Roman
history.[1]   Only one painter[2] found his inspiration in
the *Æneid*, in spite of the fact that this poem was
known and quoted everywhere.   The picture of the
she-wolf suckling Romulus and Remus is the only
one of all the themes represented which had any
connection with local legends.   All the rest come
from Greece and celebrate the adventures of Europa,
Io, Andromeda, Ariadne, Paris, Endymion, Theseus,
the slaying of the Minotaur, etc.[3]   The web into
which artists and poets wove their fancies was,
therefore, a purely exotic one.

Now it can scarcely be doubted that the house-
holders who went to the expense of having their
houses decorated in this way must, at the very least,
have known what the paintings and frescos that
covered their walls were intended to represent.   It
was, of course, characteristic of an upstart like Trimalchion that he should talk sheer nonsense when

[1] A picture representing Sophonisba, Masinissa, and Scipio.

[2] The artist who painted the picture of the wounded Æneas.

[3] This last subject has been found in the depths of Numidia, in a
group of statuary discovered at Lambæsa, and also in frescos at
Herculanum, Pompeii, etc.

he ventured on a topic of this kind, but then Trimalchion was an exception.   It is pretty certain that the middle-class citizens of the smaller Italian towns were familiar with these subjects.   Their knowledge of them was not a thing of yesterday; it was no faint memory of what they had read or been taught in childhood.   Their whole lives were passed in the midst of representations of them.   Generation after generation had had such scenes continually before their eyes; their imaginations were unable to conceive anything else; any attempt to confine them within the limits of national legend would have taken them very much aback.

We are sometimes inclined to complain of what we call " the abuse of mythology " in Latin poets. No doubt it is a fruitful source of obscurity, but in many instances the obscurity is due to our modern ignorance and would have presented no difficulty to the ancients.   True, nothing can be more pedantic than the mania of the Alexandrine poets for incessant allusion to ancient legends, many of which they themselves had only just unearthed from the pages of some forgotten commentary.   But Ovid was guilty of no obscurity when he referred to legends familiar to all his contemporaries, or when he introduced into his poems characters whose lives were told in countless paintings and whose sculptured effigies were to be found in every Greek and Roman house.   He used a language which was intelligible to all.   Where there is no mystery there can be no inner circle of the initiated.

It seems clear, however,—and here we come upon the main defect of the whole period,—that the creative faculty was dead.   The artists were little more than mere copyists; in no single instance, in no single style, have they any claim to originality.   In spite of this, however, the life of these Italians was filled and permeated with a passion for art such as is nowhere now evinced by any nation of modern times.

III

THE EVIDENCE OF HISTORY AND LITERATURE

General history and literature confirm the conclusions which we have so far based on the results of archæological research.   We take great pride in the exhibitions, which have shown during the latter half of the present century the progress achieved by the last few generations, and have placed within the view of all objects which in bygone times were guarded as secret treasures.   It may be safely asserted, however, that the life of the ancients, at any rate in so far as rich furniture and works of art were concerned, was little more than one ceaseless exhibition.[1]   The houses of private individuals, more readily accessible than they are nowadays, set their most valuable treasures before the eyes of all men. Sisenna showed his beautiful cups even to such a man as Verres.[2]   There was hardly a single festival held in any public place, in any circus, theatre, or

---

[1] The ancients were perfectly aware of this, and have told us of it themselves : *cf.* Cicero, *Tusc.*, v., 35, 102.

[2] *Verr.*, iv. (*De Signis*), 33.

ROMAN MYTHOLOGICAL PICTURE.
(Ariadne deserted by Theseus, from Pompeii.)

amphitheatre, which was not accompanied by an exhibition of works of art. The magistrate who gave the entertainment appealed to the devotion of his friends, to the generosity of all, even of mere acquaintances. Regardless of either expense or distance, he collected together everything that he thought likely to excite the curiosity of sightseers. If, therefore, the inhabitants of Rome had nothing exactly similar to the great exhibitions of modern times, they enjoyed, at any rate, a very good substitute for them.

Let us endeavour to recapitulate briefly all that ancient writers have to tell us in regard to the various articles of luxury accumulated in the private houses of their day, even in the provinces. According to Cicero,[1] before Verres became prætor there was not a single middle-class house in Sicily which did not possess, at the very least, "one or more cups for sacrificial purposes more or less large in size, with statuettes of the various divinities under whose protection the family lived, and a chafing-dish in which to burn incense; all of them of ancient workmanship and high artistic merit." They were old family heirlooms and carefully treasured by their owners.

Things must have been very much the same throughout the whole of Greece; the treasures discovered at Bosco Reale, reference to which has been made a few pages back, include the very objects described by Cicero, with the exception of the incense-dish, and there is good reason to believe

[1] *Verr.*, iv., 46.

that similar ornaments for the shrine of the *Lares* were in use all over Italy during the first century. Over the other rooms in the house were distributed precious urns, sideboards (*abaci*) filled with plate, dressing-cases (*cistæ*) with rich mirrors, personal jewellery, precious stones, gems, rings, and necklaces of all kinds. Even on the humblest tables at Rome (*in mensa tenui*) glittered what Horace calls the ancestral salt-cellar (*paternum salinum*).[1] When not made of gold it was of silver, and was often quite a work of art in its way. The testimony of Statius, of Martial, and of Juvenal is no less convincing.[2] In the very poorest houses one or two goblets, a statuette, a marble table with a carving of a centaur at its base, or some object in terra cotta of more or less artistic interest, took the place of the more costly ornaments in one of the precious metals or rare marble possessed by the wealthier classes.

The trade in these articles of luxury was a thriving one, and brought in a steady profit. The miser, in Juvenal, in reckoning up the various favours he awaits at the hands of Fortune, next to money invested at good interest and splendid plate, longs for the possession of two clever and hard-working slaves, one of whom is to carve vases for him, while the other is to paint pictures quickly and well.[3]   Among

[1] *Od.*, ii., 16, 13.   [2] Juvenal, iii., 205.

[3] Juvenal, ix., 145 :

> " Curvus *cælator* et alter
> Qui multas facies *pingit* cito."

(A carver, bending over his work, and another slave who can paint many portraits at a quick rate.)

the presents usually made during the Saturnalia, or at the end of a banquet,[1] in addition to various objects such as books, fruit, dainties, jewels, etc., we find a large number of works of art enumerated and described, a circumstance which clearly reflects the popular taste of the period.

Nor must we forget the gorgeous furniture which was so much admired by Statius in the villas and houses of his patrons.   No doubt his enthusiasm was somewhat excessive, his admiration a little indiscriminate, so that a certain allowance must be made before we can accept the praise of which he is so prodigal.   Even then, the fact remains that these houses, or villas, were simply crammed with statues in which their owners took great pride.   Now collections of this kind are never made except at a period and in a country where there is an innate taste for art, or where the feeling or fashion for things artistic obtains.   Statius tells us that at the house of his friend Vindex he saw a number of statues and statuettes in brass, antique ivory, and wax.[2]   Among the artists here represented were men like Myro,

---

[1] *Cf.* Martial (lib. xiii. and xiv.,) and the additional information given in the German text of the fifth edition of Friedlaender's *Sittengeschichte*, p. 198, at a point corresponding to p. 220, vol. iii., of the French translation.

[2] *Silvæ*, iv., 20 :

> " Mille ibi tunc *species ærisque eborisque vetusti*
> Atque locuturas mentito corpore *ceras*
> Edidici."

(There I made acquaintance with a thousand objects of antique brass and ivory, and with statuettes of wax, so true to life that one almost expected to hear them talk.)

Praxiteles, Polycletus, and Apelles. Even assuming that the works referred to were merely copies, the list is in itself a significant fact. These aristocratic collectors were not all of them ignorant men. There is no good reason why we should refuse to credit some of them, at any rate, with an enlightened passion for the masterpieces of art, and it is quite possible that Nonius Vindex was justified in claiming to be regarded as a true connoisseur in regard to the work of early Greek artists in brass, wax, and ivory.[1]

IV

ANCIENT ART AS APPLIED TO THE DECORATION OF HOUSES

So far I have confined myself to art properly so called. I cannot leave the subject, however, without first briefly reminding my readers that Pompeii has revealed to us the existence of a form of decorative art, during the imperial epoch, which was at once refined, graceful, and imaginative, and into which ingenious caricature imported that vein of humour without which no art can be said to have attained its full development. Here tiny Cupids are made to people an idealised world; and by way

[1] *Silvæ*, iv., 6, 22:

> " Quis namque oculis certaverit usquam
> Vindicis *artificum veteres agnoscere ductus*
> Et *non inscriptis auctorem reddere signis ?* "

(For whose eye is keener than Vindex's in recognising the work of the early artists, or in detecting the author of an unsigned statue ?)

of contrast, we have intermingled with them a whole host of Fauns, Satyrs, gnomes, cranes, pigmies, and animals of all kinds, whose figures the artist introduced at will. We are able to attach a meaning to many of the groups in which we find them, especially where the picture is a burlesque of some national legend (*e. g.*, Æneas carrying his father), or some well-known myth (such as the Judgment of Paris, or Jupiter and Mercury. in the house of Alcmena). Others are enigmatic or obscure; the point of the jest, more especially in the case of political caricatures, where allusion is made to passing events, frequently escapes us. The general surroundings in these pictures, whether landscape, architecture, or ornament pure and simple, are generally pleasing, and, so far as we are concerned, up to a certain point original.

V

INFERIORITY OF THE ANCIENTS IN CERTAIN RESPECTS

This superiority of the ancients has, however, a reverse side, which is not without a certain importance. There is no reason why we should do our contemporaries less than justice. Modern art-lovers or, at any rate, a good many of them, have this advantage over those of ancient times, that they are better informed ; their artistic training is more methodical, their admiration more rational and less a matter of mere arbitrary caprice.

No doubt the ancients possessed art collections; but it is very much open to question whether they were made, as we would have wished them to be, solely with an eye to artistic merit, and on purely disinterested principles.   Did they possess anything corresponding to the modern catalogue ?   It has been argued that neither the owners of these collections nor those who visited them possessed anything more than lists furnished with more or less detailed descriptions, and compiled by the professional guides.[1]   Art galleries and guides, so much we know the ancients possessed; but it is by no means certain that they had any sort of conception of what we may call the history of art.

Nor can there be any doubt that many of these would-be connoisseurs were often wofully deceived, and that they were frequently induced to buy mere copies in the belief that they were originals, or worthless rubbish as valuable antiquities.   This is one of the drawbacks which nearly always attend any wide diffusion of artistic tastes.   No sooner does a brilliant aristocracy come into existence, than it is followed by a crop of shoddy upstarts; it is a kind of procession in which the false and the mediocre are always ready to pay their homage to the true and beautiful.[2]

I ought to add—indeed, it is useless to conceal the fact—that it was a common thing among the

---

[1] Schreiber, *Rhein. Mus.*, xxxi. (1876), p. 222.

[2] Friedlaender, *Mœurs romaines* (French edition), vol. iii., pp. 286 *et seq.*

Romans to manufacture a number of roughly finished statues and keep them in stock in the same way that the modern locksmith keeps a stock of keys which only require a few finishing touches to make them fit the cheaper kind of locks. In spite of all this, however, the fact remains that during the first few centuries of our era the love of luxury and even the desire for comfort were pervaded by a feeling for art. To the Romans of the imperial epoch, art was not a mere ornament but a necessary part of their lives.

If it should so happen that I have failed to win the reader over entirely to the view put forward in the present chapter, I would simply ask him to try to imagine one of these great houses of antiquity with all the furniture, etc., that has been taken from it, restored to its place; to attempt this in the case of a palace like Hadrian's villa would be too ambitious; one of the houses at Pompeii will serve my purpose. Let the reader endeavour, with the help of engravings and written descriptions, to form a mental picture of the famous House of the Faun, with all its charming statuettes, its harmonious decoration, its choice mosaics restored to their original state and position. Or, if he prefers it, let him conjure up the beautiful House of Vettius, which has been recently unearthed, with its fine *lararium*, its vast and elegant peristyle. A single glance at such a building as this ought to be enough to convince any modern, no matter how great his admiration for the civilisation of the present day. I hope that

after such a test no one will feel any further doubt
that the denizens of the ancient world, even those
whose lot lay far from the capital and outside the
ranks of the rich and cultured classes, came nearer
than we do to living what we call an artistic life.

CHAPTER XI

THE REPRESENTATIVES OF MORAL IDEAS IN
ROMAN SOCIETY

THE reader can scarcely have failed to notice that
in imperial Rome, as here described, excesses
of all kinds were plentiful enough. Thanks to an
assured peace, and to the stream of wealth which
still flowed Romewards from every province, the
common people, the nobles, and the emperors all
alike gave themselves up without restraint to the
pursuit of pleasure. It was a community swayed
by the fashion of the hour, dominated by the spirit
of refinement and eclecticism, neurotic, easily moved
to passion, turbulent and cruel on occasion, especially when the slightest obstacle interfered with its
pleasures. We pride ourselves on being able to
understand it better than our fathers did, on showing more indulgence towards its fits of indolence
alternating with gusts of frenzy, its luxurious refinements, its passion for literary pleasures often
carried to excess.[1]

It would be unfair, however, to content ourselves
with this view of the Romans of the first century.

[1] Seneca, *Ep.*, cvi : "*litterarum quoque intemperantia* laboramus."

The practice of virtue was not unknown to them, and in this they displayed the same feverish energy as in all else. At the beginning of his *Historia*, Tacitus has drawn a striking picture of some of the noble deeds which had been witnessed in his time.[1] In evil, vice, or virtue, they always went to extremes. The only quality they lacked was a certain unity of life, a certain balance of character which more than once in their history was conspicuous by its absence.

But there is even stronger evidence in favour of the first and second centuries than the testimony of historians; works of the highest importance from which posterity—Christian no less than pagan—has derived the utmost benefit, have come down to us from this epoch. Imagine what we should have lost if the *Letters* and *Dialogues* of Seneca, the *Meditations* of Marcus Aurelius, and the *Dissertations* of Epictetus had perished in the vicissitudes of the ages. The moral life of each successive generation would have been materially impoverished thereby. In the interim Christianity has unsealed her fount-

---

[1] *Hist.*, i., 3 : "Comitatæ profugos liberos *matres ;* secutæ maritos in exilia *conjuges ; propinqui* audentes, constantes *generi*, contumax etiam adversus tormenta *servorum* fides ; supremæ clarorum virorum necessitates fortiter toleratæ, et *laudatis antiquorum mortibus pares exitus*" (Mothers accompanied their children in their flight ; wives followed their husbands into exile ; we have seen relations courageous, sons-in-law faithful, and the loyalty of slaves proof against cruel tortures ; we have seen illustrious men receive their death-warrant without flinching, and men dying deaths every whit as noble as those so highly praised in the case of former generations).

ains; mystical literature has spread from one to another, and our imaginations have been attracted by it; but all these new inspirations and mental revolutions have but added to the value of the great works which preceded them by so many years. They shine out all the more brightly in the midst of the corruption of ancient times. They differ from one another alike in language, in inspiration, and in the character of their authors; Greek rivals Latin in these internal communings; in their struggle with the vices of the time, the same protests assail us from the most widely different standpoints, from the summit of the throne, from the *cella* of the slave, and from the mansion of an ambitious, wealthy, and powerful minister who, having once attained to the highest power, realised the vanity of greatness.

I

MORAL PHILOSOPHY IN ROMAN LITERATURE

In spite of the exceptional merit of these great works, it would be unfair to separate them from other productions of the same period; Epictetus, Marcus Aurelius, and Seneca merely expressed with greater clearness and eloquence feelings which are to be found scattered broadcast over the whole literature of the first century.

At that time, as always, there were professed philosophers, whose philosophy was more theoretical than practical, and whose teaching was only adapted for show and not for use. They had no difficulty in

finding pupils worthy of them, in the houses of the
great.   We hear of one rich man whose only available time for his lesson in philosophy was while he
was being carried to and fro in his litter under the
shade of his porticos.[1]   The lady of the house was
attended by another philosopher, whose lecture had
to be delivered as she dressed, and who was liable to
be interrupted in order that his pupil might read her
love-letters.[2]   Nice teachers of morality, these! and
fitting disciples for such masters.[3]   There were
others, however, who were actuated by a genuine
desire to learn the true lessons of life, and who, in
default of any better guide, sought them in the
pages of experience.   These succeeded in infecting
even the more frivolous poets by their example.
What a difference we notice between the earlier
poems of Horace and his later works.   At first sceptical and even cynical, his poetry grows grave and
serious as years roll on.   We hardly recognise the
author of the *Epodes* in some of the later *Odes*, and
in certain passages here and there in the *Satires* and
more particularly in the *Epistles*.[4]

So, too, when we come to Horace's successors;
when we read the works of those who wrote satires
after his time, we cannot help noting that the ex-

---

[1] Seneca, *Ep.*, xxix., 4.

[2] Lucian, *Concerning those who are in the pay of the Great*, 36. The
whole of this brief treatise is full of similar passages.

[3] Seneca, *ibid.* : " *Lepidum* philosophum !"

[4] I need but mention the dialogue in *Ep.*, i., 16, 73, imitated from
the Stoic philosophers, which finds an almost exact counterpart in
Epictetus, *Dissert.*, i., 22 *et seq.*

pression of moral ideas becomes more and more un-
trammelled; it gains in sincerity and poignancy, is
nearly always instructive and dignified, and very
often extremely happy. In spite of all his obscuri-
ties and his somewhat stilted style, there are lines of
Persius which cling in the memory, and expressions
which with a very slight change might almost pass
for quotations from Holy Writ.[1] This was doubtless the reason why, even in ancient times, " his
little book " had won for him " a great name."[2]
Then, leaving on one side those of his lines which
have passed into proverbs, we have the great passages of Juvenal, those immortal tirades, of which
Jean de Müller not only noted the opening words,
but learnt off entirely by heart, " that he might be
able to read them all his life." In these passages
dealing with the respect due to the young, with the
prayers to be addressed to the gods, and the remorse
of the guilty, we have an inimitable outpouring
straight from the depths of an honest heart which
cannot fail to strike a responsive chord in the in-
most recesses of the souls of others. How many
outcries of the human soul have found their echo in
these lines! How many aspirations of humanity
has he expressed in a form which has appealed to

---

[1] *Cf.* ii., 61 :
    " O *curva in terris* animæ et *cælestium inanes !* "
(O souls bowed towards the earth, empty of all heavenly things !),
and S. Paul, Philippians iii., 19, 20, " whose end is perdition   .   .   .
who mind earthly things. For our citizenship is in heaven."
  [2] A saying of Quintilian's, x., 1, 94.

17

the emotions of generation after generation, of century after century!

Add to the force and eloquence of the poets whom
I have just mentioned, the broad and stable work
done by prose writers of almost the same period,
such as Plutarch and Lucian; the first blending
anecdotes and maxims in a pervading atmosphere
of geniality, while the keen shafts of the second
and his somewhat flippant criticism of the present
are tempered by a vague presentiment of the ages
that were to come; add all these together, I say,
and few will be prepared to dispute that at the close
of the Greco-Latin civilisation an extraordinary com-
bination of all the higher faculties of the human soul
was undoubtedly at work in the effort to raise mankind to a higher point of advancement than it had
ever previously attained.

II

THE ROMAN MORALISTS

The desire for a more active moral existence, for
a new gospel which must before all things be a practical one, was so strong at the period which we are
now considering, that in the space of a few years it
sprang up, spread and displayed itself under the
most varied forms, but always with the same intens-
sity. ·Here, if anywhere, the demand may be said
to have created the supply. Take the greatest
names of all—Seneca, Epictetus, and Marcus Aurelius: their books, in Greek and Latin, differed both

in language and in style. Nothing could have been more diverse than the positions occupied by these authors; one of them was a poor and weakly slave; another was a man of letters who had made his way into power by his talents, and also, alas! by his servility, and, it may be, by his vices; the third was an emperor who, in spite of his rank, remained a philosopher as well. Could the contrast between any three men be greater? And yet, without a doubt, their teaching can be traced to the same source of inspiration.

We find in their works all the defects usually possessed by books written with a didactic purpose. Arrangement is sacrificed in them, or rather, there is no attempt at arrangement. They simply jot down a series of reflections and dissertations one after another. They attached little value to literary form, with the exception of Seneca, whose style is always brilliant and polished, though like the others, or rather more than the others, he suffers from an unfortunate habit of repeating the same idea over and over again in different language.

Nearly all books contain some parts which cease to be interesting in the course of time: such, for instance, as the portions referring to the theories of the period in which they were written. We have to wade patiently through these shadows till we come to the words or pages which cast a radiance over all the rest. We must, therefore, bear as best we can the usual tirades of these philosophers, their panegyrics on Socrates and Cato, who, in their hands, are speedily reduced to mere puppets; in short, the inevitable stock of academic platitudes from which authors of this class seem to have been unable to shake themselves free.[1] Soon, however, the man himself appears, and begins, in penetrating accents which we might almost mistake for those of some contemporary, to tell us something we do not find anywhere else, something that touches us closely. In a word, he speaks to the heart.

Before we proceed to consider separately these three preachers of morality, I must point out one somewhat curious feature which was common to them all. Conscious of the fact that their object was a moral one, they allowed themselves to indulge in a boldness both of idea and expression, which equals if it does not surpass that of even the most licentious writers of the realistic school. In proof of this I need but mention two instances taken from the writings of Epictetus and Marcus Aurelius: others might easily be adduced.[2]

(1) *Epictetus*

In the case of Epictetus, whom I propose to take first, it will be useless to look for his best work in the *Encheiridion*. Pascal, who had an extremely

[1] Seneca, *Ep.*, xxiv., 6: "*decantata*, inquis, in *omnibus scholis fabulæ istæ sunt*" (These, you say, are tales which have been repeated over and over again in every school).

[2] Epictetus, *Dissertations*, ii., 18: the description of temptation; *cf.* in Marcus Aurelius his definition of physical love, vii., 13: "καὶ ἐπὶ τῶν κατὰ τὴν συνουσίαν. . . ."

high idea of the Greek author, seems to have read nothing but this one work of his.   In this, however, Pascal, who was doubtless influenced by his Port-Royal friends, merely followed the example of other Christian polemical writers—I refer, of course, to those of the second period, as their predecessors treated Epictetus as an opponent.[1] In our eyes, the man himself is of far more importance than his opinions, and it is in his *Dissertations* that Epictetus speaks of himself.   It is there, and on his own showing, that he appears before us in the guise of a little, lame old man,[2] whose anxiety to correct the exercises that his scholars had handed to him on the previous evening,[3] makes him wake early in the morning. Nor does our author fail to depict the surroundings amidst which he lived; the capital, where it is not safe to gossip, lest some of the emperor's secret police should fasten on an unguarded expression; the Roman ladies[4] concerning whom the philosopher cherished but few illusions.   He tells us that every second woman in Rome might be seen reading Plato's *Republic*.   It was not with a view to elevating their minds, however.   By no means.   The chief attraction which the book possessed in the eyes of the Roman ladies lay in the fact that its author there advocates a community of wives; to

[1] Schenkl, *Praef.*, pp. 13 *et seq.*

[2] Most of these biographical passages have been summarised by Schenkl in his Introduction, p. iv.

[3] Epictetus i., 10, 8 : in this obscure passage I follow the explanation given by M. Courdaveaux.

[4] Epictetus iv., 13.

their minds this was what constituted the whole essence and cream of his philosophy.'

The following passage shows how the teaching of those whom the Roman grandees affected to regard as guides and masters was sometimes received. Epictetus tells us that one of the philosophers of his day took it into his head that he would try the effect of a dialogue in the Socratic manner—then greatly esteemed in the schools—on one of his pupils, a man of consular rank. The result was not satisfactory. The wealthy personage, whom the philosopher was trying to refute and confound, cried out at last: " What do you mean, my good fellow ? Do you think you are going to lay down the law to me ?" And without more ado, he raised his fist and struck him. " I, too," adds Epictetus, " once felt inclined to try the Socratic method, but it was before I discovered the way in which it was received."²

It is clear that Epictetus besides being a philosopher was also a man of the world. He is keenly alive to the drawbacks of the scholastic profession. Although a teacher of philosophy himself, he has no prejudices in favour of " syllogisms " or even of books. On the contrary, he devotes a whole chapter of the *Dissertations*³ to rebuking those who cry out for time to read and write, as though these pursuits formed the end and aim of life. This singular indifference to everything scholastic or " book-

---

¹ *Frag.*, xv., p. 414.　　　　　² Epictetus, ii., 12.
³ Epictetus, iv., 5.

ish '' was also one of the characteristics of Marcus
Aurelius.

It is a pity that Epictetus did not go a step farther;
we can hardly understand how such a master mind
as his can have failed to anticipate the great moral
revolution which was about to take place. He was
acquainted with the Jews, with their ceremonies,
and initiatory rites. He had noted the strength of
that religious partisanship which helped them to
endure contumely and suffering. In this respect he
was every bit as shortsighted as Marcus Aurelius,
Pliny, Tacitus, and all the other great thinkers of
that period.'. And yet, we find in his *Dissertations*,
in spite of their invariably colloquial form, expressions almost entirely analogous to those that occur
in Holy Writ. So true it is that no matter how
different the hypotheses from which it may start,
the human soul cannot raise itself without entering
that one and only region where all things meet.'

¹ The name of Cicero might be added to the list. He knew the
Jews, and mentioned them in his *Pro Flacco*. But in his philosophical
treatises, and notably the *De Natura Deorum*, he has not a word
to say concerning their ideas and their religion. No doubt, in
Cicero's eyes it was little more than a vulgar superstition similar to
the religions of Egypt, Assyria, or other barbarian countries.

² Epictetus, i., 5 (p. 18): "Most of us stand in great fear of the
death of the body and do all we can to postpone it ; but *the death of
the soul* is a thing about which we scarcely trouble ourselves . . .
the death of the conscience and of the moral sense we are ready to
describe as strength of mind"; and again, i., 13: "Do you know
what you are looking at ? At the earth, at the abyss, at the miserable
laws of the dead; you do not turn to *the laws of the gods*." *Cf.* what
S. Paul says of the "Book of Life."

(2) *Marcus Aurelius*

Marcus Aurelius was introduced to the writings of
Epictetus through the medium of Rusticus.[1]   The
imperial philosopher thus hands on the tradition
transmitted by the ex-slave, which in his works becomes condensed and purified.   It is needless to
enumerate his titles, the mention of his mere name
is sufficient.   His *Meditations* form, as it were, an
indispensable supplement to Holy Writ.   He is the
first of the mystic school.   The foremost among
modern writers live on his substance.   Taine and
Paradol slept with his books under their pillows.

I purposely abstain from quotation.   These *Meditations* raise us above all academic truisms, and even
detach us from all that is transitory or perishable.
" Libraries burn: the life of man is in his conscience."   Everyone is familiar with the admirable
preface in which the imperial author scrupulously
endeavours to acknowledge all the assistance he has
derived from the works of others.   In the body of
the work I am not sure that the most incisive remarks are not also the briefest, those in which he
sums up a whole train of thought for the benefit of
the reader and of himself.[2]   Nothing can be more
expressive, more touching, or more eloquent than
the brief notes appended at the close of the first
two books which seem to us like the living signature

[1] Marcus Aurelius, i., vii.
[2] vi., 30: "ὅρα μὴ ἀποκαιϭαρωϑῆς . . ."; v., 28: οὔτε
τραγωϭός οἴτε πόρνη."

of this pagan hero, and which shed a wan light over all that precedes.[1]

(3) *Seneca*

We feel less at our ease with Seneca, for in his case we miss that harmony between theory and practice which so pre-eminently distinguishes both Epictetus and Marcus Aurelius. Nevertheless, Seneca, following the academic tradition, more than once insists on the necessity of such harmony. " Philosophy," he declares, " depends on acts and not on words; it is disgraceful to say one thing and to think or write another. The writings of a philosopher ought to be capable of application to his own conduct."[2] But when we read the pages in which Seneca writes in praise of poverty, we find it difficult to take him seriously, as we recall all that Dion tells us of the spiteful remarks of his enemies, the sixty millions at which Tacitus estimates his fortune, and the line in which Juvenal speaks of

" Et magnos *Senecæ prædivitis* hortos."[3]

[1] " Τὰ ἐν Κουάδοις πρὸς τῷ Γρανούᾳ. Τὰ ἐν Καρνούντῳ." These two books were written during the war against the Quadi and the Marcomanni. The *Granua* is a river in Hungary, *Carnuntum* a town in Pannonia.

[2] *Ep.*, xxiv., 14 and 18. Similarly Epictetus, *Dissert.*, ii., 16, 20: *Frag.*, p. 410. Epictetus, adapting the famous dictum in regard to the Lacedæmonians, "lions at home, foxes at Ephesus," tells us that the philosophers were "lions in the schools, foxes outside them"; *Dissert.*, iv., 5. Compare with this the witty reply made by Demonax to Epictetus, when the latter, a bachelor, pressed him to marry. "Very well, Epictetus, give me your daughter."

[3] x., 16: "The splendid gardens of the wealthy Seneca."

It is all very well for him to maintain that a man can despise wealth even when he possesses it,[1] and that " he is a truly great man who is poor in the midst of riches." It is but too obvious that this is merely an indirect apology on his part; his arguments are too much in his own favour, and we refuse to be deceived by his sophisms.[2]

We are, however, inclined to believe him more readily on other points; for instance, when he talks of death for which he desires to prepare himself; that day which he awaits will, so he tells us, show how far his contempt for the vicissitudes of fortune was sincere.[3] To us who know what followed, and to what " a sudden taking-off," to what a tragic end Seneca succumbed,[4] the whole of this letter, which would otherwise remind us of some academic thesis, acquires a new meaning. It is not without a certain emotion that we apply the test suggested by himself, a test far more searching than he can have imagined it would be.[5] Although there are certain details in connection with the death of Seneca of which we may not altogether approve, yet Letter

[1] *Ep.*, xx., 10.

[2] We may say of him what he says of one of the men whom he criticises and pretends to advise (*Ep.*, xxv., 3): "aliis (id) imponit, *mihi verba non dat*" (He may impose on others but cannot deceive me with words).

[3] *Ep.*, xxvi., 4.

[4] *Ibid.*, 3: "ictus et e vita *repentinus excessus.*

[5] A similar coincidence happened in the case of Cicero. *Cf.* the passage in the *Tusculanæ* (i., 104 *et seq.*) where the author foreshadows the indignities to which his own dead body was afterwards subjected.

xxxvi. will bear reading side by side with the narrative of Tacitus; it reflects nothing but credit on the
man who penned it.   It gives us pleasure to note
that his funeral was of the simplest character, in accordance with the provisions of a will made by him
when he was in the heyday of prosperity.[1]

In regard to the somewhat indelicate question
opened up by the inconsistency between Seneca's
theories and his practice, I have already indicated
the facts which may plead in his favour even with
those who refuse to excuse him on the general
ground of human frailty.   I am afraid, however,
that there are defects in his writings which it would
be useless to ignore.   M. Martha has come forward
as Seneca's champion, and holds him up to us as a
" father confessor at Rome."   Comparisons of this
kind have the advantage of enabling us to view the
world of antiquity from a fresh standpoint.   But
then how dangerous they are even to those in whose
favour they are invented!

What are the chief qualities which we have a right
to look for in a " father confessor " ?   Are they
not tact, delicacy, and scrupulous modesty both of
thought and language ?   Yet note how Seneca fails
in this respect.   In a letter of condolence addressed
to the daughter of Thraseas, on the death of her
child, he refers to the tyrant Dionysius, and although

---

[1] Tacitus, *Ann.*, xv., 64 : " ita codicillis præscripserat, cum *etiam
tum prædives et præpotens* supremis suis consuleret " (He had thus
ordered in a codicil made when he was at the zenith of wealth and
power, in which he gave instructions concerning his obsequies).

it has nothing to do with his line of argument, he must needs insist on the refinements of debauchery practised by this monarch,[1] and this too in terms which, even among men, would be considered unfit for translation.   We can scarcely refrain from applying to this singular moralist the protest which he addresses to himself later on in this very letter: " You forget, Seneca, that you are writing to a woman in order to console her."[2]   After making every possible allowance for the freedom of the Latin language, and the looseness of Roman morals, this passage can only be described as grossly indecent.   As I pointed out a few pages back, the moralists considered themselves privileged in matters of this kind, and they frequently surpass even the cynics in audacity.   But neither Epictetus nor Marcus Aurelius wrote for women, and they are never gratuitously nasty.

It may be urged, however, that this was merely a momentary slip on Seneca's part.   Let us turn to a general defect of an even more serious character. The chief qualification in a father confessor is that he should be able to adapt his precepts and advice to circumstance, and should be able to suggest an appropriate remedy for each individual evil.   But this is precisely what Seneca fails to do.   Were it otherwise, we should know all about the life of his friend Lucilius, and the occasion and motive which led him to appeal to his master.   On the contrary,

[1] Seneca, xvii., 4: "Arcesset ad libidinem," etc.
[2] xvi.

we can only hazard a guess as to the political career of this friend and correspondent of Seneca's. He was assailed by fears, we would gladly know the reason; by discouragement, but we are ignorant of its cause.

In any case, the torrent of vague commonplace with which Seneca overwhelms this friend can have done little to help him out of the moral or political difficulties in which he was involved. The whole letter reeks of academic aphorisms and copy-book headings. In almost every place, on almost every occasion, Seneca confines himself to vague generalities. A philosophic contempt for the vicissitudes of fortune is his one panacea for every sorrow and evil under the sun, and he applies it as a sort of spiritual treacle to all alike. We may rest assured that such a physician as this must often have aggravated the disease. No conscientious moralist when writing to a friend has any right to preach his sermons in the air.

In at least one instance,[1] we know this to have been one of Seneca's faults. Lucilius fears that he is about to be denounced by an enemy, perhaps by a slave (we know that under the operation of the *Lex Majestatis* such accusations were full of danger for any Roman citizen, more especially if he occupied an official position); our would-be father confessor reassures his friend by long exhortations on the contempt which we ought to cultivate for death and pain. This must have been peculiarly consoling to him!

[1] *Ep.*, xxiv.

It is evident that Seneca addresses his sermon not so much to Lucilius as to the public and posterity. His real object is to guide our conscience rather than that of his friend. From his daily observations and the scenes presented by the world of his day, he draws all sorts of morals for the benefit of those who may read him in the ages to come. Luckily for us he has also inserted numberless anecdotes of contemporary life which help to make his treatises and letters(they differ but little from one another in either style or composition) an inexhaustible mine for the literary critic and for the historian who undertakes to deal with the civilisation of the imperial epoch.

Seneca knew his period well. Thanks to the origin from which he sprang, he had passed over every rung of the social ladder from the lowest to the highest. In his early years he had been poet, rhetorician, and philosopher in turn, taking up each new calling with enthusiasm. Received at the imperial court, he seems to have been in his element there; he saw much and remembered much; a keen observer, he found no difficulty in detecting the miseries of greatness hidden behind the mask of tranquillity worn by those whom all men envied. The weariness, the loathing, and all those other mental phases which remained a mystery to the Greek philosophers of his day were to him as clear as noonday.[1] Even though his experience in affairs

[1] *Cf.* more especially the letters written in reply to requests for advice in the case of some of his friends: *Ep.*, xxv., 3 *et seq.* ; lxxv., 8 *et seq.*

of state and his residence at the imperial court may not have inspired him with a liking for worldly ways or unfailing tact, they must have taught Seneca to see things more clearly and more sanely. They helped to take him away from his books, and to make him look for life outside the petty circles of the schools, in the great world itself. He thus acquired a rich fund of experience which makes his letters, often written in haste and as a mere pastime, seem, in our eyes, far superior to his more elaborate treatises.

On the other hand, Seneca took a pleasure in writing. He possessed the most brilliant intellect of his time,[1] and he knew it.[2] His versatility increased in proportion to the difficulties encountered by him. In his moral studies he surpasses all other writers of antiquity in the skill with which he puts a case of conscience or unravels a tangled skein of complex emotions. He reproduces the most subtle gradations of feeling which, though familiar to all, no one would have attempted or believed it possible to analyse, and he reproduces them with a clearness, a preciseness, and a happiness of expression absolutely unrivalled.

His talents as a writer, his keenness of observation,

---

[1] Tacitus, *Ann.*, xiii., 3: "fuit illi vero *ingenium amœnum et temporis ejus auribus accommodatum*" (He possessed a most agreeable wit, and knew perfectly what was likely to tickle the ears of his contemporaries).

[2] *Ep.*, xxi., 3: "*notiores epistolæ meæ te facient* quam omnia ista quæ colis" (My letters will render you more famous than all the honors for which you seek). He is writing to Lucilius.

these are qualities which more than explain the admiration felt for Seneca by Montaigne and, after him, by readers of another type; in fact, by all those for whom the inner life possesses any attraction.   We may think what we like of Nero's tutor; his dialogues and letters, in spite of their dead weight of antique scholasticism, possess a peculiar and lasting value for us moderns, which tends to increase rather than diminish in the eyes of the rising generation.

(4) *The Forerunners of Seneca and Certain Philosophers Contemporary with him.*

Let us next inquire into Seneca's surroundings, and, in the first place, let us consider his young days, when his enthusiasm for philosophy led him to identify himself with one or two small groups of ascetics whom we are (quite unreasonably, as it happens) surprised to find amidst the prevailing corruption of Roman society.   At that time the future ornament of the court of Nero was a vegetarian, and shunned every form of luxury.   Let us consult the writings of the elder Seneca; from them we learn that there were " eloquent philosophers "[1] whose words delighted and disturbed their audiences at one and the same time.   The elder Seneca, who was an enthusiastic teacher of rhetoric, felt no surprise at this; he regarded it as a kind of homage paid by

[1] Cicero (*Tusc.*, ii., 9) mentions a contemporary of his named Philo, who gave lessons in rhetoric in the mornings, and lessons in philosophy in the evenings.

philosophy to the highest art of all, that of the orator. His son would probably have been more exacting, and would have refused to admit (in theory, at any rate) that philosophy did more than avail itself of the services of eloquence. As a matter of fact, the pupils of the rhetoricians looked to these men of twofold talent far more than to books for the help and example which they were advised to derive from a study of philosophy.

Foremost among the masters of this epoch we must place Fabienus, whose portrait is preserved for us quite as much in the letters of the younger Seneca as in the orations of his father. But Seneca had sat under other masters; he had attended the lectures of Sotio the Pythagorean, of Attala, who took poverty as his favourite text, of Sestius, every page of whose works inspired him with renewed enthusiasm each time he re-read them. " Great gods," he used to exclaim, " what vigour, what soul, one finds in his writings! He does not waste his time in splitting hairs; he is all life and force (*vivit*, *viget*), he is free; he is something more than human." [1] Such were the ideals aimed at by philosophers of that period.

But the very loftiness of their aims inevitably led some of the less stable minds among them astray, with the result that heroism in many cases degenerated into mere eccentricity. This was undoubtedly so in the case of Agrippinus, a man of high birth,

[1] *Ep.*, lxiv., 2.

whose extravagant caprices are recorded for us by Seneca. When this person caught a fever, he at once sat down to write a panegyric on fever; when he was exiled, he wrote an essay on exile; when news was brought to him, just as he was going in to supper, that Nero ordered him to withdraw from Rome, he merely remarked, " Very well, we will sup at Aricia." We may add as a finishing touch that, during his term of office as prætor, he took great pains to persuade those on whom he passed sentence that he was only doing it for their good. A gentle surgeon this, who consoled his patients and informed them it would be necessary to operate on them in one breath.' Exaggeration of this kind shows clearly the strength of the movement which at that time impelled Romans of every rank, and of every type of intellect, to the study of philosophy. Its influence is everywhere visible. Indeed, it is scarcely too much to say that we have here something more than that abiding moral principle, that perennial philosophy (*perennis quædam philosophia*) which is handed down from generation to generation. Marcus Aurelius and Epictetus are unconscious exponents of a doctrine which they themselves did not fully understand. We feel instinctively that even philosophy itself did not fully satisfy the aspirations of their eager souls, and that it was still less likely to satisfy those of the multitude; that we are, in short, on the brink of a new era in the history of religion. The ascetic philosophers whom we have

' Epictetus, *Fragm.*, xxi.

just been considering really acted, without knowing it, as its forerunners in the lay world.   The day was soon to dawn when the Word of Life, carried from one end of the Empire to the other, was about to illuminate the minds and stir the hearts of men. And while the world awaited the rising of the new light in the East, the coming daybreak appeared in the very centre of the Empire.   It is for this reason that the writings of Seneca, Epictetus, and Marçus Aurelius, which, in spite of their inequalities, their omissions, and their weaknesses, are yet so frequently both penetrating, soothing, and persuasive, still hold their place in our esteem, as breviaries of antiquity which mark the transition between our age and theirs.   They are still indispensable to all those of us moderns who have any care or liking for the higher moral life.

CHAPTER XII

THE ARMY IN AFRICA

I

THE IMPERIAL ARMY CONSIDERED AS A WHOLE

LET us dismiss from our minds all mere outward shows, and try to forget both the atrophied machinery of the ancient Roman constitution and the external artifices by means of which the new rulers sought to mask their power. Just as all real voice in the government rested with a single individual, so in turn the power of the Empire was entirely dependent on the army. Let us endeavour to ascertain how the imperial army was recruited and organised, and what changes it underwent from one century to another. In it we recognise the main-spring of the new *régime;* let us seek to find out its real value and what sort of life its soldiers led.

The first thing to notice is that the emperors, however much they may have differed in mind or morals, all felt and admitted that it was in the army that their real power lay. They all recognised the

ROMAN MILITARY HELMETS.
(From the House of the Gladiators at Pompeii.)

wisdom of the somewhat cynical advice given by Septimius Severus to his children,[1] and acted accordingly. At all the great crises, when the throne became vacant or an insurrection broke out, the Cæsars, their partisans and relations, at once repaired to the Prætorian camp. Even after the Prætorians had ceased to form the mainstay of the imperial dynasty, it was always to his soldiers that the Emperor turned in his hour of need. They were his comrades (*commilitones*), and he was, before all things, their leader.[2] Even the worst emperors were careful to foster the military instinct in the army, with a view, of course, to turning it to their own advantage.

Characteristic phrases expressive of this intention and of this habitual confidence on the part of the emperors are frequently met with in the works of the historians. We are told of a tribune who was mixed up in the conspiracy of Piso, that on being led out to execution, he complained at the last moment that his grave had not been dug in accordance with the army regulations.[3] Similarly, the emperors, when the insurrection which was to sound the knell of their day of power arrived, and they became the playthings of a brutal soldiery, were

[1] "Enrich your soldiers and you need not trouble your heads about anything else."

[2] Suetonius, *Galba*, 20 : "Ad primum tumultum : quid agitis *commilitones? ego vester sum et vos mei*" (At the first sign of tumult : [he would cry] What are you about, my comrades ? I am yours and you are mine). Trajan was an exception, *cf.* p. 349 note 13.

[3] Tacitus, *Ann.*, xv., 67 : "*ne hoc quidem ex disciplina.*"

wont to complain with a pathetic *naïveté* that the dignity of the general was being outraged in their persons. The unworthy Vitellius did not fail to do so.[1] Galba was more careful of the spirit of military discipline, and gave proof of greater disinterestedness when, on hearing that his rival Otho had been slain, he remarked to a soldier who boasted of the deed: " Comrade, who gave the order ? "[2]

The army owed its allegiance to the Emperor and not to the State. This was a principle jealously guarded by the occupants of the imperial throne. A senator named Junius Gallio, having seemed to disregard it in bringing forward a motion with respect to the honours to be bestowed on the Prætorian veterans, was ruthlessly sentenced to exile by Tiberius.[3]

Some of the applications of this theory were rather amusing, as when all the credit for a gallant action performed by his officers was ascribed to the Emperor. Caligula, on his own responsibility, appropriated to himself all legacies left by centurions[4]

---

[1] Tacitus, *Hist.*, iii., 85 : "tribuno insultanti, *se tamen imperatorem ejus fuisse* respondit " (When the tribune insulted him, he asked him to remember that, after all, he had been his superior officer).

[2] Tacitus, i., 35 : " *Commilito*, inquit, *quis jussit?* "

[3] Dion, lviii., 18 : " ὅτι σφᾶς (τοὺς δορυφόρους) ἀναπείθειν ἐδόκει τῷ κοινῷ μᾶλλον ἢ ἑαυτῷ εὐνοεῖν " (because he seemed to wish to persuade the Prætorians to be more devoted to the State than to the Emperor).

[4] Dion, lix., 13. *Cf.* Suetonius, *Cal.*, 38 : "testamenta *ut ingrata* rescidit " (He cancelled their wills on the plea that they were tainted with ingratitude).

to anyone other than the Emperor.   By so acting,
he claimed that he was merely doing, after the event,
what they themselves should have done in the first
place, and what they doubtless would have done of
their own accord, like the good soldiers they were.

My readers will, therefore, readily comprehend
why it was that the space devoted by historians to
military matters did not tend to diminish under the
Empire.   Even if we adopt the view of those who
regard Tacitus's treatment of these matters as the
weakest part of his *Annales* and *Historia*, yet we
must admit that his descriptions of military operations possess a life and colour which we fail to find
in any of the historians who preceded him.[1]   The
pictures he draws of the revolt of Pannonia and
Germania will bear comparison with the finest passages in Livy.   The soldiers whom he there suddenly
introduces into the foreground of his canvas are
very different from those who filled the ranks of the ·
republican army ; the portraits of them presented to
us are extremely lifelike.   Their gait, their manner
of speaking, their very accent, all stand out clearly
before us.   We seem to see and recognise a number
of military types.   There is the centurion with his
famous *Cedo alteram*,[2] the blundering fool who,
when Germanicus sought to kill himself with his

---

[1] This is the view taken by Mommsen.

[2] *I. e.*. "Here, give me another" (sc. *vitem*); the centurion in
striking one of his men had broken the vine-stock which he carried
as a badge of office, and called for another to replace it in order that
he might proceed with his castigation.

own sword, which his friends were trying to wrest from him, held out his weapon to the frenzied general with the remark, " Take mine, it has a sharper point." [1]   Then there is Pescennius, the incorrigible street-arab and *ex-claqueur*, who brought the trembling legate seemingly to the very foot of the gallows by means of a piece of make-believe which, at first, deceived all the bystanders.   But surrounding these ephemeral leaders we also see the solid though untutored mass of their followers, docile or violent by turns, bitter in their complaints at those moments when their wretchedness was forcibly brought home to them (as when the soldiers of Germanicus crowded round him feigning to kiss his hands, but really in order that he might feel their toothless gums), capable of generous feeling, yet terribly violent when they turned against their idols of yesterday; at such moments they were moved by an insatiable thirst for the blood of those whose orders they had blindly followed but a few hours before, and whose death must now atone for their misdeeds; at other times sombre and unmanageable, never at ease save in their camp or barracks, yet always ready to fight bravely when face to face with the enemy.[2]

These pictures, drawn by the hand of a master, are familiar to all, and a few words are sufficient to

[1] *Annales*, i., 35.

[2] It has been pointed out (Boissier, *L'Afrique romaine*, p. 117) that in certain collections of military inscriptions, such as those found at Lambæsa, for instance, the feelings of the soldiers are represented in quite a different light from that shown above, at any rate in so far as their own calling is concerned, and that the bitter

call them up before us.   I propose, however, to approach the subject from another point of view.   I
shall, first of all, narrow it down, and, taking advantage of a very able work which has recently
appeared,[1] shall endeavour to convey an accurate
idea of one branch of the imperial army, which
stands out clearly by itself and is fairly familiar—I
mean the African contingent.   The simplest way
will be to follow the plan adopted by M. Cagnat, and
first examine the composition of this contingent,
then the administrative system by which it was
governed, and, finally, review the camp at Lambæsa
and other military establishments.

Although the military spirit is the same all the
world over, yet everyone will admit that the life of
the soldier must have differed in the various provinces of the Empire.   It is obvious that legionaries
serving in Britain or on the Rhine cannot have followed the same system as those posted on the banks
of the Euphrates or on the confines of the Sahara.
The difference of climate alone would have presented material obstacles which no amount of energy

and threatening accent perceptible in the complaints of the legionaries, as set forth by Tacitus, is conspicuous by its absence.   But
does not this fact tend rather to show how little reliance ought to be
placed on the testimony of such inscriptions ?

[1] René Cagnat, *L'Armée romaine d'Afrique et l'occupation mili-
taire de l'Afrique sous les empereurs*, Leroux, 1892.   The best
authority among writers of antiquity is Vegetius, whose treatise has
been unjustly condemned by several modern writers.   Many of his
statements, which were formerly rejected, have been recently confirmed by the inscriptions.

or determination could possibly have overcome. The system was, therefore, gradually modified in the case of each legion permanently established on the special frontier which it was deputed to defend. As a natural consequence, habits, temperament, capacity for endurance, character, and spirit all differed in the various legions posted on the north, the south, the east, and the west. Although in theory the army constituted a single unit, it was really made up of several different battalions or, rather, legions. It was well known that, in the event of a conflict, their strength was not the same.[1] After a whole series of variations, the system finally—and inevitably—adopted, was that the ranks of each legion should be recruited from among the natives of the province in which it was stationed. Let us inquire how this change came about in Africa.

II

THE ROMAN ARMY IN AFRICA

(1) *Its Composition*

First of all, let us note that the word "Africa" is here used in its legitimate sense. The Romans had bestowed this name on the province formed after the conquest of Carthage. It became a consular

---

[1] Tacitus, *Hist.*, i., 16: "Sit ante oculos Nero, quem . . . non Vindex *cum inermi provincia*, aut ego cum una legione . . . cervicibus publicis depulerunt" (Let us remember Nero, whose yoke neither Vindex, backed only by an unarmed province, nor I, with my single legion, could succeed in throwing off).

province in the time of Augustus, and later on came to include the region known as Numidia. The proconsul, who was at the head of the civil power, lived at Carthage. On the other hand, the imperial legate, who was proprætor and commander of the military forces, resided at the place where the legion was stationed, first at Thevesta, afterwards, under Hadrian and his successors, at Lambæsa. In addition to the proconsular province there were two other provinces to the westward of it governed by *procuratores*. There were the two Mauritanias (*utraque Mauretania*): the Cæsarean Mauritania, the capital of which was Cæsarea (now Cherchel), and the Tingitanian Mauritania, the capital of which was Tingis (Tangiers).

This was the territory occupied by the African army. Its base was the littoral, its centre Carthage, a city which boasted of a civilisation but little inferior to that of Italy. The farther one went from west to south, the greater was the barbarism and absence of security. At the extreme confines of the Empire the utmost that could be done was to obtain control of the wells and caravan routes. Minor fortresses and fortified farms afforded sufficient protection to the outposts.

The nucleus of the army was formed by the legion which (save in exceptional circumstances, such as the campaign against Tacfarinas) was sufficient to safeguard Roman interests in Africa. The name by which it was most generally known was the *legio tertia Augusta*. It possessed as auxiliaries three troops of cavalry (*alæ*), ten cohorts, and two *numeri*, the total strength of the troops employed in the occupation of the proconsular province being thus raised to 12,000 men.

We know that certain distinctions existed between the soldiers of the auxiliary forces and those enrolled in the legions; the former were invariably aliens, while the latter were either drawn from the ranks of the Roman citizens or acquired the status of citizens on enlistment. Moreover, the term of service was twenty years for the legionaries, and twenty-five in the case of the auxiliaries.

The two Mauritanias were defended by auxiliary troops, who, during the first century, were reinforced by a very small number of natives. These troops were split up into cohorts, a large number of them being mounted (*cohortes equitatæ*), into troops of cavalry (*alæ*), and into *numeri* and *vexillationes*. This latter name was given to troops temporarily detached from their proper regiments and serving under a special standard (*vexillum*). In Cæsarean Mauritania there were fifteen cohorts, five *alæ* (of 1,000 men each), one *vexillatio*, and three *numeri*. According to Mommsen, the total strength did not exceed 15,-000 men, thus bringing the entire muster of the African army up to 27,000 or 28,000 men.[1]

(2) *Divisions of the Legion*

The army was at first placed under the command

[1] The present French army of occupation musters on a peace footing 48,000 men.

of the proconsul.   In A.D. 37 Caligula transferred
the command to a legate appointed by himself.   The
post soon became one of the most important in the
Empire, and was seldom conferred on any but prætorian veterans who had attained consular rank,
either on resigning the *legatio* or during their term
of office as *legati*.

The legate was supported by a staff consisting of
beneficiarii[1] (who were termed *beneficiarii legati*, or
consulares, the latter when the legate was also a consul or of consular rank), of *immunes*,[2] *singulares*,[3]
stratores (equerries), *speculatores*,[4] *cornicularii*,[5] and
quæstionarii.[6]   The duty of writing despatches and
keeping the records was intrusted to *commentarienses*,
notarii, *actarii*, *actuarii*, and *exacti ; librarii*, and
capsarii.[7]

Immediately under the orders of the legate were
the tribunes of the legion, whose office had become
a good deal less important since the time of the Re-

---

[1] A name probably derived from those voluntary helpers who accompanied the magistrates of the republic about their provinces, in
the hope of obtaining various favours at the close of their functions.

[2] Unattached officers.

[3] Detached officers.

[4] Officers employed on reconnoissance duty.

[5] Officers entitled to wear the *corniculum*, or badge of honour, on
their helmets.

[6] Officers charged with the enforcement of discipline, somewhat
analogous to the modern provost marshal.

[7] These names are all derived from substantives : *commentarii*
were day-books ; *notæ*, *acta*, were used of memoranda and written
documents of all kinds.   The *librarii* were secretaries ; the *capsarii*
were probably employed as keepers of the archives.

public, owing to the creation of prefects of the camp
and legates of the legion.   Those of the tribunes
who happened to be sons of senators were known as
laticlavii, the others were *angusticlavii*,[1] or *semestres*.
They were assisted in their functions by *beneficiarii*
(*beneficiarii tribuni*), *cornicularii*, *commentarienses*,
and *librarii*.

The prefect of the camp had to select the camping
ground and see to the victualling of the camp, the
entrenchments, and ditch (*fossa*).   He combined
the functions of a colonel of engineers and governor
of a fortress, he looked after the commissariat, the
transport service, the prison, ambulance, armory,
etc.   He was provided with a staff similar to those
of the legates and tribunes.

After these superior officers came the centurions
and decurions, the former being officers of infantry,
the latter of cavalry.   At the head of the centurions
was the *Primipilus*.   The *candidati*, whose names
were submitted by the legate to the Emperor, were
allowed to rank with the titular centurions.   Each
centurion had a lieutenant or *optio* serving under
him.   Complete lists of the centurions and *optiones*
who served at Lambæsa have been found on the
monuments.   The usual number allotted to each
legion was sixty-nine.   Among non-commissioned
officers we need only mention those deputed to
carry the eagles, flags, images, or standards (*signi-*

---

[1] *I. e.*, the *laticlavii* were entitled to wear a broad band of purple
on their cloaks, while the *angusticlavii* wore a narrow one.   The
term *semestris* denotes that they were appointed only for six months.

feri, aquilifer, imaginifer, vexillarius). Then there were the *tesserarii*, whose duty it was to carry round the *tesseræ*, or blocks of wood on which the watchword was inscribed, the picked men (*principales evocati*, afterwards known as *armatura*), and the chiefs of the non-combatant services (*architecti, pecuarii,*[1] etc.).

The cohorts and *alæ* of the legion were commanded by the prefects, tribunes, and *curatores,* the *numeri* by *præpositi* or *curatores*.

The auxiliary forces in Mauritania were placed under the orders of *procuratores* of equestrian rank, who were attended by a similar staff.

(3) *Recruiting*

The above is a brief description of the composition of the army. The question now arises, how was it recruited, and how were the soldiers maintained and fed ? What was the nature of their drill and other duties ? What do we know of their daily lives ?

Nominally, the Emperor was supposed to þe responsible for the recruiting of the army. In practice, however, this duty fell to a knight appointed by the Emperor, in the case of the imperial provinces, and in the other provinces to the proconsul. When an extraordinary levy was necessary, special agents known as *delectores* were employed.

Whence were the recruits drawn ? The answer

---

[1] Building operations and the care of the flocks fell to their charge, as their titles imply.

to this question will differ in the case of the legions and of the auxiliaries. Let us take the legionaries first. Such a copious mass of minute details concerning the recruiting of the *legio III Augusta* has been collected at Lambæsa, that M. Mommsen has been enabled practically to reconstruct the regulations in force with regard to recruiting throughout the whole Empire.[1]

His researches have led him to the conclusion that from the beginning of the first century to the end of the second, a change gradually but steadily took place in the method of recruiting the legions, the primitive organisation originally employed in the days of the Republic being transformed into a totally different system under the Empire.

At first the Emperors retained the republican customs. It had been considered good policy that legionaries should be drawn from natives of some region other than that in which the legion was stationed. The idea was that they should be purely and simply soldiers of Rome. Any other course would have been regarded as fatal to discipline. Under this general system the African contingent included soldiers drawn from almost every country, but more particularly from Gaul and other regions of the West. Thus in the time of Augustus it was the rule that all levies for the Western legions should be made in Italy and in the Latin countries of the West, while recruits intended for service in the East were levied in the Greek countries. When, how-

[1] *Cf.* his general review of this subject in *Hermes*, vol. xix., 1884.

ever, from the time of Vespasian onwards, the Italians ceased to serve in the legions, recruits for the African army were taken from the East; but a far more important point—involving, as it did, a change which became more and more strongly marked every day—was that henceforward the legion began to look for its recruits on the spot. It was no longer a question of selecting some individual African recruit as a special favour; on the contrary, African cities, from this time onward, appear more and more frequently on the lists as the birthplaces of new recruits, and we often find the note *castris* appended to a name, indicating that the soldier had been born in the camp itself.

The new system became general, and was adopted in all the provinces from the time of Hadrian onwards. Henceforward the legions were recruited on the spot. Indeed, the scheme was carried even a step farther, and a supply of excellent recruits provided for the future by organising schools for soldiers' children in the camp itself. These youngsters were placed under the charge of an officer, and had rations allotted to them, thus early becoming inured to the life for which they were intended. From a passage in Vegetius [1] we learn that, in spite of all regulations to the contrary, regiments had invariably carried about with them a horde of children (*pueri*) who, at critical moments, added seriously to the encumbrance of the baggage-train. The system indicated above had the advantage of turning this

[1] Vegetius, iii., 7.

19

drawback into a benefit for the army.   Later on,
these *familiæ militum* came to be recognised and
regulated under the Theodosian code.

An attempt had been made in this direction at an
earlier date.   Owing to the absence of any clear
legal decision on the point, the children of soldiers
could not be described as legitimate or illegitimate.
Now we find that in Africa they received the *jus
civitatis* on their enrolment in the legion.   At first
one-third, then one-half, of the recruits were drawn
from the ranks of these former children of the regiment.   Even as early as the third century they
formed the staple raw material of the legions; the
old system of levies made throughout the provinces
was thus replaced by voluntary engagements con-
tracted in the country in which the legion was
stationed.

We possess fuller information in regard to the
method of recruiting adopted in the case of the
auxiliaries.   Their names prove that these troops
were originally formed by levies made from all the
provinces, even the most distant, such as Thrace,
Britain, and Parthia.   Only one *ala* and two cohorts
were composed of Africans.   The *numeri* consisted,
so far as we know, entirely of Orientals.

The auxiliary troops were recruited exclusively
from the imperial provinces.   They were often
known by territorial names [1] ; but these names

---

[1] E. g., *ala Numidica ; ala Pannoniorum ; cohors Hispanorum,
Lusitanorum, Maurorum, Commagenorum, Chalcidenorum ; nu-
merus Palmyrenorum.*

merely indicated the region in which the regiment
had been originally enrolled. It by no means followed that they necessarily filled up the gaps in
their ranks from the country or race whose name
they bore. The name once adopted was retained
even after the recruiting ground had been changed.
It is believed that the system of recruiting the
auxiliaries must have undergone a change similar to
that which took place in the case of the legions, and
under the Severi, all or nearly all, of the auxiliaries
came from Africa. It would even appear that the
system of obtaining recruits on the spot was applied
to this branch of the army before it was tried on the
legions.

(4) *Maintenance of the Troops*

But, once enlisted, how were the troops supported ? The State provided food, clothing, and
equipment. The responsibility for this rested with
the central power. The question of victualling did
not present any great difficulty. We need but recall the fact that two-thirds of the wheat consumed
in Rome was obtained from Africa. To feed a few
thousand additional mouths on the spot where it
was grown was a very simple matter. All that was
necessary was to draw on one of the numerous
granaries that extended along the coast-line, and
were always kept well stocked with a view to insur-
ing " the security of the Roman people " and of the
Empire at large. One special feature of the African

army was that it possessed its own flocks and hunt-
ers (*venatores*).

The clothing and weapons supplied by the State
were kept in repair locally.

The money for the soldiers' pay was advanced by
the Emperor's agents, for the most part slaves or
freedmen, who deducted it from the revenues of the
provinces.   It should be noted that in addition to
the central exchequer or treasure (*fiscus castrensis*),
the *procurator* at Carthage was empowered to coin
money.

(5) *Religious Worship in the Army*

So much for food, clothing, and pay.   It may not
be amiss to add here a few words in regard to the
deities worshipped by the soldiers.   We know that
religious worship was a very important feature, and
that every legion had its gods.

M. Cagnat wisely draws a distinction between
official and private worship.   The former was obli-
gatory on all.   All adored the " Genius of the Emperor," the " images of the Emperor," attached to
the pole of the standard, the eagle, and other
ensigns, special deities of the legions; they worshipped, in addition, other deities, which strike us
as abstractions, but which they did not regard in
that light.   Among these were such gods as " Discipline," the " Genius of the Place " in which they
camped, the " Genius of the *Centuria*."   Next to
these came the major deities of the Roman Pan-

theon.   This was the official creed enforced as a
matter of discipline.

The true sentiments of both the common soldiers
and their officers must be sought for elsewhere, in
the unofficial cult.   Here we find a marked distinction between the different ranks.   While the officers
dedicate monuments to the gods of the Roman
Pantheon, and but seldom to Mithras or any of the
other Oriental deities, the common soldiers, and
even the non-commissioned officers, show a preference for the local divinities, usually worshipped by
people of their own class, such as the great Punic
deities Baal and Tanit, the *Dii Mauri*, the Nymphs,
or Hercules.

(6) *Military Exercises and Drill*

Military exercises and drill are described for us by
Vegetius.   From the earliest times the Roman
youth had preserved the traditions of these in the
Campus Martius; from thence it had spread to the
utmost confines of the Empire.   The soldier took
up his position in front of an upright stake (*ad
palos*), supposed to represent an adversary, armed
with sword and buckler of wood, twice as heavy as
the ordinary service weapons.   There he was taught
how to act effectively without exposing his own
person.   The company was paraded in double files,
in fours (*quadrata acies*), in a circle (*in orbem*), or in
a triangular formation (*in cuneum*).   Then there was
the *decursio*, in which two sections were pitted one

against the other.   The cavalry were made to prac-
tise reconnoitring and charging.   Add to this the
marching drill and swimming exercises.

In camp, especially when there was a chance of
the men being attacked at any moment by enemies
or rebels, all the sound old traditions were preserved
intact both by the army and its leaders.   I have
already mentioned the fact that the emperors did
their best to perpetuate these traditions; and con-
versely when the heads of the Empire were transported into the atmosphere of the camp, which
differed so radically from that of the capital, they
seemed at once to recover that gravity, vigour, and
dignity of bearing and accent which were too often
absent from the words and actions of their civil life.[1]

Nor was the soldier confined to exercises of a
purely military type.   He was also expected to
take his share in building operations.   He prepared
the bricks which are found in such large numbers in
Africa, marked with the name of the third legion.
He paved the roads and built triumphal arches,

---

[1] *Cf.* Hadrian's address to the *legio III. Augusta* (*C. I. L.*, viii.,
2532).   The Emperor enumerates the various burdens which have
been recently laid on the legion, and which might well have excused
some shortcomings on their part.   They had been obliged to furnish numerous escorts, and to send reinforcements to other *legiones
tertiæ :* "But," he goes on, "you have not been slack in your drill;
it has not been necessary that any excuses should be offered me on
your behalf.   You have gone through all your exercises with energy."
And to the cavalry he says : "Cavalry of the legion, military exercises have laws of their own.   Ever so little added to or taken away
from a manœuvre deprives it of all value, or else makes it too diffi-

gateways, and aqueducts. It is partly to him that we owe the baths and amphitheatres, the stately ruins of which are still to be seen.

But in order to be strictly accurate, there is one curious detail which ought not to be omitted, and this is that these very soldiers, though capable, when put to it, of doing so many things, were nevertheless prepared to transfer to a slave a part of their burdens and arduous duties—of course at a monetary sacrifice to themselves. The State author- ised this delegation of duty, and indeed encouraged it, by allowing the soldiers, by way of recompense, an extra ration or demi-ration, which was apparently intended for the maintenance of these military servants.[1]

(7) *Marriage of Soldiers*

I shall say only a few words on this subject, which is one that has furnished matter for much

cult ; now, increase in difficulty can only be attained by the sacrifice of elegance. As for you, in your exercises, which are by no means easy, you have achieved a most difficult feat ; you have thrown the javelin while fully armed with the cuirass. I not only praise you for this, I approve your valour."

When we read these virile words, which are worthy of being en- graved in stone and preserved even in our own day, we can scarcely believe that this is the same Hadrian whose finicking verses, loaded with diminutives, are preserved in the *Historia Augusta*. In place of the lover of Antinoüs, we have here the general of an army addressing his soldiers in fitting language.

[1] Soldiers who were allowed double rations were known as *duplicarii*, or *duplares ;* those entitled to a ration and a half, as *sesquiplicarii.*

controversy among students of ancient law.   I have
just spoken of the soldiers' slaves, and this leads me
naturally to those who were *de facto*, if not *de jure*,
their wives and children.   What was their position
in the eyes of the law ?   In considering this question
we must be careful about our dates, for, by a gradual
series of concessions, the emperors passed from an
absolute refusal of family privileges to the soldiers
to legal recognition of them.   Moreover, we must
distinguish between the various branches of the
service and between the common soldiers and their
officers.

There is not the slightest doubt that under the
Empire and at a very early stage in its history, officers in the army were not only allowed to marry,
but even to have their wives with them in camp.
In the inscriptions at Lambæsa,. we find the wives
of legates associated in the honours paid to their
husbands.   So, too, in the case of the auxiliaries;
as they were not Roman citizens, permission to
marry was accorded to them more freely and at an
earlier date.   It is only when we come to the rank
and file in the legions that any difference of opinion
arises.   At a very early date the children born to
soldiers during their term of military service, by
their concubines, were admitted to a sort of legiti-
macy.   Nay, more, it would seem that from the
time of Severus they were allowed to reside with
their wives, their presence in camp being required
only when on duty.   Instead of being composed,
as formerly, of a number of strangers collected from

all lands, who served for a certain period only, and
then made haste to quit the country in which they
had been stationed, the legions, at this date, consisted of native Africans employed to defend their
native land, who had wives and children in some
neighbouring town, and whose one desire, when
released from duty, was not to go too far from the
camp. The old army had thus been transformed
into a kind of territorial militia, who cared for little
outside their pay.

(8) *The Pay and Military Chest of the Legion*

The soldier was much more highly paid by the
emperors than he had been by the Republic. In
the time of Polybius he received 112 *denarii*[1] per
annum; in the time of Cæsar he was paid double
this amount, while under Domitian his stipend rose
to 300 *denarii*. This was the regular pay, exclusive
of special gratuities, which were frequent at all times,
and particularly frequent during political crises.
Cæsar gave each soldier 500 *denarii*, while Augustus
presented each man with successive donations of
2500, 500, and 250 *denarii*. The emperors who
followed them were less generous, especially Tiberius. On his discharge from the army the veteran
received 12,000 sesterces (£96).

But what did the soldier do with the sums which
he received during his period of service ? Was he
allowed to squander this money, contrary to his true

---

[1] The *denarius* was worth about eightpence of our money.

interest, and to the great detriment of the general discipline ? The emperors, faithful to the old traditions of the army, refused to allow their soldiers to carry money about with them.[1] Bread, vinegar, and bacon were the only articles to be found in their knapsacks.[2]

Moreover, a system of compulsory loans to the State was devised in the soldier's interests, with a view to keeping him out of mischief and protecting him from himself. A special fund was created into which each soldier was obliged to put one-half of the pay and gratuities he received. The sums thus paid were collected into ten purses (*decem folles*) in the case of each cohort. A further deduction was made with a view to filling an eleventh purse, which served to defray the cost of burying those who died before they had served their time. Each soldier thus received a respectable sum (*peculium castrense*) which was handed over to him on his discharge, or, in the event of his death, was paid to his heirs. His civilian relatives took care to remember this. Juvenal[3] draws a picture of a father paying court, not without a certain trepidation, to his soldier son, in order that he may not be forgotten in his will.

This arrangement, while it benefited the soldier, was also profitable to the State, for it tended to keep the men faithful to their colours. Those who had a

---

[1] Spart., *Pesc. Nig.*, x., 7.

[2] *Avid. Cass.*, v., 3. Niger's soldiers clamoured for a dole of wine ; he replied, "You have the Nile, and yet you ask for wine !"

[3] Juvenal, xvi., 56.

good round sum waiting for them in the regimental
chest were not likely to feel any great desire for
either mutiny or desertion.   It is Vegetius who is
responsible for this remark, but it is one that remains
equally true in every age.

(9) *Military Guilds and Corporations*

Being thus released from anxiety in regard to the
status of his family, and the safety and transmission
of his savings, the soldier had leisure to think about
his funeral. We know what an important matter
this was in the eyes of the ancients, even of the
poorer sort.   I need but recall the Roman burial-
clubs and the *columbaria*.   Let us see how the
Roman soldier managed to free himself from this
last care, thanks to certain provident societies,
which at first sprang up spontaneously, then developed into associations tolerated and encouraged
by the authorities, and were finally placed upon a
regular, official footing.   We shall find that, owing
to ever-increasing concessions on the part of the imperial authority, the soldier was at last completely
reassured on all these points, and ended by not
merely tolerating, but actually loving his profession.

From a very early date there must have existed
in every regiment *collegia*, or guilds, which guaranteed a tomb and honourable burial to all their members.   These associations gradually expanded and
turned their attention to other objects besides

funerals.   They offered various advantages suitable to their rank both to soldiers and officers.

The inscriptions at Lambæsa furnish us with details concerning associations of this kind (*scholæ*) which existed among the non-commissioned officers of various grades (*optiones, cornicularii, tubicines,* etc.).   They organised sacrifices, and probably gave banquets as well, which were attended by members of the guild; they endeavoured to provide for the future of the members in all sorts of different ways. Thus, if one of the associates left the legion, a certain fixed sum was handed over to him; a smaller, though still fairly respectable sum was payable to him should he have the misfortune to be degraded. One of the guilds voted his travelling expenses to a member who was going to Rome with a view to obtaining promotion (*ad spem suam confirmandam*). What more could a soldier's heart desire ?[1]   There was one further object of ambition in certain individual cases.   Native-born Italians who had be-

---

[1] *Cf.* the prayer offered by a prefect at Lambæsa, *C. I. L.*, viii., 2632 :

> "Leiber Pater bimatus. . . .
> Ades ergo cum Panisco :
> Facias *videre Romam*,
> Domini munere *honore*
> *Mactum* coronatumque."

(Liber, mighty God, born of two mothers [I translate this word as though it were a corruption of *bimatris*, a term applied to Bacchus by Ovid in allusion to the legend that he was concealed in Jupiter's thigh after the death of his mother, Semele], come, then, with Pan ; let me see Rome once more and receive honour and a crown by the favour of the master.)

come naturalised as provincials for the sake of promotion, longed not merely to see Rome again, but to be reinstated in their native country.[1]

No doubt this habit of co-operation lasted on even after the term of military service had expired. Veterans, whether members of these guilds or not, had numerous favours granted to them by the State. They installed themselves not far from the camp— probably on land given to them by the government. They were always the favoured candidates at municipal elections, and the central power reserved for them all the titles (such as that of *curator reipublicæ*) and privileges at its disposal.

III

THE CAMP

I must now say something about the stationary camps in which the legions were permanently quartered. At first, constructed in accordance with a traditional plan, like other military institutions, they underwent a gradual transformation. Their temporary buildings were slowly replaced by edifices of stone, and embellished by porticos and triumphal arches. Even in the third century, after the soldiers had ceased to live in the camp itself, the authorities

[1] Bücheler, *Carmin. Epig.*, i. 19, 8, (Prayer of a *procurator Augustalis* of the Narbonnaise):

> " Tu (Silvane) *me meosque reduces Romam* sistito,
> Daque *Italia rura* te colamus præside."

(O thou, Silvanus, bring me and mine back to Rome, and grant that under thy protection we may cultivate the Italian fields.)

took care that they should find there everything that might benefit their health or conduce to their pleasure.   At Lambæsa they had assembly rooms, magnificent public baths, and, very probably, an amphitheatre.   I purposely abstain from going into details.   A brief study of M. Cagnat's little guide-book to Lambæsa, or a glance at the photographs reproduced in his *Armée d'Afrique*, or even at the cuts contained in Duruy's book, will supply the reader with any information he may desire much more quickly and agreeably than whole pages of description.

Both officers and men did their best to make their camp an agreeable place to live in.   We have no difficulty in forming some idea of what it was like from the remains of great buildings which still exist. Ancient writers[1] tell us that soldiers sometimes laid out their camps in a most luxurious style, with gardens, arbours (*topia*), covered ways, and porticos —doubtless as a protection against the heat.   In fact, they possessed too many of these luxuries. The military emperors, with their stringent ideas on the subject of discipline, lost no time in introducing reforms in this direction, and promptly demolished a number of these useless buildings.   Their maxim was that an emperor " was feared by his soldiers only so long as he showed that he was not afraid of them," and they certainly acted up to it.[2]   Hadrian

[1] Spartianus, *Hadrian*, x., 4.
[2] *Cf.* the letter from Severus in *Niger*, iii., 11 . "quem (militem) *quamdiu non timueris, tamdiu timeberis.*"

had already set them an example in this respect, for he never shirked hardship or danger, and though he watched over the well-being of his soldiers and veterans, he took care not to allow them to impose on him.[1]

IV

THE VARIOUS OTHER LEGIONS

The military institutions which I have described, and the changes which we have noted in the history of the African contingent, were certainly not confined to this particular branch of the Roman army. Each detachment of two hundred thousand men, or so, who were employed to guard the tranquillity of the Empire, was, of course, obliged to adapt itself to the climate of the region in which it was stationed.   This led to necessary differences of occupation.   In Germany the soldiers made embankments and dug canals for drainage, whereas in Africa they had to go in search of springs, convey their waters to the camp by means of splendid aqueducts, and carefully store them in vast reservoirs.   In the one country they had to fight against

---

[1] The following anecdote is recorded in his biography (xvii., 7): Hadrian came upon a veteran in the public baths who, for lack of any other assistance, was obliged to rub himself against the wall ; he thereupon gave him slaves to attend on him.   The next day, at the same baths, he found a number of old soldiers, all of whom industriously rubbed themselves against the wall as the emperor passed by.   The device failed, however, as he merely remarked that they had better set to work and rub one another.

the sun; in the other they were obliged to contend against cold and damp. The proportion of cavalry to infantry varied in different localities, and even the weapons with which the men were armed were subject to divers modifications.

But these minor differences did not affect the main organisation of the various forces. The same principles were applied in north and south alike. The emperors did not adapt themselves to circumstances. They merely bowed to a necessity, which became daily more and more imperative, when they decided to recruit the legions from the native races, and when they rendered the conditions of the soldier's life more and more tolerable and pleasant by a gradual extension of his privileges. The result was obvious. Before it fell, the Empire had conceded to officers and men all that they wanted, and there is nothing to show that either the one or the other had any desire left unsatisfied.

CHAPTER XIII

FACE TO FACE WITH THE BARBARIANS ON THE NORTHERN FRONTIER

COMMUNITIES are like pictures, or like some vast plain. In order to get a good view of them, we must go some little way off, and, standing at a distance, look at them, if not from an eminence, at any rate from the outside. In order, therefore, to form an unbiassed judgment of the Roman community during the first and second centuries, we will go outside the Empire, and, stationing ourselves on its northern fringe, on that *limes* which archæologists have taken so much trouble to trace, we will try to make out what is taking place on either side of the frontier. It was here that the Empire first began to totter, and it was in this direction that it was eventually destined to fall.

Our first care in this general survey will be to ascertain the attitude of the Romans towards these barbarians, with whom they were henceforward to be in permanent contact, and who, though repeatedly defeated, were never finally conquered. We will next try to distinguish between the barbarians of various epochs, separating those of the first centuries from those of the great invasion, and will endeavour to estimate the relative value of the various sources of information at our disposal, contrasting the *Germania* of Tacitus with the works of Ammianus Marcellinus and other historians.

I

THE BARBARIAN WORLD

For a detailed description of the barbarian world, I must refer the reader to the histories on the subject.[1]   In the present work I am obliged to content myself with enumerating some of the races who dwelt beyond the natural frontiers of the Roman Empire.   Seneca tells us that in the first century there were, beyond the Ister, the Dacians; to the north of the Strymon and Hemus, the Thracians; to the north of the Danube, the Sarmatians, whose excellent cavalry made them specially formidable; while beyond the Rhine lay the Germans, whose principal strength lay in their infantry.[2]

To simplify matters, we may leave on one side the eastern frontier, where the Arsacides constituted a continual menace to the Roman supremacy, and where the humiliations to which a captive emperor

---

[1] Apart from Duruy's *Histoire romaine*, every one is familiar with the remarkable contributions on this subject which have appeared in France during the last fifty years.   I need but mention the names of Amédée Thierry, Littré, Geoffroy, and Fustel de Coulanges.

[2] Seneca, *Quæst. Nat. Prol.*, 8.   So, too, in one of Martial's epigrams, *Epigr.*, *lib.* 3 (or *De Spectac.*), we find all the principal races of the ancient world collected with references to their different customs and dress.

was subjected foreshadowed the decline of the Empire. On the north, the struggle continued almost without interruption on both banks of the two rivers. On the Danube, the Quadi and Marcomanni managed to place Rome in a position of terrible danger, from which it required all the energy of Marcus Aurelius to extricate her. On the west every illustrious son of Rome—emperors, generals, and writers—hurried to fight for her, or guard her on the banks of the Rhine. After Cæsar, after the princes of the imperial family and the future emperors, came Agricola, Pliny, and Tacitus. It was here that Julian first rose into prominence. The struggle between Rome and Germany was not destined to cease until the moment came when the barriers raised against barbarism were broken down, and Gaul, the north of Italy, and the whole Empire were overwhelmed by the flood of invasion.

Rome defended her territory there in accordance with her usual methods. The system of fortification varied. In the best days of the Empire, this frontier, which extended over a distance of six hundred leagues, was guarded by eight legions in the two Germanies, stationed in permanent camps; there were two more legions in Pannonia and two in Dalmatia, and a whole chain of fortresses connected by ramparts and wooden palisades.

It would be a mistake, however, to suppose that these fortifications constituted an insurmountable barrier between the two peoples. These two worlds, the civilised and the barbarian, were not entirely

closed against each other.   More than one Gallic
or Italian merchant ventured far into the interior
with his merchandise, and brought back with him
the produce of the country, such as furs and amber
from Germany.   On their part, the barbarians
crossed the frontiers and came to besiege the Roman
markets, and to initiate themselves into customs and
a mode of life with which they eagerly desired to be
acquainted, however much they may have affected
to despise them, though, as usually happens in such
cases, they succeeded in assimilating only the vices
of their conquerors.

Other nations bearing other names were soon to
appear on the banks of the great boundary streams;
the Goths at the beginning of the third century;
then the barbarians of the great invasion; but both
the boundaries and the area of the struggle remained
practically the same.   At different periods and
under different emperors, Rome employed artifice
and main force in turn against her enemies.   At
one moment she domineered over them, robbed
them, decimated them, and threw them as a prey to
the beasts in the arena; at another she took them
into her pay, armed them, and taught them.   In
short, she treated them as a clumsy trainer treats the
monster which is one day destined to devour him.

II

ROMAN IDEAS IN REGARD TO THE BARBARIANS

If soldiers and generals when they reached the
frontier did not omit to scan the country beyond it,

neither were the pure-blooded Romans—those who
never quitted the capital—any less curious about all
that concerned the barbarians and particularly about
the rumours that were current in regard to their
manners and customs.[1]

The inhabitants of the Seven Hills only occasionally caught sight of the barbarian captives, real or
fictitious, who were led before the chariots of victorious generals; their sole knowledge of these distant
countries was derived from the somewhat confused
narratives of soldiers returned from foreign service,
or from the scarcely less confused accounts to be
found in the ever-increasing library of books dealing
with the foreign wars of the Empire, or containing
descriptions of Britain or of Germany. Meanwhile
the popular conception of the barbarians was, even
in the early days of the Empire, reduced to a con-
crete form on the monuments, where they began to
occupy a larger and larger space, especially on
triumphal columns, in bas-reliefs, and the groups of
statues by which the city was adorned.

(1) *The Barbarians as Depicted on the Monuments*

Let us take this last source of information first,
and see what the monuments have to teach us.
Here we need not expect to find any very accurate
representation; the artists may have exaggerated

---

[1] Seneca, *De Otio*, v., 32 : "Hæc res (cupido ignota noscendi) . . .
populos . . . cogit . . . *mores barbarorum audire gentium*" (The desire for information concerning the things of which they are ignorant
impels nations to listen to what is told concerning the customs of
barbarian races).

certain features, and the Roman sculptors, influenced by the Greeks who were their masters in the art, and who possessed a barbarian type of their own which they were accustomed to treat in a conventional manner, may have idealised the likenesses they placed before their contemporaries. Moreover, it is probable that they flattered the prejudices of their time. Still, seeing that the Romans possessed occasional opportunities for inspecting the originals, their artists were probably obliged to adhere much more closely to the reality than those of Greece. What, then, do we find in the monuments?

In every single instance, the barbarians are represented in the hour of defeat. The emperor, his officers, and his soldiers, always have the best of it; whereas, the barbarians invariably look sombre and dejected. Juvenal, in describing the trophy raised in honour of a victorious general, adds as a final touch:

" et summo *tristis captivus* in arcu." [1]

Ever since the Romans had conquered the world, captive and barbarian had come to be synonymous terms. They are represented with long hair, either curly or matted, a fact which renders them distinguishable from the Romans at the first glance. [2] Their appearance alone shows the native ruggedness

[1] x., 13: "and at the top of the arch [of triumph] a prisoner of sombre mien."

[2] Tacitus, *Arg.*, 39: "Domitianus . . . emptis per commercia, quorum habitus et *crines* in *captivorum speciem* formarentur" (Domitian having bought in the market a number of slaves whose hair and external appearance were similar to those of captives). .

of their character, and even a certain sullen stupidity. On the other hand, it would not do to lessen the credit due to those who had conquered them; they are therefore depicted as strong and valiant, with a courage often bordering on heroism.

In accordance with a convention borrowed from Greek art, but which, as it happened, was partly true to life, the barbaric warrior, whether German, Gaul, or Briton, is generally represented naked or almost naked.[1] The artists took advantage of the opportunity thus afforded them to show their knowledge of anatomy and make display of a skill which necessarily lay dormant when dealing with the draped portions of the human body. This explains the frequent introduction of barbarian figures and the magnificent specimens of this kind of work which are to be found in our museums.[2]

In like manner, the artists made capital out of traditional characteristics ascribed to the barbarians. They were said to be impatient of all restraint, very jealous of their independence, always anxious to be first where honours were concerned, and inclined to view the splendours of the Empire with assumed indifference or contempt.[3] Even when defeated,

---

[1] They went into battle *bare-sark* to show how little they were afraid of wounds. Ammianus (xiv., 4, 3) thus describes the Saracens of the Nile: " bellatores *seminudi, coloratis sagulis pube tenus amicti* " (half-naked warriors, clothed to below the waist in bright-coloured cloaks).

[2] *E. g.*, the Gallic warrior in the Capitol Museum, erroneously described as the " Gladiator."

[3] Tacitus, *Ann.*, xiii., 54.

they still showed themselves insolent and un-daunted, except when they adopted a suppliant at-titude, in which case they proved themselves false and treacherous. These qualities furnished the artist with plenty of well defined material and a host of widely different emotions which enabled him to vary his subjects and throw them into any form he pleased.[1]

As the barbarian warriors were introduced into groups as pendants to the legions, where the general and his officers were represented side by side with the auxiliaries and common soldiers, it became ne-cessary in the case of the barbarians, as in that of the other group, to distinguish the chiefs and princes by giving them a different dress and armour. These bas-reliefs and columns, which had to stand the criticism of those who had been eye-witnesses of the subjects they depicted, must necessarily be fairly true to life, and Boeckh is probably not far wrong in asserting that the exact representation of barbar-ians and legionaries developed into an orginal branch of Roman realistic art.

In the battle scenes which we find at the base of the triumphal arches, each member of the enemy's forces has his own particular dress, weapons, and facial characteristics; their wives often appear beside them; Dacians, Sarmatians, Quadi, Marcomanni, all are clearly differentiated one from the other, each race retaining its own peculiar cast of counten-ance. If we have a difficulty in following the dif-

[1] Ammianus, xvi., 10, 16, and xxiii., 6, 82.

ference between them, the fault is not so much due to the artist as to our own imperfect knowledge of barbarian antiquities.   It is only at a later period, when less care was taken with work of this kind, that we come upon a more conventional type, similar to that which occurs so frequently in Greek statuary.

III

THE BARBARIANS IN LITERATURE AND IN HISTORY

From the artists we now pass on to authors and historians.   In dealing with the references to the barbarians by Roman writers, we must, first of all, note that there are two epochs and sources, or rather series of sources, which differ widely from one another.   On the one hand, we have Tacitus and the writers at the end of the first century; on the other, the historians of the succeeding centuries and the information obtainable from far less trustworthy sources, such as the *Historia Augusta*, Sidonius Apollinaris, and Ammianus Marcellinus.

(1) *The Germania of Tacitus*

We will first examine the *Germania* of Tacitus, a veritable " Golden Book " and a storehouse of inexhaustible wealth; all other works on the subject are little more than a detailed commentary, frequently hypothetical and contradictory in character, on the forty-six chapters of this work.[1]

---

[1] Gibbon's verdict still holds good.   This treatise of Tacitus's, which contains, perhaps, more ideas than words, has been and still

The breadth of view which distinguishes his survey
of the region beyond the frontier, was, perhaps,
neither so rare nor so exceptional in ancient times
as is generally supposed.[1]   It seems so to us, simply
because all the accounts of the wars of Germany
written by Roman historians have been lost.   A far
rarer quality, near akin to genius, is the author's
power of penetration, his continual effort to attain
accuracy in every detail and to bring the truth
plainly before the eyes of his readers.   No other
writer has ever displayed a better knowledge or
more perfect control of his subject.   Let me try to
bring this clearly home to my readers.

In spite of all that has been said to the contrary,[2]
this little book forms a distinct work, with a definite
end and purpose of its own; it contains, moreover,
in accordance with the author's usual method, an
exordium and peroration.   The introduction is an
imitation of the opening chapter of Cæsar's *De Bello
Gallico*, the conclusion is at once abrupt[3] and in-

continues to be, annotated by numberless scholars, and still taxes
the genius and penetration of philosophic historians.

[1] Geoffroy, *Les Barbares*, p. iv.

[2] Anyone who wishes to convince me that the *Germania* is merely
a detached portion of the *Historia* of Tacitus, will have to prove (1)
that the *Germania* contains a single sentence which clearly connects
it with the larger work ; (2) that there is any parallel instance in the
works of Tacitus of a digression in forty-six chapters.   A contrary
view has been advanced afresh by M. Brunot in his *Un fragment
des Histoires de Tacite, étude sur le* "De Moribus Germanorum,"
Paris, Picard, 1883.

[3] " Quod ego ut incompertum in medio relinquam " (As we have
no definite information on these points it is useless to say more).

tentionally disdainful, such as we should expect
from a writer who concerned himself with facts and
not with legends.

The date at which the work was written is indicated in cap. xxxvii., where there is internal evidence
to show that it must have been composed after the
second consulate of Trajan (98) and before the third
(100).

The arrangement of the contents is clearly indicated by one of the closing sentences of cap.
xxvii. In the preceding chapters the author has
been dealing with the origin and customs of the
Germans considered as a whole (*in commune*); in the
chapters that are to follow Tacitus is about to speak
of the institutions and usages of the various German
races taken separately (*singulæ gentes*). He proposes
to single out their characteristic features and to note
those of them which made their way into Gaul.

Now the first question that arises—and it is mani-
festly an important one—is whether Tacitus is communicating to us the results of direct personal
observation or whether he speaks on the authority
of others. The former hypothesis, which harmonises
better with the high esteem in which his *Germania*
is universally held, has prevailed until quite recently;
an important argument in its favour was supplied
by the researches of Borghesi in regard to the life of
Tacitus. M. Fustel de Coulanges has since, however, keenly disputed it.[1]

---

[1] *Histoire des institutions politiques de l'ancienne France*, vol. ii.,
l'Invasion, pp. 237 *et seq.*

Montesquieu's brilliant dictum in regard to Tacitus, " who abridged everything, because he saw everything," [1] is therefore, apparently, no longer true of the *Germania* unless it be taken in a purely figurative sense.   No doubt Tacitus has greatly condensed his material in this work, but it is possible that he had not actually *seen* a great deal of what he writes about.   To be on the safe side, let us adopt a negative hypothesis and say that where he had no personal observation to go upon, Tacitus collected an enormous mass of second-hand information of all kinds.

Another much debated question is the precise meaning to be attached to the somewhat enigmatic sentence at the end of cap. xxxiii.[2]   Tacitus did not fail to realise, and indeed here explicitly admits, that in the struggle of the nations it is might, not right, that is the final arbiter of their fate.[3]   Did he, then, really feel doubtful concerning the superiority of the Roman power over that of the enemies who assailed it ?   Does his reference to the Empire being hard pressed by fate (*urgentibus imperii fatis*) prove

---

[1] *Esprit des lois*, xxx., 2.

[2] " Maneat, quæso, duretque gentibus, si non amor nostri, at certe odium sui, quando, *urgentibus imperii fatis*, nihil jam præstare fortuna majus potest quam hostium discordiam " (I pray that there may remain and continue among these peoples, if not the love of Rome, yet at least their hatred of one another, at this time the Empire is pressed so hard by fate, that we can look for no greater good fortune than discord among its enemies).

[3] Cap. xxxvi. : "*ubi manu agitur*, modestia ac probitas *superioris sunt*" (In a hand-to-hand conflict, moderation and justice are always on the side of the stronger) ; *i. e.*, might makes right.

that Tacitus foresaw the danger of a general barbarian invasion ? In more than one passage he lets
us see that he realised how much the Roman
victories hitherto obtained over such enemies had
cost, and how much—or how little—they were
worth.[1] The struggle against them had again and
again to be undertaken afresh. A part of the territory formerly conquered had been lost.[2] The barbarians were able to boast that they had inflicted as
many defeats on the Romans as they had suffered
at their hands,[3] and thus had re-established a sort of
equality between the two peoples.

In my opinion, however, it would be a mistake to
interpret the sentence under discussion too literally,
either one way or the other. It is easy for us moderns
to be wise after the event. Tacitus does not need
adventitious merits to be ascribed to him. If he
really foresaw the invasion, it can only have been as
a remote contingency. The habitual acerbity of
his style may have led him to express his apprehensions in exaggerated language. It was quite in ac-

---

[1] Tacitus, xxxvii. : "*tam diu Germania vincitur* . . . ; proximis
temporibus *triumphati magis quam victi sunt*" (For a long time
past we have been conquering Germany . . . ; but of late years we
have triumphed over them oftener than we have defeated them).

[2] *Ibid.*, xli. : "Albis, flumen inclutum et *notum olim, nunc tantum
auditur*" (The Elbe, a celebrated river, and once familiar [to the
Roman legions], now little more than a name).

[3] *Ibid.*, xxxvii. 9: "multa *invicem* damna." Cf. *Hist.*, i., 1 :
"*nobilitatus mutuis cladibus* Dacus" (The Dacians, illustrious from
the fact that their wars with Rome have resulted in defeats on both
sides).

cordance with his ideas in regard to the progress of
events to reserve a place for the obscure workings
of destiny[1] ; it is one of his favourite literary devices.   But it is very doubtful whether his patriotism
would ever have allowed him to admit that the
downfall which ultimately took place was inevitable.
In spite of Gibbon and his supporters, we must
adhere to the text of the best MSS. and read
urgentibus.[2]   Assuredly fate was pressing the Empire hard, since after a period of growth and conquest, it now found itself on the down grade.   Yet
this is in no way equivalent to saying that it was
within two or three centuries of its end.

On the other hand, M. Fustel de Coulanges borders on paradox when he tries to make out that
Tacitus was far from entertaining any feeling of
anxiety in regard to the future of the Empire.   This
is merely running to the opposite extreme.   It is
a view which presupposes great blindness on the
part of the historian, and reduces this and other
similar passages in his writings to the level of mere
rhetorical effects of style.   Neither of these conclusions seems to be justified.

It was from Rome that Tacitus described the
Germans, and he judges them from the Roman
standpoint.   On the other hand, he is writing for
the benefit of his contemporaries, and is not sorry
to find a text from which to preach them a sermon.

---

[1] Cf. *Ann.*, vi., 22.

[2] In preference to *vergentibus*, the reading suggested by Justus Lip-
sius on the authority of an inferior MS.

In reading this highly original book we must try not to forget this double point of view from which its author wrote.[1]

From what sources did Tacitus obtain the facts which he has handed down to us ? This is an important question which it is impossible to answer as explicitly as one would wish to do. The only ancient writers mentioned in the *Germania*, or who have dealt with the subject of which it treats, are Cæsar[2] and Pliny.[3] Pliny seems to have been the principal source to which Tacitus was indebted; he was a well informed man, who was able to speak of the Germans with the authority of an eye-witness. But the Roman literature of an earlier period may also have furnished the historian with details concerning the barbarians. It is believed that Sallust, in dealing with the Mithridatic war, had spoken of the barbarians settled in the basin of the lower Danube, and that Livy in his 140th book had narrated the history of the German wars down to the death of Drusus. Among the various generals who took part in these wars, and the politicians who followed the history of that period, it is very probable that more than one may have left memoirs and histories which are lost to us.[4] Finally, there was a

---

[1] The words *interpretatio Romana*, in cap. xliii., 14, furnish an apt summary of his attitude. They apply to the work as a whole and not merely to the writer's remarks on religious questions.

[2] Mentioned in cap. xxviii. of the *Germania*.

[3] Mentioned in the *Annales*, ii., 69, in the following terms: "C. Plinium *Germanicorum bellorum scriptorem*" (Pliny, the historian of the Germanic wars). [4] *Cf.* Geoffroy, *Les Barbares*, p. 84.

very abundant oral tradition, from which a man in the position of a senator ought to have found little difficulty in sifting out the true and the false.

We can readily understand the attraction which the subject possessed for Tacitus. In the first place, there was the curiosity aroused among the Romans by certain natural phenomena peculiar to Germany, such as the production of amber, a substance to which the natives had attached no value until the luxury and caprice of a foreign nation caused it to rise in their estimation,[1] and, above all, the extreme shortness of the summer nights. Tacitus, like other Romans, believed[2] that in Germany one came literally to the end of the world.[3]

When he reaches the moral side of his subject Tacitus throws a flood of light on all the more characteristic features of German institutions and customs. He points out that they did not worship in temples, but in the solitude and seclusion of groves consecrated to the gods (ix.); that they had no towns, or even villages, their houses standing isolated

---

[1] Cap. xlv., 14.   [2] *Ibid.*

[3] *Ibid. :* "Illuc usque, *et fama vera, tantum* natura" (It is thus far only that the world extends, the rumour to this effect being a true one). *Cf.* the chapter on Drusus (xxxiv.). Tacitus, like Suetonius (*Claud.*, 1), admits that the son of Tiberius was stopped by divine intervention : "*obstitit Oceanus* in se simul atque in Herculem inquiri. Mox nemo tentavit *sanctiusque ac reverentius* visum de actis deorum credere quam scire" (The Ocean prevented him from exploring its depths. No one ever dared to renew the attempt afterwards : it was thought to be more pious and respectful to believe what is told us of the actions of the gods than to seek a more exact knowledge concerning them).

from one another (xvi.); that there were no courtesans or faithless wives among them. Then he
notices the peculiar status of their women (xix.); the
contrasts observable in the character of the men,
who though brave and indefatigable in war, were
lazy and inert at home (xv.); the devotion of the
clansmen to their chieftain (xiii.); the system of
compensation enforced in the case of most crimes
(xii., 7)[1]; the terrible punishment inflicted on cow-
ards (xii., 3); the *baritus* (iii., 3); the cries and crash
of lances by which the warriors signified their approval or disapproval of the harangues of their leaders (xi.); the attachment of the soldiers to their lances
and war-horses (xiv., 2, and xviii., 8). Then he deals
with local customs as well, such as those of the
Chatti, who never clipped their horses or shaved
their beards until they had killed their first foe; or
of the *Harii*, worthy ancestors of the " Hussars of
Death," who endeavoured to intimidate their adversaries by means of their black shields, blackened
bodies, and other gruesome equipments (xliii., 19).
Here we find a whole host of lifelike touches, man-
ifestly based on reality, which faithfully reproduce
for us the characteristics of a bygone age.

As might have been expected from so thoughtful
and sincere a writer in dealing with a subject of
this kind, Tacitus rarely misses an opportunity of
contrasting Roman vices with certain virtues possessed by their enemies. It is true that the *Germania* was not written simply as a vehicle for these

---

[1] The German *Wehrgeld*, or system of compounding crimes.

epigrams, but neither do they seem out of place in
its grave and trustworthy descriptions.　Hence the
allusions to the corruption of Roman morals (xix.),
to the senseless extravagance of Roman funerals
(xxvii.), to the shameless practices of legacy-hunters
(xx.), to the insolence of the emperors' freedmen
(xxv., 8), and to the baseness of those who flattered
the wealthy and powerful.　He gives what is practically an ironical summary of this undesirable existence in a passage where he contrasts it with the
hideous and savage poverty of the Fenni (xlii.),
which he seems to consider preferable to the gilded
luxury of Rome.　It is evident that there is a certain straining after effect here, and that the contrast
is somewhat overdrawn.

(2) *The Barbarians as Represented by Later Writers,
such as Ammianus and Sidonius*

In the following pages I propose to give a few
definite and picturesque details in regard to the
barbarians who surrounded the Empire on all sides,
and were, one day, destined to overrun it.　In
doing so, I shall not take all my facts from any one
author, nor will they all refer to one and the same
epoch.　Once we leave the *Germania* of Tacitus [1]

[1] To anyone desirous of estimating the true value of the *Germania*,
even when viewed in one of its less important aspects, I would
recommend the following test : Compare the geographical details
given by Tacitus, which are so clear that one can easily follow them
on the map, with descriptions of a similar nature furnished by the
historians who preceded him, even the very greatest of them, and

behind us, we feel that our sources of information are much diminished in volume. It is therefore needless further to restrict our opportunities by the adoption of hard-and-fast methods which cannot here answer any useful purpose.

The first thing to be noted is that in the centuries immediately succeeding the age of Tacitus, a number of important changes have taken place in the barbarian world. New names come to the front (Franks, Alemanni, and Goths, while races which formerly loomed large in history have entirely disappeared. The juxtaposition of the old and new names is very frequent in the *Historia Augusta*, in Ammianus, and in all the historians of that age [1]; it must therefore have been necessary. Very probably M. Fustel de Coulanges [2] is right in believing that these races grew up and destroyed one another with great rapidity. It will be sufficient to recall, in passing, the two great movements which took place on the frontier. The first of these was the invasion by the Quadi and Marcomanni towards the close of the

with those found in subsequent writers (especially Ammianus); or, if a still stronger contrast be desired, compare the description in Tacitus's *Germania* with the chapters devoted to the same subject by Pliny the Elder (iv., 96); and yet Pliny had seen the barbarians in their own country, and it is believed that in compiling the descriptions in his natural history, he had access to a chart of the world copied from the celebrated map of Augustus.

[1] "Franci *olim dicti* Germani" (the Franks, formerly called the Germans); "Halani *veteres* Massagetæ" (the Halani or ancient Massagetæ); "Saraceni *eidem qui* Scenitæ Arabes" (the Saracens who are identical with the Scenite Arabs).

[2] P. 119.

second century (162–180), which Marcus Aurelius at length succeeded in repelling. Rome then made an effort of which she would later on have been incapable. At the beginning of the fifth century, the final gap was made and Rome succumbed.

Among these barbarians there were two main groups. First come the Germanic races; they dwelt for the most part in fixed abodes, at any rate for some time together; they wore a close-fitting dress, and their infantry was especially formidable. On the other hand, we have the nomadic races of Eastern origin, who lived in tents, changed their quarters incessantly,[1] and wore loose flowing robes. Their cavalry, armed with long lances, and wearing cuirasses ornamented with pieces of horn and linen, knew not what it was to be weary. Mounted on their Hungarian chargers, which were sometimes made to carry two riders, they caracoled and curvetted in the most brilliant fashion. Nor must we

---

[1] Ammianus, in speaking of the Saracens, xiv., 4, 5, declares that "*alibi* mulier nubat, *in loco* pariat *alio*, liberosque *procul* deducat, nulla copia quiescendi permissa" (A woman may marry in one place, become a mother in another, and carry her children on with her to a third, without being permitted to rest) ; and of the Huns he says (xxxi., 4, 5) : "Nullus apud eos interrogatus respondere, unde oritur, potest, *alibi conceptus, natusque procul et longius educatus* (Not one of them could tell to what country he belonged : conceived in one place, born in another far distant, and educated in a third). Napoleon's remark to Dorsenne during his Egyptian campaign, "You were born in camp, you have been brought up in camp, and, if I live, you shall die there," might have been applied to these races, not in a spirit of exaggeration, but as a sober statement of fact.

forget to mention that Gothic monarch defeated by Aurelian, whose chariot was drawn by four reindeer.[1]

In order to stave off the invasion by which they were continually threatened, the Romans adopted the policy of trying to stir up the barbarians against one another, and, following the desire expressed by Tacitus in regard to the Germans,[2] made capital out of the feuds existing between the Goths and Vandals, the Franks and Burgundians. But this was a remedy which did not long retain its efficacy. The temporary alliance sought for by the emperors, the enrolment of native auxiliaries who were quickly added in a mass to the regular legions, all these expedients only served to bring into greater prominence the ever-increasing weakness of the Empire. When Suevi, Rugii, Ostrogoths, and even Vandals came to be promoted to posts of command in the Roman army, it must have been clear to all eyes that the Empire of the West was nearing its end.

Let us consult two of the most celebrated writers of the fifth century and find what they have to say concerning the barbarians whom they saw intermingling with the Roman society of their day.

Ammianus Marcellinus

Ammianus was a soldier who detested courtly intrigues and the populace of great towns. He judges the barbarians from the point of view of an adver-

---

[1] Vopiscus, *Aurel.*, 34, 3, says that they were stags (*cervis*).

[2] *Cf.* p. 316, note 2, *Maneat, quæso*, etc.

sary.   Faithful to the old tradition, he refuses to recognise in these foemen on the Rhine and the Danube anything more than so much raw material which afforded scope to the Romans for the exercise of patience and courage.   In spite of rhetorical defects of style, his remarks are sometimes shrewd and well expressed.   I have already quoted what he says of the Saracens and Huns; elsewhere he describes the Quadi swearing on their daggers, which they regarded with almost the same respect as that paid by them to the Deity (xvii., 12); then he draws a picture of the *Cornuti* and *Bracchiati*, who accompanied Julian in his expedition against the Alemanni singing their national war-song (xvi., 12, 43), while, on their side, the Alemanni posted on the islands of the Rhine, or on steep slopes having enormous tree trunks, poured forth dismal howlings and insults against the Romans and against Cæsar (xvi., 11, 8). Their king wore a flame-coloured plume in his helmet; he rode at the head of his men confident in his strength, clad in shining armour, and brandishing a huge javelin, on a foam-flecked steed, towering high above the rest by reason of his lofty stature (xvi., 12, 24).   According to Ammianus, the Huns were the most terrible of all the barbarian races '; from their youth up their cheeks were scored with iron in order that the scars might stop the growth of the hair; thus, though beardless, they looked old, and none of them had the slightest pretension to beauty; they were like eunuchs, thick-set and strongly

---

[1] Ammianus, xxxi., 2, 2.

built, with huge heads, "monstrous and terrifying shapes, who might at first sight be mistaken for two-legged animals, or for those statues which are employed as piers for bridges, blocks cut into a dim resemblance of the human form."

Ammianus, perhaps following the example of Tacitus, is here and there unable to resist the temptation to mention some horrible custom, as where he tells us that the Geloni, after flaying their enemies, used their skins as a covering for themselves and for their horses (xxxi., 2, 14).

Sidonius Apollinaris

Sidonius was a poet and rhetorician, of Gallo-Roman birth, with a taste for magnificent villas, fine speeches, and well turned verses and letters. His success and talent in this direction obtained him a brief lease of power. Around him we find a bevy of provincial nobles of the same kidney, whose whole attention is absorbed by games and festivals; punctilious on questions of etiquette, exceedingly ambitious, jealous of each other and ever ready to run one another down before the master of the hour[1]; all of them absolutely blind to the coming danger, and powerless and stupefied when it finally burst on them. Before long the country was invaded and ruined; Sidonius, formerly a consul, now became a captive and a hostage, compelled to pay court to a Visigoth king. His vengeance lay in his tablets and

[1] *Ep.*, i., 11.

in the letters which he wrote to friends as unfortunate as himself. One of his favourite themes is a description of the blunders and brutality of his new masters. He watched and observed them closely; compelled to endure familiarities, he finds some consolation in poking fun at them behind their backs, earnestly hoping that they may never find him out. According to Sidonius, the proper way to treat them is to laugh at them, to despise them, and to fear them.[1] The last item in this programme seems to leave but little scope for the other two.

Let us borrow from Sidonius the following description of a Gothic council held after the manner of the ancients:

" In spite of their green old age, burdened with years, they stand upright; on their lean backs hang dirty, greasy linen garments; the great skins that cover them scarcely reach as far as their calves, while the horse-skin gaiters round their legs are secured by a single knot."[2]

This is how he describes the hordes of Scythia:

" On foot they seem to be of average height; on horseback they are tall, and very tall when seated. The child has barely left his mother's apron-strings when he takes his first lesson in riding. It almost seems as though their limbs were soldered to the backs of the animal they bestride, so firm is their seat. Other men are carried on the backs of their horses, these men live there."[3] " They have broad chests and fine shoulders,

[1] *Ep.*, iv., 1, 4.   [2] *Pan. Avitus*, 452.
[3] *Pan. Anth.*, 260 *et seq.*

the paunch drawn in at the groin." [1] " The faces even of their children inspire horror. Their bodies are a round mass surmounted by a narrow head; under their foreheads are two caverns from whence they see without eyes. . . . Their noses are purposely flattened so as to provide room for their helmets." [2]

At the court of King Euric, Sidonius met Saxons with blue eyes and hair shaved to the roots, Heruli with bluish cheeks, and Burgundians seven feet high. [3] A friend having asked him for a set of Fescennine verses, Sidonius replies that it is impossible to write them when one lives in the midst of shaggy hordes,

" amid the sounds of the Germanic jargon, when the sated Burgundian sings, his head well greased with rancid butter. . . . Happy thine eyes and ears, happy thy nose, to escape the smell of garlic and odious onions, the unfailing sequel to a dinner of ten courses indulged in overnight." [4]

It is pretty plain what Sidonius thought of the giants who had made themselves masters of his country. He little imagined that of all his verse and prose, in which each word is weighed and measured with such scrupulous care, the passages in which he speaks of these very barbarians, and the details he gives concerning them, would prove more interesting to posterity than all the rest.

---

[1] *Pan. Anth.*, 258.

[2] *Ibid.*, 246.

[3] *Ep.*, viii., 9, 21 *et seq.*

[4] *Ad Catull.*

Sidonius loved his country, invaded and ruined though it was, but he draws no distinction between the Gauls and the rest of the Empire; he reserves his whole admiration for Rome: " The home of law, the school of letters, the *curia* of dignities, the head of the world, the fatherland of liberty, the only town in the world where provincials feel themselves at home and where barbarians and slaves alone are foreigners."[1] In this passage we recognise the provincial still dazzled by the splendours of the metropolis, the consul of yesterday; the first half of the sentence recalls a state of things which was already past and gone, while the latter half is rather a pious aspiration than a statement of fact. However it may have been with the slaves, the barbarians who had captured and recaptured Rome intended to return thither; they felt so much at home there, that something like a century passed before they thought of leaving. And down to the time of the Renaissance it was—for other reasons, it is true[2]— a matter for remark that at Rome foreigners were, so to speak, entirely in their element, whereas at Venice, though nominally free, they could not help feeling that they were but passing guests.

[1] *Ep.*, i., 6, 2: " in qua unica totius orbis civitate soli *barbari et servi peregrinentur.*"

[2] Montaigne, *Voyage*, 4to ed., p. 168.

CHAPTER XIV

A TYPICAL ROMAN OF THE EMPIRE, PLINY THE YOUNGER

DURING the earlier centuries of the Empire, there were a certain number of writers whose attraction for modern readers is due quite as much to their character and personality as to their writings. Plutarch and Lucian have been widely studied and still find attentive readers. Then, too, we have that worthy Emperor Marcus Aurelius and his band of philosophers, Epictetus, and, in a lesser degree, Seneca also. Add to these the satirists, whom we value—yet distrust—for all the evil they tell us of their contemporaries. If, however, we seek to combine in a single portrait of some one Roman of imperial times all the typical characteristics of the Roman society of that period, we shall find no one more truly representative of it than Pliny the Younger. His origin, his family connections, his relations with politicians and literary men, his rank, the career in which he won a certain distinction, his

prejudices, even his respectability and talent, all
contribute to make him, more absolutely and entirely than any other, a true Roman of the first
century.[1] The pupil of Quintilian and friend of
Tacitus, honoured by Trajan with his confidence,
and intrusted by him with the discharge of exalted
functions—these facts alone afford sufficient proof
that Pliny has some claim to be singled out from
the common run of his contemporaries. He is perfectly willing to talk about himself—indeed, in his
letters, he seldom talks of anybody else. But, if
not troubled by modesty, he is honest and sincere.
In the previous chapters of this book we have taken
up various standpoints from which to form some
idea of Roman society during the first century; let
us here endeavour to view it as a whole through
Pliny and around him.

I

LIFE OF PLINY—HIS CHARACTER—HIS COUNTRY-
HOUSES—PLINY AT PUBLIC READINGS

His life, family, and fortune are well known. His
uncle, the naturalist, who adopted him, took pains
to teach him the value of time by instilling into him
a love for work and study. Pliny the Younger was

[1] On the accession of Trajan, the more prominent Romans who
represented the preceding age quickly disappeared ; thanks to the
political crises which rapidly succeeded one another, a few years
sufficed to carry off the whole generation to which they belonged.
Pliny mentions this circumstance (iii., 7, 9) with a certain regret,
apropos of the death of Silius Italicus, the last of Nero's consuls.

chiefly attracted to literature by the nimbus of
celebrity which awaits the successful writer; to
secure this was his pet ambition, and he spent his
whole life in endeavouring to make a name for himself that might go down to posterity. We seem to
miss in him the activity which distinguished his
uncle, but neither did he share his ruggedness, his
eccentricity, nor his prejudices.[1]

One merit we must concede to him. He knew
how to gain the affection of those who surrounded
him. His third wife, Calpurnia, was an enthusiastic
admirer of his writings. She sang his verses to the
accompaniment of a *cithara ;* when he gave a public
reading, she listened behind a curtain, or, if she was
unable to be present at his triumphs, she kept her
slaves running to and fro every moment in order
that she might learn the number and warmth of the
plaudits he obtained.[2] It is no small thing to be
able to inspire such an affection as this.

A quæstor at twenty-seven, Pliny was appointed
consul by Trajan in the year 100 A.D. at the age of
thirty-eight; eleven years later he became imperial
legate in Bithynia.

His modest fortune, if we may believe his own
account, consisted mainly of landed estates and
vineyards. His practice as an orator was quite as
much in the courts as in the Senate, and he prob-

---

[1] iii., 5, 8 : " *acre ingenium*, incredibile studium, summa vigilan-
tia " (A mind full of energy, with a marvellous passion for study, and
of the utmost vigilance).

[2] iv., 19.

ably received a good many important legacies in return for his labours on behalf of his clients, in accordance with the custom of the time.[1]   Had he not been a rich man, he could scarcely have made those presents of one hundred, three hundred, and even five hundred thousand sesterces to several of his friends, to which he refers in his letters.[2]

It was his success as an advocate in civil actions that first brought him into prominence.   " My battlefield," he says (arena mea), " is the tribunal of the centumviri."[3]   His victories in this arena were numerous.[4]   He tells us how the judges at first listened to him with great gravity; then, overcome by emotion, they were no longer able to contain themselves, but suddenly, vanquished by his eloquence, rose to their feet and burst into prolonged applause.[5]   Successful advocates of our day cannot hope for similar triumphs.

Nor was he less successful in the Senate.   The provincials whose cause he championed, more especially the inhabitants of Betica,[6] commissioned him to proceed against defaulting magistrates.   In other cases he was employed by the Senate itself either to proceed against or to defend men who had filled the

---

[1] Cf. supra, Chap. VII., p. 175.   [2] £800, £2400, and £4000.
[3] vi., 12, 2.   [4] ix., 23.

[5] Our admiration for Pliny's success would be greater were it not for the fact that we seem to have heard something very similar to this told of Cicero in connection with his oration Pro Cornelio (Quintilian, viii., 3, 3).

[6] iii., 4, 2: he appeared on behalf of Betica against Classicus, a consul who had died.

posts of prætor or consul. Pliny pretended reluct-
ance to undertake these cases, but when the suit was
a promising one and likely to do him credit, he
ended by yielding.

I have spoken of Pliny's success as an orator,
and no doubt it was genuine enough. But he
does not attempt to conceal the fact that many of
the forensic triumphs of his day were very hollow
affairs. The chief merit of many of his contemporaries lay in their skill in organising an efficient
claque, and in posting its members in good positions.
In such cases the ability of the orator was generally
in inverse ratio to the amount of applause he received. Quintilian gave Pliny[1] an account of the
way in which this evil first made its appearance in
Rome. Domitius Afer was one day pleading a
cause with much gravity, when applause of an un-
usually pronounced and exaggerated character was
heard close by, the first applause which owed its
origin to " organisation." Domitius paused in his
speech and sorrowfully exclaimed, " *Centumviri*,
our art has received its death-blow."

Pliny did not resort to expedients of this kind.
His sole artifice consisted in cultivating the affection
and admiration of the rising generation; he gave
them good advice,[2] helped them in the early stages
of their career,[3] and was consequently regarded by
them as a model of excellence, even in poetry, a
fact which causes us some surprise. In the eyes of
these young supporters of his " Pliny was worth all

[1] ii., 14, 19.   [2] vi., 29, 3.   [3] vi., 23, 2.

the ancients put together.'' [1]   This speech would be charming if it were recorded by anyone but Pliny himself.[2]   Pliny was a thoroughgoing man of letters, to whom purely business details were intolerable; as president of a tribunal, he had to sign large numbers of documents.   He complains bitterly of this.   What is the good, he asks, of all this scribbling, of this unliterary literature ? [3]

The greater part of his time was spent away from Rome in his country-houses.   He possessed villas in some of the most celebrated parts of Italy, at Tusculum, at Tibur, at Præneste.[4]   He had two special favourites among them, however,[5] which he has described at great length, and to which we have already had occasion to refer.   One of these was in Tuscany, at Tifernum (now Città di Castello, in Umbria), the other at Laurentum.

These villas certainly did not belong to the class of luxurious resting-places (*deversoria luxuriæ*) described by Seneca, which were placed on the summit of some mountain, with a vast panorama of sea

---

[1] iv., 27, 4 : '' *Unus* Plinius *est mihi priores*.''

[2] The literary activity of that period, if not brilliantly successful, was none the less respectable and worthy of attention.   An inscription in verse (Bücheler, *Carmina Latina Epigraphica*, i., No. 97, p. 53), which cannot be much later than this date (we only know definitely that it is later than the time of Trajan), indicates that a certain Bassulus had translated some of the comedies of Menander, and that he had written comedies himself ; and in one of Pliny's letters we learn that a contemporary of his, Vergilius Romanus, had written comedies in imitation of Menander which rivalled the works of Plautus and of Terence.

[3] i., 10, 9.   [4] v., 6, 45.   [5] Chap. VIII., pp. 191 *et seq.*

and land extending in front of them, or near some
bay which served as setting for the splendid buildings which formed a long fringe on its shores.[1]
Neither did they resemble those houses first described by Cato, and after him by Varro, whither
the owner came frequently and busied himself in
calculating the amount of his expenditure and receipts, his regard for his property being similar to
that of a peasant for his holding. Pliny looked on
the country as a place for bodily repose, where he
desired, however, to reserve, or if possible to create
opportunities for mental exertion. In a previous
chapter[2] I have had occasion to point out that in
the long list which he gives of the various rooms
and chambers in his villas we find a very large number of studies mentioned. I can scarcely believe
that Pliny had a different one for every evening like
the famous Sicilian tyrant; still, there can be little
doubt that he spent the best part of his time in them.

Even when he goes out he still continues to work.
When he takes an airing in his litter, or goes on a
journey, he spends his time either in reading or
writing. If he goes to help in the vintage, he is
careful to take a book with him, as he is thus quite
certain in any event to " pick up something."[3] If
he starts out to hunt the wild boar, Pliny finds that
his tablets are quite as necessary as his hunting
spears, and it sometimes happens that the boar has
been good enough to walk into the net prepared for

---

[1] lxxxix., 21. [2] Chap. VIII., p. 198.

[3] An untranslatable pun on the word *legere* = to read, to pick.

22

him while Pliny is filling his tablets in the throes
of literary composition.   He is thus able to bring
home a double booty.   It is in a letter to Tacitus [1]
that we find this story.   The villa at Laurentum
consisted of a house, garden, and a fine extent of
sandy beach.   No farm, however, brought in a richer
harvest to its owner; for even if his prune-trees did
not produce much fruit, Pliny was always able to
fill his tablets at Laurentum. [2]

Pliny carefully guarded his moments of literary
inspiration, and did his best to prevent any of them
from being wasted; sometimes he awaited them, as
Buffon did after him, at the top of some high tower;
at other times he buried himself in a study from
which all sounds were excluded, and where the
chatter of his slaves, the roar of the waves, and even
the noise of the tempest could not penetrate: even
the daylight could not enter, once the shutters were
closed. [3]   There he passed his time in plaguing the
Muse, or rather the Muses, for he wrote far more
prose than verse.   He kept continually revising
what he had written, and held long and animated
conversations with his books and tablets. [4]   Although
he was perfectly well aware that too much revision
is often hurtful, [5] he was incessantly on the watch
for hidden defects in his works.   He knew that
posterity concerns itself only with writings that are
perfect and complete, a fact which he repeats more
than once. [6]

[1] i., 6.   [2] iv., 6.   [3] ii., 17, 21.   [4] i., 9, 5.   [5] vii., 12, 1.
[6] v., 8, 7. He is good enough to tell us all about the trouble he

But to go back to his country-houses. Not only did he manage to get through a lot of work there; the places themselves furnished him with subjects. Pliny, like other writers of his time, prided himself on his powers of description. Even the most commonplace subjects did not come amiss to him. He can make " copy " out of an inundation of the Tiber and its tributaries,[1] or out of a visit to the source of the Clitumnus.[2] On one occasion he takes a longer flight and one which proves more interesting to the modern reader, when, in a letter to a friend, he enters on a long rhapsody in praise of his villas, and indeed of his whole Etrurian estates.[3] He combines the vanity of a man of letters, anxious to display his talent (42 *et seq.*), who never doubts that the perusal of one of his letters will serve quite as well as a visit to the place he describes (41), with the self-satisfaction of a landed proprietor pointing out the various beauties of his domain, its fountains and grassy vistas, its quaintly trimmed shrubs, its drawing-rooms and dining-rooms, its baths and porticos, cryptoporticos and covered galleries, its hippodrome and—I know not what else.[4] He dwells, as is but natural, at somewhat greater length on the

took over the arrangement and revision of his Panegyric (iii., 13, 3). He polished up his speeches and made large additions to them (ix., 28, 5). Elsewhere he tells us how he sent one of his books to Tacitus in order that he might have the benefit of criticisms on it (vii., 20, 1 *et seq.*).　　　[1] viii., 17.　　[2] viii., 8.　　[3] v., 6.

[4] 40 : " Nisi proposuissem *omnes angulos* tecum epistula circumire " (Unless I had proposed in this letter of mine to take you round over every nook and corner of the villa).

works of art or decorations and landscape paintings
(trees and birds: 22), on the *columellæ* (36) and the
marbles.   But here, we cannot help feeling how
widely Pliny's taste differs from ours; he lingers
lovingly over his shrubs trimmed into animal shapes,
over his plants arranged so as to form letters which
produce the name of the owner and that of the landscape gardener.   He does not attempt to conceal
the fact that he had superintended this splendid
piece of work himself, and that he is rather proud
of his share in it (41).

Pliny and Public Readings

In the intervals between these periods of rest and
seclusion, when he was not occupied by his duties
in the courts or the senate-house, Pliny's chief delight lay in attending public readings, either in the
capacity of reader or as one of the audience.   Where
were these readings held at Rome ?   Pretty nearly
everywhere.   Pliny applauds[1] certain nobles, the
Pisos among others, who had conceived the idea of
establishing *auditoria* in their own houses.   He
mentions[2] that he had been present when the
younger Piso read some exceedingly fine couplets,[3]
and is careful to bring forward this fact as a healthy
sign of the times.[4]   It proves, in his opinion, that
the aristocrats are not content to rest on their ances-

---

[1] v., 17, 2.   [2] *Ibid.*

[3] *Ibid.* : " Recitabat καταστεριόμων eruditam sane luculentam-
que materiam " (He read a learned and brilliant essay on the con-
stellations).   [4] *Ibid.*, 6.

tral *imagines ;* they seek to establish their credit and
perpetuate their memories by noble foundations
which command universal admiration.

Very probably some of the minor theatres, such
as the small covered theatre at Pompeii, or the Greek
theatre in Hadrian's Villa, were utilised for the purpose of these readings. It is also very likely that
there were one or more lecture-rooms attached to
the library on the Palatine.[1] These rooms and the
people who collected there are never long absent
from Pliny's mind. They were the judges who sat
as a court of first instance to try the value of each
new literary work. Pliny, though his bookseller
assures him that his works are widely read, accuses
himself of laziness. He is always puzzling his head
about the next book he is to give to the world, and
what line he is going to take up this time, what
model he is to follow.[2] As a precautionary measure,
he makes a number of preliminary drafts in various
styles (ix., 21, 1). Once the work is finished, he
first reads it to a small circle of two or three intimate
friends; he then carefully weighs any objections
they may have raised with another set of friends
(vii., 17, 7); with a view to disarming the scruples
of those critics who are disturbed by his boldness of
thought or language, he dutifully omits the passage
objected to and substitutes another and simpler,
even if feebler, version in its place (vii., 12, 4), so
keen is his anxiety to meet the views of those who
are to be his listeners or his readers.

[1] Lanciani, *Anc. Rome*, p. 113.   [2] i., 2.

At last the great and long-looked-for day of the public reading arrives. Pliny's misgivings and disquietude increase in proportion to the number of his auditors. By the time he gets on his legs, the author has lost all confidence in himself. He begins to wish that he had treated, not merely a part, but even the whole of his book in quite a different manner (vii., 17, 9). So great is the effort involved on these occasions, in Pliny's eyes, that he believes this to be of all others the surest means of bringing one's works to the highest pitch of perfection. "To have the fear of the great public, more particularly the educated section of it, continually before our eyes, this is the most drastic of all remedies that can be applied to cure us of our defects." [1] The mere thought of the final public reading is a corrective in itself; amendments begin to suggest themselves as one enters the lecture-room, pale and trembling, with eyes that glance apprehensively in all directions. We suspect that Pliny is here writing on the morning after a success; he is incapable of questioning the sincerity of the applause with which the reading of his discourse was received; it is only the friends or clients of such a man as Regulus who ever feign an unreal enthusiasm on such occasions (iv., 2, 4 *et seq.*). In his case it was all genuine, and Pliny modestly compares this memorable day with that other famous occasion when Æschines read his own oration and that of Demosthenes to a Rhodian audience (iv., 5).

[1] i., 13 : "timor est, timor *emendator asperrimus.*"

After appearing in the character of reader, Pliny is quite ready to take his turn as a listener. In this capacity his zeal and enthusiasm are no less conspicuous than in the other; he applauds a great many of those whose reading he goes to hear. Literature has lost much of its ancient lustre. It is, therefore, all the more incumbent on those lovers of the art who still survive to mutually praise and support one another.[1] At any rate, this is the view taken by Pliny. This practice of reading literary works to an audience seems to us to have largely contributed to the decay of literature, but Pliny, on the contrary, regarded it as one of the most effective methods of arousing the public from their indifference. Tacitus was more clear-sighted than this.[2]

Nevertheless, Pliny does not attempt to hide from us the seamy side of that " world of boredom " which was not unknown even in ancient times. He tells us how the friends who were to sit in judgment on the aspiring writer arrived late, and often stood about outside the lecture-room employing a slave to keep them informed concerning the progress made

---

[1] We find the same sentiments expressed by Statius in his preface to the First Book of the *Silvæ :* " Manilius certe Vopiscus, vir eruditissimus et qui præcipue *vindicat a situ litteras jam pæne fugientes* " (Manilius Vopiscus, a most learned man, and one who avenges literature for the state into which it has now fallen, being as it is, practically dead amongst us).

[2] *Cf.* the tone adopted by Aper (*Dial.*, ix., 15) in describing a poet who works day and night for a whole year " in order that he may at last beg his friends to be so good as to come and listen to him " (" ut sint *qui dignentur audire* ").

by the reader, and how towards the end of the
reading they all trooped in together (i., 13) and displayed an enthusiasm which made up in noisiness
what it lacked in sincerity.   Pliny protests against
such conduct, but he would probably have protested
still more loudly if his listeners had remained silent
and motionless.   A nice way this would be of spending a day consecrated to the interests of a friend!
It was a positive duty to applaud the reader, no
matter what your private opinion of his merits as a
writer or your real estimate of his capacity might
be.   Is he your superior in talent ?   If you are niggardly of your praise, what sort of reception can
you expect when your own turn comes round ?   Is
he your equal or inferior ?   Then clearly it is to
your interest to place those whom you equal or
surpass as high as possible.   This was Pliny's
theory in the matter, and we can readily believe
that he carried it into practice.

Other writers than Pliny have handed down to us
some of the humorous incidents which occurred
during these readings.   For instance, we have the
fat man who excited great merriment by breaking
down one seat after another during a reading given
by Claudius, this merriment being still further increased by the reader's clumsy references to its
cause.[1]   But the facts recorded by Pliny constitute

[1] Suetonius, *Claud.*, 41 : " Cum initio recitationis, *defractis com-*
pluribus subselliis obesitate cujusdam, *risus exortus* esset, ne sedato
quidem tumultu, temperare potuit (Claudius) quin ex intervallo
subinde facti reminisceretur cachinnosque revocaret " (At the begin-

our main source of information in regard to the history of public readings during the first century. I need but quote the anecdote related of a descendant of Propertius who began a set of elegiac verses with the words " *Prisce, jubes* [1] . . ." when a celebrated lawyer of that day, named Priscus Javolenus, who happened to be present, broke in on him with the remark, " *Ego vero non jubeo.*" [2] The laughter which greeted this interruption may be imagined.

II

PLINY AND TRAJAN—LETTERS TO TRAJAN AND PLINY'S PANEGYRIC

Chief among the correspondents of Pliny we must place the Emperor Trajan. Now, let us see what impression is produced on the modern mind by what is known as the Tenth Book of Pliny's Letters (in other words, the collected letters of Pliny and Trajan). And first of all, I should like to say a few words about the *Panegyric* and about a certain celebrated letter of Pliny's.

In this letter (vi., 31), Pliny tells how the Emperor invited him to his villa at *Centumcellæ* (Civita

---

ning of the reading, several seats gave way under the weight of a very fat man, which gave rise to peals of laughter ; when the uproar had subsided, Claudius could not keep himself from recalling the incident more than once, and this led to a renewal of the laughter on each occasion).

[1] "You ask me, Priscus . . ."

[2] " Not at all, I ask you nothing " (vi., 15).

Vecchia).   He mentions the principal questions discussed in the council; Pliny had evidently taken his
duties as councillor seriously and is anxious that we
should know it.   Only one of the affairs which occupied Trajan and his advisers is of any interest to
us, this being a case of what the French call a *crime
passionnel*.   It appears that the wife of a tribune had
been guilty of adultery with a centurion.   Her husband had denounced her to the legate, and the centurion had been cashiered and dismissed the service.
The tribune, however, actuated by a lingering regard
for his wife, took her back, and it was no easy matter to make him understand that his guilty spouse
must share the punishment meted out to her para-
mour.

After business came pleasure.[1]   Considering that
the guests were dining at the table of an Emperor,
their meals were of a very simple character.   They
listened to music and spent the night in talk.   Pliny
is full of admiration for the site on which the villa
stood, and for the strand which it overlooked, especially the fine harbour, the mouth of which was to
be guarded by an artificial island, with which the
engineers were then making visible progress.   On
leaving the villa the Emperor presented his council-
lors with gifts.

The Panegyric

As a rule, the *Panegyric* is never mentioned except
in uncomplimentary terms.   Few critics see anything

[1] § xiii.

in this written speech but that " flattery which speaks to vanity." [1] Alfieri tells us [2] that the first time he began to read it he stopped after the first few pages, and in a gust of indignation flung the book away, and, seizing his pen, exclaimed aloud: " My dear Pliny, if you were really a friend, a rival, and an admirer of Tacitus, this is how you should have spoken to Trajan," and in the heat of inspiration he filled four long pages.

These severe criticisms apply, I think, not so much to the work of Pliny as to the class to which it belongs, a class which Pliny is unjustly accused of having founded. In fact, Pliny is here made to suffer for the sins of Gallic rhetoricians, such as Constantine and his successors, who paid him the compliment of imitating him. There is a tendency to hold him responsible for the irritation aroused in us by more than one passage in the funeral orations of the classical age. The friend of Trajan, however, was merely conforming to a well-established usage, when he proceeded to enumerate, in flattering terms, the various acts of the Emperor's reign in their chronological order. The parallel review of the blunders and crimes of Domitian which accompanies it does not, in our opinion, atone for the general feebleness of the composition. But here again, Pliny was doubtless following a fixed rule. Instead of wasting our time in criticising the general form imposed by the nature of the subject, we

[1] Fénelon, *Dial. Eloq.*, i., p. 158 (Despois).
[2] Memoirs, *Virility.*

shall be better employed if we follow in the footsteps of those scholars who have recently set themselves to weigh Pliny's studied expressions and to
grasp as far as possible the drift of his allusions.   In
so doing we shall speedily find that the *Panegyric*
furnishes us with much detailed information concerning the constitution and political institutions of
the first century, and that it is a veritable mine of
wealth to all those who seek for the facts and customs that underlie its coating of rhetorical varnish.

The Tenth Book, or Correspondence of Pliny and Trajan

We now pass on to the letters of Pliny and Trajan.[1]   In a double series of this kind, consisting, as
it does, of letters and replies, the reader can scarcely
refrain from comparing them one with the other,
and we find in this old-world correspondence a feature which is noticeable in the published letters of our
contemporaries.   The editors of modern works of
this kind are often surprised and disappointed with
the result.   It frequently happens that the reader
refuses to give the principal credit to the person in
whose interest the letters have been published.   So,
too, in the case of these letters, which must have
been edited by the family or friends of Pliny, few

---

[1] I intentionally leave the question of the authenticity of the whole
or a part of these letters on one side.   It is one which has been
fully discussed by Hardy in his edition (Macmillan, 1889), and by
M. Wilde (Leyden, 1889).

modern readers will be ready to admit that Pliny
has in any way the lion's share of credit.

Even his rhetorical graces cannot conceal his
weaknesses; our sympathies at once go out to
Trajan and remain with him. We cannot but ad-
mire his curt replies, so full of good sense and,
sometimes, of high moral feeling. We know from
the *Panegyric* [1] that the courtly style of writing was
even then in fashion, and are therefore in no way
surprised when we find Pliny celebrating Trajan's
birthday and recounting to the Emperor all the
vows which he had offered up on the occasion, for
we feel convinced that Pliny was quite sincere. But
why does he persist in consulting his master on so
many paltry points of administration ? Trajan is at
length obliged to protest—gently and indirectly, it
is true—against the repeated requests in which his
legate asks that an architect and an engineer may
be sent out to him in Bithynia, just as though Pliny
did not know perfectly well that the Romans imported these craftsmen from Greece and Asia. [2] The
Emperor admonishes him to adhere to the principles
of sound administration, especially in all that concerns the finances of his province and the discipline
of the army. [3] He is quite conscious that the imperial government is not entirely free from abuses,

---

[1] Pliny addresses the Emperor as *Dominus* (Lord), and *sanctissi-
mus* (most holy); he speaks of his *indulgentia*, of his *pietas*, of his
magnitudo, of the *felicitas orbis*, etc.

[2] xviii. and xxxix., xxiv. and xl., 2. (I quote the numbering of
the letters from Keil's edition throughout.)

[3] xx. and xxii.

and it was' precisely in order that he might set them right that Pliny had been sent to this particular province.[1]   When the courtier legate feels it to be his duty to submit to the sovereign some doubtful case, in which he thinks the provisions of the *lex majestatis* might be applied, Trajan protests.   This is his attitude in the case of a certain Dion whom an enemy had sought to ruin by disclosing the fact that he had erected a statue of the Emperor in close proximity to the tombs of his wife and son.[2]   The offence seemed a very serious one to those who had lived under the rule of Domitian; but Trajan cannot understand how Pliny, who knows his views, should have hesitated or considered it necessary to consult him.[3]   So, too, he tells Pliny to pay no heed to anonymous denunciations.[4]   It is only with difficulty that he can be persuaded to allow statues of himself to be erected in a temple.[5]   He will have no special indulgence shown to the imperial freed-

[1] xxxii.

[2] xxxi. and lxxxii., 2.

[3] *Ibid.* : " *Potuisti non hærere*, mi Secunde carissime . . . cum propositum meum optime nosses, *non ex metu* nec terrore hominum aut *criminibus majestatis* reverentiam nomini meo acquirere " (You should not have hesitated, my dear Secundus. . . . You know very well that I do not intend to make men pay due respect to my name from motives of fear or terror, or by prosecutions for petty treason).

[4] xcvii. : " *sine auctore* vero *propositi libelli* in nullo crimine locum habere debent " (Information which is lodged anonymously is to be disregarded).

[5] ix.: " Quamquam ejus modi honorum *parcissimus*, tamen patior " (Though I am as a rule very chary of sanctioning honours of this nature, yet I allow it in this case).

men.[1] The days of Nero are now past and done with.[2] He adopts a similar course in regard to a scheme for a compulsory loan which it was sought to impose on the decurions of a town in Asia.[3]

I need but refer, in passing, to the famous letter in regard to the Christians (xcvi.). It is rather a shock to our feelings to learn that Pliny considered it necessary to put two poor serving-maids to the torture in order to ascertain the whole truth (§ 8), and we find it difficult to understand how he could send steadfast Christians to their death with such an easy conscience.[4] But Pliny is honest, he tells the Emperor all that he has discovered, or rather admits that he has found no evidence in support of the odious accusations levelled against the Christians. We need not be surprised at his absolute failure to understand their doctrines, if we reflect that other Romans such as Seneca, Tacitus, Epictetus, and Marcus Aurelius, who might have been expected to be better informed and more capable of grasping the drift of this new teaching, remained equally ignorant. It is easy to be wise after the event, and the mere fact that the lapse of ages has placed us beyond the possibility of error, does not warrant us

[1] At *Centumcellæ* (Book vi., 31, 9).

[2] *Ibid.* : "*Nec ille Polyclitus est nec ego Nero*" (He is not Polyclitus [one of Nero's freedmen] nor am I Nero).

[3] lxv. : "Invitos ad accipiendum compellere *non est ex justitia nostrorum temporum*" (It does not fit in with the justice of our times to compel people to borrow against their will).

[4] 3 : "Perseverantes *duci jussi*" (Those who were obstinate I ordered to be led out to execution).

in expecting an equally clear prevision of the future on the part of the ancients.

III

OTHER LETTERS OF PLINY

We may now pass on to the other letters. They have all been edited or rewritten; scarcely a single one of the letters in the collection contains any of those details which abound in the letters of every-day life, but which are only of interest to those who either write or receive them.[1] What Pliny gives us has undergone a process of pruning. He has con-sidered the effect on his readers throughout, and has retained nothing which he feared might fail to at-tract them. Pliny's idea of interesting his readers is to talk incessantly of himself, of his cases in the courts, his readings in public, his presents, his minor verse, even of his witticisms, which he retails for their benefit.[2] It is all very well to make allowances for an author's vanity; in Pliny's case there is alto-gether too much of it, and the reader cannot help feeling that he has worn his matter threadbare.

On the other hand, we owe a debt of gratitude to the author of the letters for all that we are able to learn, by his agency, about those among whom he lived; especially about his uncle, whose habits he describes, and whose tragic death he records for the benefit of Tacitus, together with an account of

---

[1] I can only recall one letter (vi., 30) to which this remark does not apply.

[2] Pliny, ix., 26, 1 : '' *Dixi de quodam oratore.* . . .''

all he saw and all that he knew of the famous eruption.   We have to thank Pliny for a complete list
of his uncle's writings (vi., 16), together with the
order in which they were written (iii., 5).   It is from
him too that we obtain a whole series of anecdotes
which throw a vivid light on Domitian and his
times.   I propose to quote two of these, partly to
make my meaning clearer, partly in order to induce
the reader to look up the others for himself.

Domitian, who prided himself on his religious
devotion, desired on one occasion to show how zeal-
ously he watched over the eternal fire of Vesta and
the chastity of her priestesses.[1]   He proved this, in
an eminently characteristic manner, by impeaching
the chief Vestal, a certain Cornelia, and causing her
to be buried alive (iv., 11, 16).   She vehemently declared her innocence up to the very last, and we are
told that as she was in the act of descending into
her living tomb, her dress caught on something, and
she was obliged to disengage it.   The executioner
held out his hand to aid her, but she avoided him
with a rapid movement, anxious to preserve her
person from the degradation of such hateful contact.[2]

The Emperor, feeling that public opinion was

---

[1] Statius, *Silvæ*, i., 1, 35.

[2] *Ibid.*, 9.   A somewhat similar story is told of the Princess of
Monaco.   Before she perished at the scaffold on the 9th Thermidor,
she cut off her hair with a piece of glass and begged Fouquier-
Tinville to hand it to her children ; she particularly desired that it
should not reach them through the hands of the executioner.   " It
is the only legacy I have to leave to my children," she writes, "*and
I am anxious that it should escape defilement.*"   (M. Aderer.)

23

against him in this matter, was anxious to prove himself in the right. He therefore made secret overtures to an ex-prætor, Valerius Licinianus, who was one of those charged with complicity in Cornelia's crime, owing to the fact that he had harboured one of her freedwomen in his house. All that was required of this supposed accomplice was that he should confess himself guilty. If he refused, his doom was certain. Valerius, who felt that his case was hopeless, no matter how he acted, agreed to do as the Emperor wished. Domitian thereupon joyfully exclaimed: '' Licinianus absolves us." He allowed the self-confessed criminal to take such part of his property as he chose, merely condemning him to nominal banishment, a sentence which Valerius afterwards completed in Sicily.. There, the ex-prætor turned teacher of rhetoric, and took his own misfortunes as a subject for his first lesson. He came to his class clothed in the pallium, in place of the toga, being no longer entitled to wear this latter garment. '' O Fortune," he began, '' how strange are thy vagaries; thou makest senators into professors and professors into senators." The subtly distilled bitterness of this speech, says Pliny, almost leads us to believe that the unfortunate Valerius took up the calling of teacher for the sole purpose of delivering this opening sentence. The whole business, including the pressure brought to bear upon the accused, is eminently characteristic of the time of Domitian; but this final comment is curiously typical of Pliny and his tastes.

The following incident throws a light on the next epoch of Roman history. The Emperor Nerva, who tried to show universal leniency, found it necessary, at the very beginning of his reign, to protect certain persons who had been magistrates and all-powerful favourites under Domitian, against the attacks of a consul and others. He was dining on one occasion with his friends at the house of one of these persons, a man who was said to have made his money as an informer. The conversation turned on one of Domitian's tools, L. Valerius Catullus, that terrible blind man whom Juvenal had described as " one of the monsters of the time." [1] Instances of his malevolence and bloodthirsty deeds having been mentioned, the Emperor chanced to remark: " I wonder what would have become of him if he had lived." One of the other guests at once replied: " Oh, he would be dining with us now " (iv., 22).

Pliny's Friends and Enemies

Seeing that Pliny talks so much about himself, it is only natural that we should learn a good deal concerning his friends and enemies from his letters. Among the latter may be mentioned the two defaulting magistrates whom he was commissioned to proceed against, Marius Priscus, formerly procurator of Africa, and Cæcilius Classicus, formerly procura-

---

[1] Juvenal, iv., 114: " Grande et conspicuum nostro quoque tempore monstrum " (That great and striking prodigy who, even in these degenerate days, deserves the name of monster).

tor of Betica.   Pliny's pet aversion, however, was
the informer Regulus, a man who had done his best
to ruin him, had laid traps for him, and denounced
him.   Pliny is never at a loss for something disagreeable to say about him.   There are other persons as well whose blameworthy actions are recorded
by Pliny, either directly or indirectly.   Unfortunately his discretion does not allow him to give their
names, and we are therefore, in the majority of instances, unable to identify them.

Chief among Pliny's friends was the famous Ver-
ginius Rufus, who more than once refused the
purple; after him come several of the best writers
of that day, such as Silius Italicus and Martial,
Suetonius and Tacitus; among the less well known
I may mention Vestricius Spurinna, one of Otho's
generals who had two or three times served as consul, a hale old man in spite of his eighty years, who
led a life of pleasant leisure.   Pliny noted the
system by which he regulated his daily existence,
and describes it in detail; he thus enables us to see
how a Roman grandee spent his days after age had
compelled him to retire from the cares of office.[1]

Of Pliny's other correspondents we know but
little.   Mommsen, in his valuable index, has managed to trace the career and *cursus honorum* of a
good many of them.   But in reading the letters
many of these names convey little more meaning
than so many algebraic symbols.   For all literary
purposes these friends of Pliny's might just as well

[1] iii., 1, 4 *et seq.*

be anonymous; they file past the reader like a troop of shadows, no single one of which leaves any permanent impress on the memory. It is one of the penalties of the method adopted by Pliny, which he considered so ingenious. Moved by literary scruples, he decided to suppress the topical portions of the genuine letters before including them in his collection. The literary element is all that remains of them. The genuineness of the names and facts does not prevent them from seeming every bit as unreal as though the author had invented the whole thing from beginning to end.

Pliny's Failings and Virtues

But, after all, Pliny remains an eye-witness and typical representative of Roman society in the first century. He has his faults, of course, not the least of which is his vanity. At the same time, he would have been the last to dispute this; and his friends willingly forgave him his shortcomings, though, to tell the truth, some of his weaknesses are of a kind which causes us no little astonishment. Take his credulity, for instance; he believed that the future is disclosed to us in dreams, the only difficulty being to interpret them correctly (i., 18): on the death of Curtius Rufus he recalls the fact that his brilliant career had been predicted to him by an apparition, and he follows this up by a highly ornate version of the story told concerning some phantom or other which has been exorcised from a haunted house by the philosopher Athenagoras (vii., 27).   The various bizarre hypotheses put forward by Pliny in an attempt to explain the phenomenon of the periodical rise and fall of the waters of Lake Como, prove clearly enough that his mind was incapable of viewing such questions from a scientific standpoint.   His perfectly genuine passion for literature is often carried to excess and threatens to become sheer monomania; when he assures us that on the death of his friends, or when his wife is ill, or his dear ones in peril, he can always find consolation in his books, he seems to be quite unconscious that such a confession as this must necessarily tend to lower our esteem for the character of him who makes it.

Moreover, he displays undoubted narrow-mindedness on certain subjects.   Indeed, this defect is occasionally so obvious, that many people might for this reason alone refuse to recognise in Pliny the typical representative of a century which included so many generous spirits, so many vigorous and far-seeing minds.   What strange ideas, for instance, Pliny seems to have had in regard to history and the responsibilities of the historian (v., 8).   No doubt, in the passage referred to, he merely gives expression to the academic theories of his time, but we may be certain that his uncle, with all his faults, would never have written such a letter as this.   It is a very singular thing, that though Pliny fully realised the superiority of Tacitus, he was incapable of analysing the cause to which it was due; and he little suspects that this same letter, which leads us to couple their two names together, necessarily involves a crushing condemnation of his own views.

It will be seen that the list of Pliny's failings is a long one,[1] but, nevertheless, we can and, indeed, ought to overlook them.   In the first place, because some of them are really almost merits in the eyes of the modern reader who is desirous of learning all he can about the social life of that time.   If it be urged that Pliny is continually posing and attitudinising in these letters of his, even this defect has its value, since it shows us what these Romans wished men to think of them.   Pliny talks a great deal about himself, and shows both himself and his friends in the best possible light; he thus reveals the view which he desired posterity to take of him; this was the ideal of a Roman man of letters as conceived by Pliny, and, doubtless, also by many of his contemporaries to whom these letters are addressed and whose sympathies must, therefore, be more or less reflected in them.

On the other hand, we cannot refuse to credit him with qualities which amply made up for any defects

---

[1] Since I have not attempted to conceal them, I may be allowed to protest against the unfairness of certain modern critics, such as Doudan, himself a Pliny of the nineteenth century, who thus makes merry at the expense of the real Pliny (*Lettres*, iv., 32, April 3, 1861): "I should very much like to know what Cicero would have thought of this young advocate who had been brought up in cotton-wool by the best masters of his time.   What would that stormy petrel, who had breasted the tempests of civil strife, have said to this pretty little canary singing in his cage all sorts of pretty airs that he had learnt about liberty, virtue, etc.?"

he may have possessed. There can be no question about his learning and that when he pleased he could be very witty; he was well informed on many subjects, and very sincere; and, above all, he was good-natured, a virtue rare enough in his time, or indeed in any other, and one which always deserves a place in the front rank. Pliny was naturally good-natured; this quality is apparent in every habit of his life, in every position in which he finds himself; in his own house he was an indulgent master to his slaves[1]; as a magistrate he could not help feeling pity for those unfortunate wretches who had been condemned to death but not executed, their sentences being commuted to public slavery (x., 31), and who were legally deserving of punishment; or for slaves found guilty of having enlisted in the legions (x., 29). To a father who is inclined to be too hard on his son he writes a letter (ix., 2), which is primarily remarkable because of the change it indicates in Roman ideas concerning family relations, but which could only have been written by a man whose mind was open to every kind of humane and generous feeling.

In this respect Pliny is in harmony with our own secret preferences, and a fitting type of one of the finer aspects of the social life of his day.

IV

CONCLUSION

Before I lay down my pen, I should like to take a rapid survey of this society, some salient aspects

---

[1] v., 19: πατὴρ ὡς ἤπιος ἦεν (He was like a father to them).

of which I have here endeavoured to depict. We can scarcely refrain from comparing it with that of our own day, and the first thing that strikes us is the many and wide differences between the Romans and ourselves. We find amongst them certain hateful institutions, such as slavery, a moral scar of which they were unconscious, and which they regarded as a necessity. Their political life may have been more intense than ours, but it was marked by alternate spasms of unparalleled license and horrible despotism. Their religious ideas are so far removed from ours, that our minds refuse to enter into them and we can only realise the emptiness and absurdity of their creeds. In their customs and even in their entertainments, we shudder at cruelties which they periodically looked forward to with delight. Both high and low lived in an atmosphere of feverish excitement. The refinements of lust, the mad pursuit of pleasure, these are features of Roman society which make it compare very unfavourably with that of our own day.

Nevertheless, we must not lose sight of the fact that we also have a great deal in common with the Romans, and that our debt to them is a heavy one. Let us leave on one side those elements which are common to human nature and which, for good or ill, have persisted for the last eighteen centuries; even in what remains we shall find that we have dutifully submitted to countless influences and have religiously preserved unnumbered traditions. In art, in literature, in language, and in learning, our

models come to us from Rome, and we all admit it.
The sole aim of the Renaissance was to bring back
into existence that antique life, in which it was felt
that love for the arts was more widely distributed
and perfection more frequently attained.   Our literature, in which order and perspicuity are regarded as the highest qualities, owes its chief
inspiration to the Roman spirit.   Nor is this less
apparent in our political debates, in which questions
of principle are everything and which are nothing if
not logical.   Our laws are little more than a modern
adaptation of Roman legislation, an imitation of
Roman judicial sagacity.   And, after all, is our
vaunted moral superiority really beyond dispute ?
Ought not our moralists rather to content themselves with continuing the tradition handed down
by Epictetus and Marcus Aurelius ?

As a matter of fact, our modern present is largely
made up from the Roman past.   Let us leave the
question of superiority on one side, and thus avoid
the absurdity inherent in an academic discussion of
this nature.   In the words of Ovid [1]:

" Laudamus veteres, sed nostris utimur annis."

The latter half of this verse is well exemplified in
the practice of our daily lives, and there is little
fear of our being weighed down by the dead past;
we are too keenly alive to the advantages which we
share with our contemporaries to allow our own

[1] *Fasti*, i., 225 : " We praise the ancients, but this does not prevent
us from taking full advantage of our own times."

individuality to be crushed by the weight of that heritage of art and literature which has come down to us from Rome; nevertheless, I hope the reader of the present book will agree with me in thinking that it would be both unfair and ungrateful on our part if we failed to apply the first part of Ovid's verse to Rome.   Let us pay her our tribute of praise and admiration with an unsparing hand.

INDEX

A

Acclamationes, 76

Actors, 107

Africa, army in, 282–304

Agriculture, writers on, 185

Agricultural superstitions, 188

Agrippinus, a moralist, 273

Ammianus Marcellinus, 325–327

Amphitheatre, 109–116 ; barbarians in the, 114 ; *De Spectaculis*, 110 ; gladiatorial combats, 113 ; gymnasts, 112 ; hunting spectacles, 113 ; mythological tableaux, 111 ; naval engagements, 6, 111

Antoninus, poverty of, 85

Apophoreta, 129–132

Apotheosis of Emperor, 142

Arbela, battle of, 18

Arena, *see* Amphitheatre

Army, Roman, 276–304 ; Imperial, 276–282 ; Tacitus, description of, 279–281

Army in Africa, xi., 282–304 ; benefit societies, 300 ; burial clubs, 299 ; camp, the, 301 ; children, soldiers', 290 ; disposition of, 283 ; *Donativa*, 86, 297 ; drill, 293 ; gifts to soldiers, 86, 297 ; *Legio III. Augusta*, 283 ; legion, divisions of, 284 ; maintenance of troops, 291 ; married soldiers,

295 ; military guilds, 299; pay, 297 ; promotion of barbarians, 325 ; provinces, the three African, 283 ; recruiting, 287 ; religious worship in, 292 ; *testamentum in procinctu*, 161, 165 ; veterans, colonies of, 301; will-making in the, 161

Art, Roman, 234–252 ; *Asarota*, 21 ; Bosco Reale, find at, 239 ; catalogues, 250 ; decoration of houses, 15, 248 ; diffusion of, general, 241–244 ; exhibitions, 245 ; forgeries, 250 ; historical pictures, 18 ; inferiority of ancients, 249 ; landscape in Roman, 204–208 ; mosaics, 18, 238 ; multitude of works of, 234–241 ; mythological paintings, 16, 242 ; in Roman provinces, 234, 245 ; public monuments in, 235–238 ; treasures in Pompeii, 237, 248, 251 ; Vindex, the connoisseur, 248

Asarota, 21

Augustus, buildings on Palatine, 64 ; *Decennia*, 97 ; funeral of, 143

Authors, difficulties of ancient, 232

B

Banquets, gifts at, 130 ; funeral, 140

365